W9-BLL-920

*The Local Service
Airline Experiment*

Studies in the Regulation of Economic Activity
TITLES PUBLISHED

Studies in the Regulation of Economic Activity

The Local Service Airline Experiment

GEORGE C. EADS

The Brookings Institution / *Washington, D.C.*

Library of Congress Cataloging in Publication Data:
Eads, George C   1942–
  The local service airline experiment.
  (Studies in the regulation of economic activity)
  Includes bibliographical references.
  1. Air lines, local service—United States.
I. Title.   II. Series.
HE9785.E2   387.7'42'0973   72–141
ISBN 0–8157–2022–X

9 8 7 6 5 4 3 2 1

Foreword

SOON AFTER the end of the Second World War, the Civil Aeronautics Board authorized a group of "feeder" or "local service" carriers to provide scheduled air service to the nation's smaller and more isolated communities. In the succeeding twenty-five years the federal government provided to these carriers $1 billion in direct cash payments and substantial amounts of indirect aid in order to accomplish this purpose. While the local service carriers have established themselves as an important part of the nation's air transport network, it is appropriate to ask whether the original goal of the program has been achieved. This question is particularly timely because subsidy payments, after moving downward throughout the mid- and late 1960s, have turned upward again and may reach a record $90 million in fiscal year 1972 if the requests of the local service carriers are granted.

In this study of the local service airline industry, George C. Eads concludes that performance has fallen far short of the goal established by the Civil Aeronautics Board. He traces the blame for much of this failure to faulty government regulation, contending that the primary result of twenty-five years of regulation and subsidization of these carriers has been to create a group of "junior trunklines" that supplement the service already being provided by the larger trunklines. Yet the quality and quantity of airline service provided to the smaller communities that depend solely on the local service carriers has deteriorated over the past ten years, while the per passenger cost to the federal government of providing this service has not fallen substantially and may have increased.

Mr. Eads concludes that on economic grounds a strong case can be made for ending the local service subsidy altogether, since in most cases the service now being provided appears to offer little improvement over existing transportation alternatives. If, however, a political decision is made to continue to subsidize local air service, he urges that a new scheme of subsidization—involving competitive bidding for the right to provide local air service—be tried. This, he believes, would encourage the use of more efficient aircraft and would provide better service to the smaller and more isolated communities, at significantly lower cost to the government.

Mr. Eads, who is an associate professor of economics at George Washington University, prepared this study as a member of the associated staff of the Brookings Institution. The study is one of a series of Brookings Studies in the Regulation of Economic Activity, which are devoted to analysis of issues of public concern in the field of economic regulation. Supported by a grant from the Ford Foundation, this research is directed by Joseph A. Pechman, who heads the Brookings Economic Studies program, with the assistance of Roger G. Noll of the economics staff.

The author wishes to express his gratitude to James C. Miller, Charles H. Berry, Uwe Reinhardt, Robert F. Wigmore, J. Dawson Ransome, Robert W. Simpson, Roger G. Noll, Richard Quandt, Samuel L. Brown, Frank M. Lewis, and William Raduchel for providing assistance and advice during the writing or for commenting on portions of the manuscript. He is particularly grateful to Evelyn Fisher and Catherine Haverkamp of the Brookings staff for their thorough checking of the data. The manuscript was edited by Virginia C. Haaga; the index was prepared by Joan C. Culver.

The views expressed in this book are those of the author and do not necessarily represent the opinions of the trustees, officers, or other staff members of the Brookings Institution or of the Ford Foundation.

KERMIT GORDON
President

May 1972
Washington, D.C.

Contents

Tables

Figures

CHAPTER ONE

Introduction

THE CIVIL AERONAUTICS BOARD, the agency charged with the economic regulation of the U.S. air transport industry, announced on July 11, 1944, that it was initiating an "experiment" to expand air service to the smaller and more isolated communities of the country, in spite of the fact that "the traffic potential at small cities is not encouraging."[1] It proposed to accomplish this expansion, not through the sixteen certificated air carriers then in existence, but by creating a new group of "feeder," or "local service," carriers that would specialize in providing short-haul, low-density air service. The first of these carriers was Essair (later called Pioneer Air Lines), which began operations on August 1, 1945, flying a single round trip each day over a route linking Houston and Amarillo, Texas, with intermediate stops at Austin, San Angelo, Abilene, and Lubbock. The company used the 9-passenger Lockheed L-10 Electra, an aircraft designed specifically for short-haul, low-density operations. By the end of 1945, Essair had carried 4,452 revenue passengers. Twenty-five years later, in 1970, nine local service carriers as a group were serving 453 cities and carried 27 million passengers annually. They flew aircraft with an average seating capacity of 70, the smallest in general use being the 40-passenger turbo-prop-powered Fairchild F-27. Concerning this quarter century of growth, *Flight Magazine*, an industry trade publication, editorialized:

Any way you cut the picture for analysis you come up with the final conclusion that the "experiment" to expand our scheduled air transport services into the smaller communities of the nation 25 years ago has been a monumental success—a classic case of enlightened Federal policy in partnership with typical U.S. businessmen operating under the most productive free enterprise system in the world.[2]

It is the thesis of this book that the primary "success" of the local service experiment has been not the provision of efficient short-haul, low-density

1. *Civil Aeronautics Board Reports*, Vol. 6 (July 1944–May 1946), p. 2.
2. "Needed: Jet Age Decisions," *Flight Magazine*, Vol. 58 (June 1969), p. 21.

air service, but the creation of nine relatively weak trunkline carriers. This "success" has cost the U.S. taxpayers approximately $1 billion in direct subsidy payments to the local service carriers;[3] yet the creation of additional trunklines, if that is a worthwhile goal, could have been accomplished at little or no cost to the taxpayer merely by relaxing the Civil Aeronautics Board's prohibition of direct entry into the trunkline ranks, which has allowed no entry since the passage of the Civil Aeronautics Act in 1938. This book argues that the service provided to the smaller and more isolated communities of the nation has been more costly and of lower quality than was necessary and that this is in large measure the result of the regulatory policies of the CAB. This analysis leads to the proposal that subsidy to the local service carriers be phased out rapidly and that the carriers be allowed to drop flights to any points they do not want to serve. In the relatively few cases where federal subsidy for local air service could be justified because of the geographic isolation of some small communities, service could be provided either by air taxis under subcontract with local service carriers or by carriers that contract directly with the federal government to perform specified services in return for lump-sum subsidies. Adoption of these proposals should reduce substantially the total amount of local service subsidy while improving the quality of air service to smaller communities. It would end the CAB's economically inefficient (and as yet unworkable) policy aimed at internalizing the local service subsidy by using profits generated on longer-haul routes to cover losses incurred on shorter, lower-density routes. This would eliminate one of the major reasons for continued control of entry into the airline industry and would remove some of the pressure that is building for regulation of the now unregulated scheduled air taxis.

One point should be made clear at the outset. The term *subsidy*, as used in this book, refers to direct cash payments made by the federal government to the local service airlines. It does not include such indirect forms of subsidy as the provision, at no cost or at user charges considerably below cost, of airport and navigation facilities to the local service airlines. This is not to say, however, that such "indirect" subsidy is negligible. For example, a recent Department of Transportation report estimated that the average federal share of annual jet runway construction costs, at a sample

3. Before 1953, subsidy was paid as a part of compensation by the government for the carrying of air mail. At the direction of Congress, this practice was stopped, and subsidy subsequently was separately identified. Throughout this book the terms "mail pay" and "subsidy" will be used interchangeably.

of thirteen local service airports where jet landings and takeoffs are very infrequent, is approximately $12 per departure with a range from $0.75 to $338.00 per departure.[4]

It is important also that the reader be familiar with certain other terms that will be used throughout. By *local air service* is meant air service of a short-haul, low-density nature, operated generally between smaller outlying communities and major traffic hubs. It does not refer to a specific group of air carriers, but to a type of service.

The *local service carriers* are the air carriers that were created by the Board during the immediate post-World War II period for the specific purpose of providing local feeder air service,[5] though they are by no means the only carriers offering such service. Figure 1-1 summarizes the history of this carrier group over the last twenty-five years. It can be seen that of the nineteen carriers that have been certificated as local service air carriers and have engaged in flight operations, two have disappeared altogether as a result of the refusal of the Board to renew their certificates. One carrier whose certificate was allowed to expire, E. W. Wiggins Airways, had many of its routes taken over by a surviving local service carrier, Mohawk Airlines. Six carriers were acquired by other local service carriers, and one was acquired by a trunkline. These mergers occurred largely during two periods—the early 1950s and the late 1960s. Nine of the original nineteen carriers had survived as of the end of 1970. However, in mid-1971, Mohawk, severely weakened financially by an extended strike of its pilots (caused in part by a dispute over job security for pilots affected by the transfer of routes to air taxis) sought CAB permission to merge with Allegheny Airlines, the largest of the local service carriers.[6] As of the time when this book went to press, the merger had been approved by a hearing examiner and was before the full Board, whose approval seemed assured.

The *trunk carriers* are those that were certificated in 1938 under the "grandfather" provisions of the Civil Aeronautics Act. Under Section 401(e)(1), any carrier that could show that it had been operating continuously between May 14, 1938, and the effective date of the act was to be granted a permanent certificate. Many of these carriers at the time of their certification were little larger in terms of their size and of the strength of their routes than were the local service carriers the Board later created.

4. Department of Transportation, "A Statement on National Transportation Policy" (1971; processed), pp. 20–21.

5. The local service carriers were originally called "feeder carriers."

6. *Flight Magazine*, Vol. 60 (June 1971), pp. 27 and 35.

Figure 1-1. Development of the Local Service Air Carriers, 1945–70

Arrows denote mergers

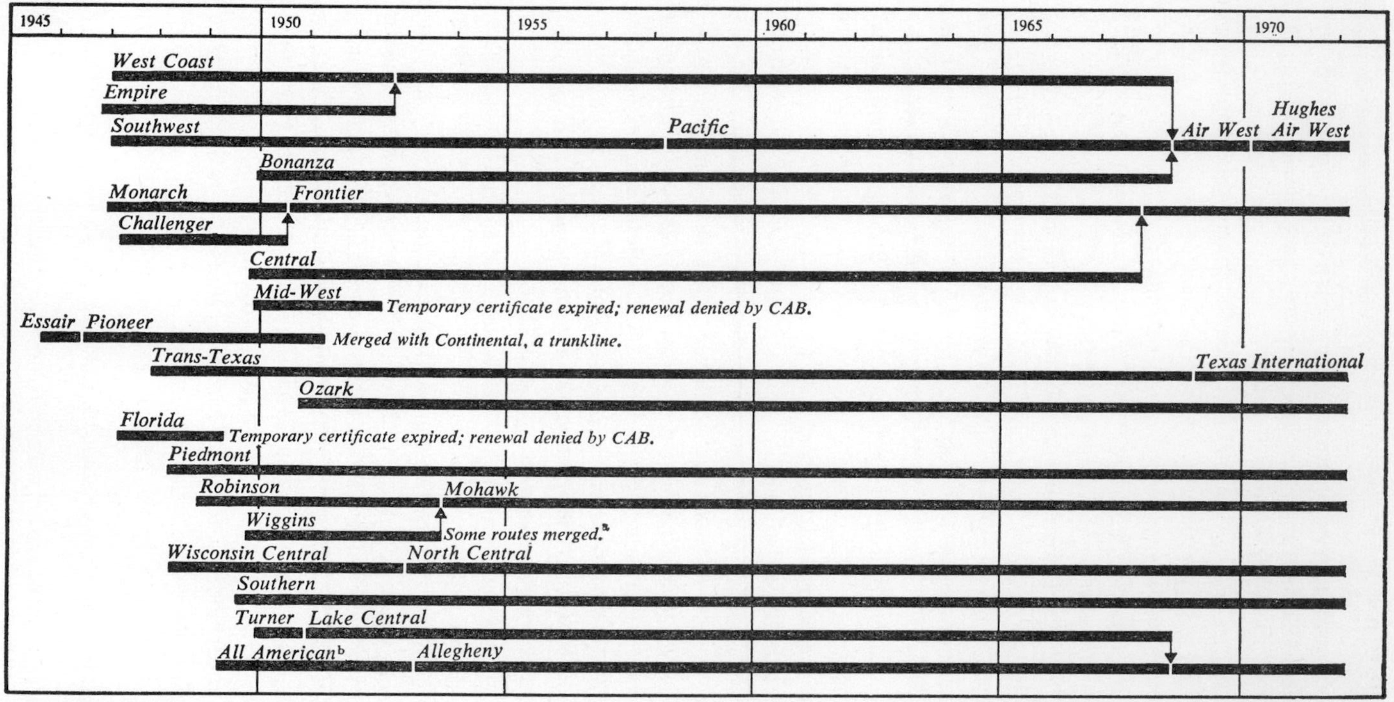

Sources: Civil Aeronautics Board, *Annual Airline Statistics*, various years; *Handbook of Airline Statistics, Calendar Years, 1949–1956* (1960); *Handbook of Airline Statistics, 1969 Edition* (1970), pp. 503–6; CAB, *Aircraft Operating Cost and Performance Report for Calendar Years 1969 and 1970* (August 1971), Vol. 5, pp. 99–100; and relevant preceding issues.
a. The certificate of E. W. Wiggins Airways was not renewed, and some of its routes were taken over by Mohawk.
b. All American Aviation operated a certificated mail pick-up service for several years before initiating passenger service on March 7, 1949.

4

However, the possession of a permanent certificate entitling each of them to provide scheduled air service over a certain route proved to be a valuable asset, and none of the trunk carriers disappeared from the industry except through merger with another carrier. From a high of sixteen, the number of trunks had fallen by the end of 1970 to eleven.[7] After nearly a decade of stability in numbers following the 1961 acquisition of Capital Airlines by United, a merger fever has now struck the industry, and applications to merge from American and Western, Delta and Northeast, and National and Northwest are before the CAB as this book goes to press. Mergers involving Braniff, Eastern, and Continental have also been mentioned within the industry. Thus it is not impossible that within a year or two, mergers will reduce the number of trunklines to six or seven.

The terms *scheduled air taxi, air taxi, commuter air carrier,* and *third-level carrier* are all used to designate carriers operating scheduled service under Part 298 of the CAB's Economic Regulations.[8] This provision, known as the "air taxi exemption," in general exempts all air carriers operating aircraft whose maximum gross takeoff weight is 12,500 pounds or less from federal economic regulation and from most of the data-reporting requirements of the Board. (The gross takeoff weight is the weight of the aircraft, fuel, crew, and payload at the moment of brake release for the takeoff roll.) These carriers can begin and terminate operations at will, subject only to state regulations. They can fly wherever they choose and charge whatever fare they like. While several thousand nonscheduled air taxis have operated since the air taxi exemption was established in 1952, the number of *scheduled* air taxis was relatively small until the mid-1960s. In January 1964 there were only 12 such carriers, operating a total of seventy-two aircraft,[9] but a survey reported by *Flight Magazine* in December 1968 revealed that there were by then more than 200 scheduled operators.[10] In the years that followed, this segment of the airline industry experienced a severe "shake-out"—a phenomenon quite common to industries that have had rapid growth and a substantial amount of entry. By the end of fiscal

7. These were American Air Lines, Eastern Air Lines, Trans World Airlines, United Air Lines (usually referred to as the "Big Four"), Braniff Airways, Continental Air Lines, Delta Air Lines, National Airlines, Northeast Airlines, Northwest Airlines, and Western Air Lines.

8. *Code of Federal Regulations, Title 14, Part 200 to End* (1971), pp. 364–78.

9. Department of Transportation, Federal Aviation Administration, *Scheduled Air Taxi Operators as of October 1967* (1968), p. 4.

10. E. H. Pickering, "Survey Shows Growth for Commuters," *Flight Magazine,* Vol. 58 (December 1968), p. 33.

1971, the number of passenger-carrying scheduled air taxis offering at least five round trips a week had declined to 126. However, the number of passengers carried rose by 3.2 percent between fiscal 1970 and fiscal 1971, and by the latter year had reached 4.35 million.[11] This is more passengers than were being carried by the local service carriers as a group as late as 1958, their fourteenth year of operation.[12] Slightly over 90 percent of these 4.35 million passengers were carried by the 50 largest scheduled air taxis.

This unstructured evolution of the scheduled air taxi segment of the airline industry in a largely unregulated environment provides an interesting contrast to the planned evolution of the closely regulated local service carriers. A strong case can be made that these small, unsubsidized carriers have been more successful in tailoring their services to the needs of the short-haul, low-density air transport market than have the local service carriers. Yet their success may be their undoing, for pressure is building to end the exemption from economic regulation that these carriers have enjoyed thus far.[13] The ability of scheduled air taxis to attract traffic away from the local service carriers in areas where the two compete directly is considered by some to be a liability rather than an indication that the unsubsidized service they provide is considered by the public to be superior to the subsidized service provided by the local service air carriers. Furthermore, the severe financial problems that many of the scheduled air taxis have faced have been pointed to as proof of the "destructive" nature of competition in this segment of the airline industry, although no convincing evidence has been offered that the public is injured by this competition. Calls for "route protection" have been heard from the air taxi industry itself.

The reasoning advanced for extending detailed economic regulation to the scheduled air taxis is reminiscent of the arguments heard during the 1920s and 1930s for extending Interstate Commerce Commission regulation to common carrier trucking. It is hoped that the growing consensus among economists that regulation of motor trucking is against the public interest and should be abandoned,[14] coupled with the history of the effects

11. "Commuters Decline But Traffic Increases," *Aviation Week and Space Technology*, Vol. 96 (Jan. 24, 1972), p. 27.

12. Civil Aeronautics Board, *Handbook of Airline Statistics, 1969 Edition* (1970), p. 54.

13. See, for example, "Joint Petition of the Local Service Air Carriers for Amendment of Part 298," CAB, Docket 24123 (Jan. 14, 1972).

14. See, for example, Alfred E. Kahn, *The Economics of Regulation: Principles and Institutions* (Wiley, 1971), Vol. 2, pp. 178–93. Kahn concludes: "What is inconceivable,

of regulation on the cost performance and growth strategies of the local service airlines detailed in this book, will provide an adequate warning of the need to avoid economic regulation of the scheduled air taxi industry unless an overwhelming case to the contrary can be made.

Some idea of the relative sizes of the three types of air carriers just discussed is given by Table 1-1, which shows 1969 traffic and employment data for the trunks, the local service carriers, the largest (in revenue passenger-miles) and second smallest[15] trunks (United and Braniff), and the largest and smallest locals (Allegheny and Southern Airways), and the average air taxi. It is apparent that while the local service carriers have been growing rapidly in size due to mergers and awards of new route authority, the largest local service airline remains considerably smaller than the smaller trunklines. The merger of Allegheny and Mohawk may change this, however, unless the smaller trunks themselves merge with each other or with larger carriers.

This book is in three parts.[16] Chapters 2 and 3 deal with factors affecting the demand for short-haul air service and with the costs of providing this service. Chapter 3 also discusses two important cost-related questions that have an obvious impact on the regulation and subsidization of local service carriers: first, the importance of the small size of the local service carriers relative to the trunkline carriers in explaining their higher costs, and second, the possible impact on local service costs of direct competition between local service and trunkline carriers—on both competitive and noncompetitive routes.

The next section (Chapters 4–6) outlines the policies of the CAB concerning the routes of the local service carriers and their subsidies. Chapter 4

---

given the basic economics of this industry, is that deregulation could indeed usher in a long period of chronic sickness. Or that firms capable of providing reliable, efficient, and diversified service would be faced with the choice of either adulterating their product or going bankrupt. The industry simply lacks the essential prerequisites of destructive competition. What is equally inconceivable is that performance would not improve in vital respects" (p. 193).

15. The smallest trunkline in 1969 was Northeast Airlines. Although classified as a trunkline, since it was certificated under the grandfather provisions of the Civil Aeronautics Act, it has always resembled a local service carrier with a few trunk routes appended.

16. Data collected for this book sometimes differed among the various sources consulted. Wherever possible, consistency checks were performed to determine the reason for the discrepancy. Occasionally, however, the reason for the difference could not be established, and in these cases the author has had to make his own judgment as to which source to use.

Table 1-1. Traffic and Employment Data for All and Selected Large and Small Individual Trunk and Local Service Air Carriers and for Air Taxis, 1969

Description	All trunk carriers	All local service carriers	Largest and second smallest individual trunk carriers		Largest and smallest individual local service carriers		Air taxis, average[a]
			United	Braniff	Allegheny	Southern	
Revenue passenger-miles (thousands)[b]	90,393,401	6,473,531	21,313,486	3,169,240	1,321,547	377,473	3,868
Revenue aircraft-miles (thousands)[c]	1,672,967	231,152	386,291	68,078	44,644	14,679	660
Originating passengers (thousands)[d]	116,671	23,388	25,876	5,476	4,567	1,440	33
Average available seats	107.6	64.9	106.9	95.9	70.8	58.8	n.a.
Average revenue passenger load[e]	54.0	28.0	55.2	46.6	29.6	25.7	5.1
Passenger load factor (percent)[f]	50.2	43.1	51.6	48.5	41.8	43.8	n.a.
Average stage length of plane (miles)[g]	532	145	590	399	170	132	n.a.
Average on-line passenger journey (miles)[h]	775	277	824	579	284	262	142
Originating passengers per route-mile[i]	556	256	854	491	433	199	n.a.
Number of employees	220,716	26,360	50,609	8,374	4,661	1,750	40

Sources: *Aviation Week*, Vol. 92 (March 2, 1970), pp. 38–39; Civil Aeronautics Board, *Reports to Congress, Fiscal Year 1969*, pp. 88, 93; *Flight Magazine*, Vol. 58 (December 1969), pp. 32–33.

n.a. Not available.

a. Air taxi data are averages for those air taxis responding to a *Flight Magazine* questionnaire. The original data, which referred to only a single month, were multiplied by twelve, where appropriate, for this table.

b. A revenue passenger-mile is generated by flying a paying passenger one mile.

c. A revenue aircraft-mile is generated whenever an aircraft (regardless of size) flies one mile in revenue service.

d. The average number of paying passengers boarding aircraft at the point of original enplanement on the reporting carrier's system. A return portion of a round trip counts as a separate origination.

e. Average number of paying passengers aboard an aircraft.

f. Average number of paying passengers divided by average number of available seats.

g. Average distance covered between takeoff and landing while in revenue service.

h. Average distance traveled on the routes of the indicated airline.

i. Route-miles are as of June 30, 1969.

examines the Board's decision in 1944 to establish the carriers as a separate group and examines their early operations and subsidization. It concludes with a study of CAB decisions in the late 1940s and early 1950s concerning the renewal of the carriers' temporary certificates of public convenience and necessity.

Chapter 5 traces the CAB's efforts to "strengthen" the local service carriers while still preventing them as much as possible from competing with the trunklines. The Board removed certain restrictions on the operations of these carriers, transferred to them a large number of the trunklines' stations, instituted a policy of allowing local carriers to drop weaker stations, and undertook to improve the financial position of the carriers by raising subsidy payments and allowing a higher rate of return so as to permit them to modernize their aircraft fleets.

Chapter 6 concentrates on post-1966 policies, which abandoned the general policy of discouraging direct local service–trunkline competition and attempted to reduce subsidy payments by internalizing the subsidy. Chapters 4–6 also examine the impact of CAB route and subsidy policies (and of the pattern of their evolution) on the cost performance of the local service carriers, particularly as reflected in equipment choice. It is argued that these policies have encouraged local carriers to base their equipment purchase decisions on their longer, denser routes, and that this equipment has proved to be totally inappropriate for shorter, low-density routes.

In the final section, Chapter 7 examines the level of service being provided today to the communities that depend entirely on the local service carriers for their scheduled certificated air service. This service is found to be of such low quality that in a large number of cases it obviously does not provide any real improvement over other available modes of transportation. On the other hand, the cost to the government of providing this service is found to be substantial, and it is suggested that this cost may not have declined and may even have risen over the past fifteen years. In view of these findings, Chapter 8 suggests four options open to the government in its future policy toward support of local air service and the local service carriers: (1) to end all support for local air service; (2) to provide the support needed to compensate the local service carriers fully for the level of service they currently provide; (3) to encourage the local carriers to subcontract service at existing marginal locations to air taxi operators; or (4) to contract directly with air carriers (primarily air taxis) to provide specified services in return for lump-sum subsidy payments at the relatively few points where continued federal support of local air service is deemed worthwhile. The book concludes by suggesting the criteria on which the government should base its choice among these options.

While this book was in press, the CAB announced that it would seek permission from Congress to introduce a limited direct competitive bidding scheme, such as is outlined in Option 4 in Chapter 8. As support for its proposal, it released in late March 1972 a three-volume study entitled

Service to Small Communities, prepared by the staff of its Bureau of Operating Rights. The CAB study, conducted independently of the present volume and not available outside the Board prior to its official release, identifies the same problems with the current method of subsidy payment and reaches many of the same conclusions as to what can be done to improve the subsidy program.

CHAPTER TWO

The Demand for Short-haul Air Service

FACTORS AFFECTING the demand for short-haul air service and the relative importance of those factors will be discussed in this chapter. Most of the studies that are reported here have used data from the denser short-haul markets that until recently were served primarily by the trunklines. In generalizing these results to all short-haul markets of both high and low density, it is assumed that the relative impact on each of the factors affecting demand is similar. Any available evidence on short-haul, low-density markets is also presented.

An alternative would be to estimate separate demand functions for trunk and local service carriers and to consider the local service demand function to be representative of the low-density markets. A major objection to this approach is that the carrier-group identity of the carrier in a specific market often is an historical accident or a reflection of CAB policy concerning the proper division of functions between trunk and local carriers. Many of the markets once served by trunks are now served exclusively by local carriers; and there have even been a few cases where the reverse has occurred.

One important distinction between the two carrier groups is that the government has established a basic "demand" for service in the lowest-density markets served by the local service carriers by subsidizing such service. How the government has chosen the basic level of service it will support and how variations in this "demand" have affected the carriers is discussed in Chapters 4–6.

The Demand for Passenger Transportation

Much of the current research on the demand for travel suggests that it is a mistake to consider in isolation the demand for any single mode of transportation, such as air travel. The classic gravity model in its simplest form hypothesizes that total travel between any two points increases in proportion to the product of the populations at the two points and decreases in proportion to the square of the distance between them. Additional influences on total travel are assumed to include such factors as the cost of travel and the frequency and quality of service. Increases in the population of either locality, or improvements in the quality of the transportation network linking them, serve to increase travel. Similarly, reductions in the cost of service (including both ticket price and travel time, with the latter reflecting the opportunity cost of a traveler's time) are assumed to have a stimulating effect on travel.

More complex models, such as the abstract mode model of Quandt and Baumol, suggest that the choice of travel mode is determined solely by the characteristics of each relative to those of other modes. Examples of these characteristics are the price (again including the implicit value of the traveler's time), frequency, and timing of the service. Travelers are assumed to have no inherent preference for any one mode of travel.[1] Taken together, these models indicate that an attempt to determine the factors affecting the demand for air travel solely as a function of such variables as the price of air travel, its frequency, and so on, must proceed under a strong and somewhat unrealistic *ceteris paribus* assumption concerning all other travel modes. Conclusions from studies of a single mode, therefore, should be interpreted with some caution.

Unfortunately, demand studies using gravity models, while they are useful in explaining the total amount of travel between two points, do not tell much about the demand for any particular mode of travel, at least as they have been formulated up to now. On the other hand, abstract mode models are still in their infancy. Therefore, it will be necessary to rely to some degree on single-mode studies in spite of their limitations.

The Size of the Short-haul Air Travel Market

For purposes of this chapter, a *short-haul airline market* is defined as one that is less than five hundred miles in length, unless otherwise specified. In

1. Admitting that some travelers are reluctant to fly, Richard E. Quandt and William J. Baumol try to correct for it by using dummy variables. See "The Demand for Abstract Transport Modes: Theory and Measurement," *Journal of Regional Science*, Vol. 6 (August 1966), pp. 13–26. See also Richard E. Quandt (ed.), *The Demand for Travel: Theory and Measurement* (D. C. Heath, 1970).

Table 2-1. City Pairs, Passengers, and Passenger-miles, Short-haul Air Markets and All Air Markets, 1968

Domestic one-way trip length (miles)	City pairs		Passengers		Passenger-miles	
	Number	Per-cent	Number (thousands)	Per-cent	Number (thousands)	Per-cent
Short-haul air markets						
0–49	150	0.3	77	0.1	3,120	a
50–99	620	1.1	1,373	1.3	113,341	0.1
100–149	976	1.7	4,422	4.3	551,212	0.6
150–199	1,373	2.4	7,806	7.5	1,441,149	1.7
200–249	1,642	2.9	8,504	8.2	1,945,725	2.3
250–299	1,831	3.2	6,691	6.4	1,884,981	2.2
0–299, total	6,592	11.6	28,873	27.8	5,939,528	6.9
300–349	1,931	3.4	5,227	5.0	1,754,572	2.0
350–399	1,961	3.4	5,130	4.9	1,934,585	2.3
400–449	2,079	3.6	5,170	5.0	2,240,559	2.6
450–499	2,072	3.6	4,224	4.1	2,090,882	2.4
0–499, total	14,635	25.6	48,624	46.9	13,960,126	16.2
All U.S. air markets	57,060	100.0	103,746	100.0	85,939,318	100.0

Source: Civil Aeronautics Board, *Handbook of Airline Statistics, 1969 Edition* (1970), p. 386.
a. Less than 0.05 percent.

some of the studies referred to, however, markets of more than three hundred miles are classified as medium-haul. Although the airplane generally is thought of as a means of long-distance transportation, Table 2-1 shows that the markets classified here as "short-haul" constitute a substantial portion of the total market for air transport.

In 1968, the year to which the data in Table 2-1 refer, the local service carriers originated 22 million passengers. Since in 1967, 92 percent of all local service carrier on-line originations were for trips of 400 miles or less,[2] it seems that the locals carried only about half of the short-haul air passengers. Local carrier participation in many of the most lucrative short-haul markets, such as Boston–New York (190 miles, 2.4 million passengers), New York–Washington (216 miles, 1.9 million passengers), and Los Angeles–San Francisco (354 miles, 1.7 million passengers) was minimal. However, there were relatively dense markets in which the locals participated to a significant degree; two examples are Philadelphia–Pittsburgh

2. Eastern Airlines, "Eastern Airlines' Proposal for a Revised Fare Structure" (Eastern, July 1969; processed), p. 6.16.

(268 miles, 292,000 passengers in 1968), of which Allegheny Airlines carried about half, and Albany–New York (138 miles, 169,000 passengers), of which Mohawk Airlines carried 85 percent.

A Portrait of the Short-haul Air Traveler

The Census Bureau's *National Travel Survey*, together with relatively meager information made available by the carriers themselves, provides a portrait of the short-haul air traveler. More than half of all air travel is still for business reasons, though this proportion is declining. In 1967, 51 percent of all commercial air trips were made either for direct business purposes or to attend conventions.[3] Business is the reason for at least as large a proportion of short-haul air travel. Surveys taken in the 1960–62 period by Ozark Air Lines showed that 80 percent of its passengers were traveling on business. A similar survey taken in 1961 by Central Airlines found that 56 percent of its passengers were traveling on either private or government business, and 16 percent were traveling under military orders.[4]

These data refer to trips, not travelers, and this distinction is important. American Airlines, in a travel survey made in 1963, found that only 10 percent of its travelers took 57 percent of the airline trips.[5] The median number of airline trips per year, per passenger responding to the Ozark survey, was about ten. Two-thirds of Ozark's passengers had traveled by air more than five times in the previous year; more than one-fourth had made between six and seventeen trips; another fourth had made between eighteen and sixty-five air trips; and about 11 percent had made more than sixty-five trips by air in the preceding year.[6] One would assume that most of these frequent travelers were traveling for business purposes.

Although business is the predominant reason for short-haul air travel, most short-haul business travel is done by automobile. In 1967 only about 1 percent of all trips of less than 200 miles were made by air, while almost 95 percent were by automobile. The importance of air travel rises sharply

---

3. U.S. Bureau of the Census, *Census of Transportation, 1967: National Travel Survey*, TC67-N1 (1969), p. 21.

4. "Study Pegs Local Air Markets," *Airlift, World Air Transportation*, Vol. 25 (November 1961), p. 19; and "Exclusive: Ozark's '62 Travel Study," *Airlift*, Vol. 26 (November 1962), p. 21; *Flight Magazine*, Vol. 49 (June 1962), p. 60.

5. American Airlines, Bureau of Travel Analysis, "A Profile of the Air Traveler" (American Airlines, 1963; processed), p. 3.

6. "Study Pegs Local Air Markets," p. 19.

as the length of trip increases; 12 percent of all trips in the 200–499-mile range were by air.[7] Yet during 1967 the average length of on-line passenger trips for the local service carriers was only 227 miles, and 92 percent of local service on-line passenger originations were for trips of 400 miles or less.[8] Ozark asked its passengers in 1960 how they would have traveled had Ozark's service been unavailable. Significantly, only 8.2 percent said they would not have made the trip. Automobile travel was the alternative for 40.2 percent; 37.1 percent said they would have taken a train; 6.9 percent designated private airplane; 6.1 percent would have ridden a bus; while 3.7 percent listed other means.[9]

Thus, the average short-haul air traveler is likely to fly relatively frequently and to be traveling on business. He generally has alternative modes of transportation available to him. He chooses air travel presumably because of its relative cost, speed, and convenience; changes in these factors could be expected to affect his choice.

Factors Affecting the Demand for Short-haul Air Service

Perhaps the best statement of the problem faced by the local service carriers in attracting traffic was made by the CAB in its original decision to create this class of air carriers:

In connection with this relatively low traffic potential [of smaller cities] we believe it is desirable to emphasize constantly the fact that in attempting to develop this potential, local air carriers will be competing with the most highly developed rail and highway transportation systems in the world. The highway system not only provides a network of motor bus lines but also the roadway for the private automobile. We must assume that this vehicle will continue to carry the vast majority of all short-haul passengers, as in the past, and perhaps increase the proportion somewhat after the war. The further development of these surface systems will also be intensified with increased emphasis after the war, and they will also reap the benefits of technical developments and improvements. These systems have their greatest utility in short-haul services.

7. U.S. Bureau of the Census, *National Travel Survey*, p. 21.
8. Eastern Airlines, "Proposal for a Revised Fare Structure," p. 6.16.
9. "Study Pegs Local Air Markets," p. 19. This evidence is in conflict with American Airlines' 1963 survey (cited above), which found that 94 percent of business air travelers (found to be 50 percent of all air travelers) traveling "near" distances (not otherwise defined) said they could not have made their trip except by air. During 1963 the average on-line passenger journey was 837 miles on American, but was only 190 miles for Ozark. This may help to explain the discrepancy.

The airplane, on the other hand, has had its greatest utility in the longer distance transportation market. In this market its outstanding characteristic of high speed gives it a great competitive advantage, and permits the fullest exploitation of its inherent characteristics. But this inherent competitive advantage diminishes sharply, with conventional type aircraft, as the length of the trip is reduced. Even in the long-haul market its speed advantage becomes less effective as the number of intermediate points at which landings must be made on each flight is increased.

Thus, in going into the small-city, short-haul market, the airplane will be faced with the most intense kind of competition, with its principal selling point, speed, greatly diminished in value. While it will still have advantages to offer, the differential in fare that it now appears will be necessary will counterbalance them to some extent. Five cents per mile, the figure generally considered as the prospective passenger fare, is approximately three times the average fare for motor bus transportation. In addition there are many other factors . . . which will affect the traffic potential, such as the distance between the airport and city center, the time of day at which service will be scheduled, the frequency and regularity of schedules, the mail departure requirements, the extent to which reservations will be necessary, and many other details which will vary according to the locality and the city size.[10]

Price

It is generally believed that the price elasticity of demand for air travel varies with the length of trip and that demand is relatively inelastic for short-haul trips. This view is shared by the local carriers. Robert E. Peach, president of Mohawk Airlines, in testifying about the industry's problems before a congressional committee in 1966, said:

It is our contention, based on 20 years of experience that a 5- to 10-percent reduction in short-haul fares will not stimulate traffic more than a minor amount—if at all—that short-haul air passengers are primarily business oriented. They respond not to a dollar or so fare reduction but [to] the frequency and timing of flight schedules, quality of reservations services, and the like.[11]

In 1966, Mohawk's average revenue per passenger was $17.98. The average length of its passenger on-line trip was 222 miles. These two figures imply that Mohawk's "yield" (average revenue per revenue passenger-mile) was 8.10 cents. (The average yield for the local carriers as a whole

10. *Civil Aeronautics Board Reports*, Vol. 6 (July 1, 1944–May 1946), pp. 2–3.
11. In *Review of the Local Air Carrier Industry*, Hearings before the Aviation Subcommittee of the Senate Committee on Commerce, 89 Cong. 2 sess. (1966), p. 413. See also "Eastern's Response to the Civil Aeronautics Board's Questions Regarding a Domestic Fare Structure," in Civil Aeronautics Board, Bureau of Economics, Rates Division, *A Study of the Domestic Passenger Air Fare Structure* (1968), p. 174; also, Eastern Airlines, "Proposal for a Revised Fare Structure," sec. 6.

during 1966 was 7.64 cents per revenue passenger-mile.) A 10 percent cut in Mohawk's average fare would have meant a saving to the passenger of only about $1.80, a fraction of the hourly salary of most businessmen. More significantly, the chief alternative mode of short-haul travel, the automobile, also costs about 8 cents a mile to operate;[12] and a rental car costs a flat daily rate of ten dollars or more, plus a mileage charge usually greater than 10 cents a mile, though this is offset to some extent by commercial discounts given by rental car agencies. Thus, most firms prefer that their executives and salesmen fly whenever any significant amount of time will be saved.

Gronau's work on the effect of travel time on the demand for passenger transportation emphasizes this point.[13] While these results should be treated with some caution, they do shed new light on this important topic. Gronau explicitly expanded the concept of travel cost to include what he refers to as the "price of travel time." Presumably this price reflects the opportunity cost of an individual's time. His results indicate that even when this price is presumed to be zero, for a single individual the automobile is a more expensive mode of transportation than the airplane for trips of more than 590 miles. As the "price of time" rises, the length of trip for which the automobile is the cheaper form of travel drops rapidly. At a price of time of only $4 an hour, the automobile is cheaper only for trips of less than 119 miles. However, increasing the price of time further does not serve to shorten appreciably the length of trip for which the automobile is the cheaper mode. Even at a price of travel time of $10 an hour, the switching distance is as high as 87 miles. Gronau's results are appreciably different if more than one person is making the trip. For a family of two adults and two children, the automobile is the cheapest mode for trips of 2,500 miles, even if the price of travel time for the family as a whole is approximately $4 an hour. Gronau, however, did not include the cost of food and lodging en route.

As for the switching distances between modes of public transportation,

12. The average rate of reimbursement for automobile travel by companies is 8 cents a mile. See Reuben Gronau, "The Effect of Traveling Time on the Demand for Passenger Transportation," *Journal of Political Economy*, Vol. 78 (March/April 1970), note 13, p. 387.

13. Reuben Gronau, *The Value of Time in Passenger Transportation: The Demand for Air Travel*, Occasional Paper 9 (Columbia University Press, for National Bureau of Economic Research, 1970). A critique of Gronau's work is provided in Philip K. Verleger, Jr., "A Point-to-Point Model for the Demand for Air Transportation" (Ph.D. thesis, Massachusetts Institute of Technology, 1971), pp. 36–48.

Table 2-2. Distribution of Person-Trips,[a] by Distance and Mode of Travel, 1967
Percent

Distance[b] (miles)	All modes				Public modes		
	Auto-mobile	Bus	Train	Com-mercial air	Bus	Train	Com-mercial air
Less than 50	95.2	2.3	1.0	0.1	67.5	29.2	3.3
50–99	95.9	2.6	0.7	0.1	76.7	20.5	2.8
100–199	93.5	2.6	1.1	1.8	47.3	20.0	32.7
200–499	80.6	3.1	1.6	12.2	18.3	9.5	72.2
500–999	61.9	2.3	4.3	27.8	6.6	12.5	80.8
1,000 and over	55.5	1.5	3.2	36.6	3.7	7.8	88.6

Source: Bureau of the Census, *Census of Transportation, 1967: National Travel Survey*, TC67-N1 (1969), p. 21. Percentages may not add to 100 due to rounding.
a. For a definition of "person-trip," see *National Travel Survey* (mentioned in Source, above), p. 2.
b. One-way straight line miles.

Gronau concludes that air travel saves no time at all relative to rail travel for trips of less than 135 miles.[14] The public transportation modes in use for trips of less than 135 miles are rail (for higher-income passengers) and bus (for lower-income passengers).

For distances of more than 135 miles, air travel begins to cut sharply into the rail market, squeezing it out entirely at 176 miles. For trips of 176 miles or more, either air or bus is used. If a person's price of travel time is less than $4.70 an hour, he uses the bus for trips of up to 176 miles. If it is above that, he flies. The price of time necessary to induce a person to fly drops rapidly beyond 176 miles, becoming almost flat at about $2 an hour at 400 miles. Only if his price of travel time is less than $1 an hour will a person always take a bus rather than fly, regardless of the distance.

The choices of modes actually made by travelers in 1967 correspond roughly to those predicted by Gronau's model. For trips of less than 100 miles, air travel is used very little relative either to the automobile or to other modes of public transportation. In the 100–199-mile range all three modes of public transportation are used approximately equally, but the automobile predominates overall. Beyond 200 miles, air becomes the dominant public mode and begins to capture a major share of the total market (see Table 2-2). The importance of the automobile for trips of more than 1,000 miles presumably reflects the fact that in 1967 only 19.8 percent of all

14. Gronau does not comment on the use of helicopters by some businessmen. His rail data are for the year 1963, and his city pairs are centered on New York. These facts presumably account for the relatively good showing of rail transportation.

Table 2-3. Domestic Air Fare Structure for Jet First Class and Jet Coach, 1965
Cents per mile

Distance (miles)	Jet first class fare		Jet coach fare	
	East–West	North–South	East–West	North–South
100	17.71	18.89	11.26	14.34
200	12.03	12.74	8.51	9.95
300	10.14	10.69	7.59	8.48
400	9.19	9.67	7.14	7.75
500	8.62	9.06	6.86	7.31
600	8.24	8.65	6.68	7.02
800	7.77	8.13	6.45	6.65
1,000	7.49	7.83	6.31	6.43
1,300	7.22	7.54	6.18	6.23
1,600	7.06	7.37	6.10	6.10
1,900	6.95	7.24	6.05	6.02

Source: Civil Aeronautics Board, Bureau of Economics, Rates Division, "A Study of the Domestic Passenger Air Fare Structure" (CAB, 1968; processed), p. 232.

automobile trips were made by only one person, while 52.8 percent were made by groups of three or more.[15] The typical short-haul air passenger, as indicated by the survey data presented above, also is consistent with these results.

The pricing policies actually followed by the airlines have supported the theory that short-haul air travel is relatively price inelastic. Until 1952, the fare per mile was virtually constant, regardless of trip length, and air fare changes were made on a percentage basis. In that year, however, there occurred the first of several "dollar-per-ticket" fare increases by the trunk carriers, which raised the per-mile fare for short trips relative to that for long ones. These increases led to an increasingly sharp downward slope in the air fare structure over the years. The data in Table 2-3, which were taken from the CAB's domestic air fare structure study published in January 1968, show the taper in the fare prevailing in 1965. The study recommended that this downward slope be increased, a recommendation that echoed Peach's testimony in the hearings cited above. That the two fare increases approved during 1969 were aimed at doing just that is shown by the fact that the local service yield (average revenue per passenger-mile)

15. According to Gronau's figures, if a party of three traveling by automobile included two adults and one child, and if the price of time for the party was less than about $3 an hour, the automobile would be the cheaper mode in terms of total cost, even for trips of more than 2,500 miles.

rose by 15.1 percent during the fourth quarter of 1969, while the trunkline yield rose by only 9.2 percent.[16] The fare on Eastern's popular New York–Boston air shuttle, a service marketed on the basis of its convenience and frequency of service, rose from $15.24 to $20, an increase of 31 percent.

The belief by the local carriers that businessmen—their most important customers—are relatively insensitive to price has not blinded them to the price sensitivity of other significant groups in the public. The chronically low load factors of the local airlines have led them to be among the most innovative in tailoring new fares to attract price-sensitive travelers while making sure that businessmen did not qualify for them. The locals have been strong supporters of the youth fare and have led in making it a purely price discriminatory device. While most of the trunks have required youths to accept a no-advance-reservations service in return for their discount, many of the locals have had full-reservation youth fares since the early 1960s. In order to tap the other end of the age spectrum, Mohawk introduced in 1961 a "golden-age" excursion fare, which offered a one-third discount on fares to men over 65 and women over 62 who paid a $5 membership fee and agreed to fly between midnight and 1 p.m.

In the fall of 1966 Frontier Airlines tried to introduce a special ladies' fare, which would have provided a 50 percent reduction for a fifteen-day round trip ticket usable throughout Frontier's system. Complaints by Western Air Lines, Northwest Airlines, and Trailways Bus System led the Board to disapprove the proposal as "unduly discriminatory." In 1967 Frontier reintroduced its proposal, this time reducing the discount to 40 percent and seeking to place the fare into effect for 3 months and then only on routes over which it did not compete with other air carriers. The proposal was again rejected. Frontier had originally proposed the ladies' fare when it found that only 20 percent of its passengers were women and that most women travel for personal rather than for business reasons. Frontier's president was quoted as saying: "This, in itself, presents an untapped source of personal travel without serious dilution of existing revenues. . . . Instead of being discriminatory, men as a class would benefit from this reduced fare, since the ladies' fare would generally be paid for by husbands or other relatives."[17]

Another device with which the local carriers have attempted to tap price-sensitive submarkets is the off-peak fare.[18] For example, the fact that

16. *Aviation Week and Space Technology*, Vol. 92 (April 27, 1970), p. 35.
17. "Ladies' Fare Filed Again by Frontier," *Air Travel*, Vol. 23 (June 1967), p. 70.
18. Off-peak fares are not discriminatory in an economic sense but serve to even out capacity utilization. See Oliver E. Williamson, "Peak-Load Pricing and Optimal Ca-

such a high proportion of their customers are traveling on business has meant that the local carriers are subject to severe declines in traffic on weekends. In order to generate weekend traffic these carriers early adopted liberalized family plans that were applicable all week rather than, like the trunkline family plans, only on weekdays. Some also adopted "weekends unlimited" fares that allow unlimited weekend travel on their systems for a flat charge.

The local carriers also have been leaders in promoting the use of standby fares that give substantial discounts to persons willing to come to the airport without a reservation on the chance that seats will be available. Furthermore, they have taken the lead in extending such fares to all passengers—not just young persons and military personnel.

The behavioral evidence concerning local service pricing policies is thus consistent with the statistical evidence and the a priori belief that a major portion of short-haul air travel—business travel—is relatively insensitive to price, but that traffic can be increased through price discrimination or other devices designed to tap price-sensitive, nonbusiness markets.[19]

Improvements in Speed

It was argued above that when one takes into account the value a traveler places on his time, the airplane often is the cheapest mode of travel, even though the fare charged is usually higher than that of other modes of transportation. This suggests that, other things being equal, increasing the speed of air travel should increase the demand for this mode relative to that for other modes and should also have a positive impact on the total demand for travel.

The time spent in air travel consists of two parts: the time it takes to get to and from the air terminals and the time required for the actual flight, including that for intermediate stops and connections. For less than a certain distance (estimated by Gronau at 135 miles), an airplane saves no time relative to bus or rail. An example of this was indicated by a Mohawk

---

pacity under Indivisibility Constraints," *American Economic Review*, Vol. 56 (September 1966), pp. 810–27.

19. In 1967 over 40 percent (852,000) of Frontier's 2,000,000 passengers traveled under some sort of special fare arrangement. The family plan was used by 280,000; standby fare was next (no number given); and youth fare was third, attracting 116,000 users. "Frontier's Special Fares Build Volume," *Flight Magazine*, Vol. 57 (June 1968), p. 99.

Table 2-4. Best Cruising Speed and Flight Time by Length of Hop, Selected Aircraft, 1969

Type of aircraft	Best cruising speed (miles per hour)	Flight time (minutes)[a]			
		50-mile hop	100-mile hop	200-mile hop	400-mile hop
Douglas DC-3	167	22.6	40.7	76.8	149.2
Convair/Martin[b]	280	20.1	33.4	60.0	113.1
Convair 580	340	16.4	25.8	44.5	81.4
Douglas DC-9	560	16.4	22.8	35.0	61.1

Sources: *Aviation Week and Space Technology*, Vol. 84 (March 7, 1966), p. 199, and Vol. 91 (March 10, 1969), p. 149; Civil Aeronautics Board, "Local Service Air Carriers' Unit Costs, Year Ended March 31, 1969," Attachment A, pt. 1, p. 1; pt. 2, p. 1; pt. 5, p. 1; and pt. 4, p. 1.
a. Does not include ground taxi time, which is roughly the same for all types of aircraft.
b. Convair 240 and 340/440 and Martin 202 and 204.

Airlines executive in 1953. He observed that while a businessman seeking to go from downtown Buffalo to downtown Rochester, a distance of 55 miles, could fly between the two airports in only 28 minutes, the added time required to get to and from the airports raised the total travel time to 1.8 hours and reduced the average overall speed to only 37 miles an hour.[20] In 1953 Mohawk was flying DC-3s, but as Table 2-4 shows, even if DC-9s had been used on the route, the problem would not have been alleviated. The time required to get an aircraft into the air and down again varies little with its speed, and for short flights it is this time and not the time spent at cruising speed that matters.

This also shows why the local carriers are particularly sensitive to such factors as air traffic congestion that tend to increase trip time. In 1968, the average local service hop of 130 miles required only 34 minutes. A delay of 15 minutes due to air traffic congestion at the hub terminal from which a flight originates would increase the total flight time by almost 50 percent and reduce the average airport-to-airport speed from 232 to 160 miles an hour. A delay of one hour, not uncommon today during peak traffic periods at New York, Chicago, or Washington, would lower the average speed to 84 miles an hour, not substantially faster than the speed attainable in an automobile on an interstate highway. The apparent success of the high-speed Metroliner on the 228-mile Washington–New York railroad run is further evidence that for short distances the fastest way to travel is not always by air.

20. David E. Postle, "The Transport Helicopter in Local Service Operations," *Flight Magazine*, Vol. 39 (June 1953), p. 34.

Another factor that cuts down the inherent speed advantage of the airplane for short distances is the need to make intermediate stops. In 1968 the average local service passenger traveled 248 miles. Since the average length of hop was about 130 miles, this means that he was required to make one stop en route. Suppose that the passenger in question was traveling on a DC-9. A 250-mile nonstop flight on a DC-9 takes 42 minutes, which implies a speed of 357 miles an hour. A single 20-minute stop midway through the flight, that required no diversion from the original line of flight, would reduce the effective speed to about 210 miles an hour. These times do not include time spent traveling to and from the airports and are based on the assumption that a flight is ready to leave whenever the passenger desires.

If an airline were free to vary the type of flights it offered, it would offer nonstop flights whenever there was enough traffic. Intermediate stops would be made only if the additional traffic they generated more than offset the loss of passengers resulting from the lower quality of service offered and the additional operating costs incurred in making the stops. A carrier might choose to operate smaller, lower-cost equipment in a skip-stop pattern (landing at different intermediate points on each flight and thereby increasing the average stage length) if the improvement in service quality generated enough traffic. As will be seen below, the local carriers have not generally been free to make such scheduling decisions. The Board has placed restrictions of varying stringency on their scheduling in order to prevent trunk–local service competition in certain markets and to assure the provision of a certain minimum level of service to marginal communities. The efforts of the local carriers to modify these restrictions and the effect of the restrictions on local service operations will be discussed in detail below. At present the point to be illustrated is that factors that add to total travel time, such as congestion and intermediate stops, reduce the attractiveness of short-haul, much more than long-haul, air travel. While carriers in long-haul markets can overcome such problems to some extent by using faster equipment, this solution is of limited benefit in short-haul markets.

While air carriers operating in short-haul markets have been able to increase effective aircraft speeds by only a limited amount, improvements in other modes of transportation (generally excluding the railroads) have increased the average speed of their closest competitors. Since World War II the United States has undertaken massive federally financed road building, of which the Interstate Highway System is the main example. Federal aid highway mileage increased from 233,000 in 1945 to 911,000 in 1967. The improvement in roads raised the average speed of automobiles and buses from 45.0 and 45.5 miles an hour, respectively, in 1945 to 59.5 and 59.4 miles an hour in 1967.[21] This represents an increase of about 33 percent since the end of World War II. In 1947 express bus service between New York City and Washington, D.C., was scheduled at 7.5 hours. In 1965 better roads and improved equipment brought the same trip down to 4 hours and 10 minutes. (In 1948 a nonstop DC-6 flight between New York [La Guardia Airport] and Washington was scheduled for 1 hour and 20 minutes. In 1968 the same flight was scheduled for 50 minutes [American Airlines, Boeing 727] to one hour [Eastern, DC-9], but actual elapsed times were running considerably longer due to congestion.)

Louis Kohlmeier recently provided an even more graphic example of the impact on short-haul, feeder-type air service of improvements in alternative modes of transportation. In 1957 Rockford, Illinois, a city of 135,000, provided 80 passengers a day for Ozark Airlines. At that time Ozark flew six flights a day each way between Rockford and Chicago, a distance of 70 miles, offering good connections with flights from the Chicago airports. The flying time of a DC-3 was 38 minutes. The opening of the Northwest Tollway reduced the driving time between Chicago and Rockford to approximately one hour. (The Tollway connects directly with Interstate 90, which in turn passes close to O'Hare Field, Chicago's busiest airport.) As if this did not create enough problems for Ozark, the improvement in the roads prompted the Rockford Chamber of Commerce to sponsor an express bus service offering six round trips a day between O'Hare and Rockford. The price of a one-way trip, which required 90 minutes, was $5.00—half of Ozark's fare. Ozark's response was to reduce the frequency of its service. By 1965 Rockford's average daily passenger originations had fallen to 22. By 1969 the city was generating only 9 passengers a day.[22]

Frequency and Timing of Service

Another factor having an obvious impact on the demand for short-haul service is the frequency of the service provided. Of the 124 exclusively

21. U.S. Bureau of the Census, *Statistical Abstract of the United States, 1969*, p. 543, No. 809, and p. 547, No. 817. These figures are based on the actual speed of each vehicle on tangent sections of main rural highways during off-peak hours.

22. Louis M. Kohlmeier, Jr., *The Regulators: Watchdog Agencies and the Public Interest* (Harper & Row, 1969), p. 180. Kohlmeier lists several other cases in which highway improvements have had a direct adverse effect on short-haul air traffic.

served local service stations where traffic fell off between 1968 and 1969, flight frequency had fallen at 101 of them. The average reduction in the number of flights per station per year was 11.1 percent, from 2,240 to 1,968. On an average, traffic at these stations dropped by 11.0 percent, from 16,802 in 1968 to 14,944 in 1969.

For a person using short-haul air transportation in getting to a final destination, high frequency makes it more likely that he can depart at a preferred time. For a person using short-haul air service to connect with a long-haul flight, high frequency means that airport waiting time will be minimized. In the area of frequency, short-haul air service faces its chief competition from the automobile—either owned or rented. Theoretically, the frequency of this travel mode is infinite. Put another way, the reciprocal of frequency—the mean expected time until the next departure—is zero. Gronau's results, cited above, take no explicit account of the frequency of service offered. Gronau implicitly assumes that for every mode a vehicle is ready to leave at the request of the passenger. The fact that his data covered thirty-eight city pairs, all centered on New York, probably means that all the modes in his sample offered the maximum frequency of service to be found.

A recent study provides some interesting findings concerning the direct impact of frequency on the demand for air service and how this impact varies with trip distance.[23] This study covered bus, automobile, and vertical/short takeoff and landing (V/STOL) aircraft. There appears to be no problem in generalizing the result slightly to cover conventional aircraft. The main effect of this would appear to be to lower the market share obtainable by air transport in proportion to the time required in traveling to and from a conventional airport. Comparisons throughout the study were based on a bus service offering twenty departures a day, and the automobile departing when the traveler wished. The average speed of both automobile and bus was assumed to be 36 miles an hour (probably a valid assumption if urban driving is included). The V/STOL aircraft was assumed to average 400 miles an hour.

Figure 2-1 summarizes the results and shows that even for a high speed V/STOL aircraft, where distances are short and travel alternatives are of high quality, a very high frequency of air service is required to capture an

23. R. W. Simpson and M. J. Neuve Eglise, "A Method for Determination of Optimum Vehicle and Frequency of Service for a Short-Haul V/STOL Air Transport System," Report R-68-1 (Massachusetts Institute of Technology, Flight Transportation Laboratory, May 1968).

Figure 2-1. Share of Potential Market Attainable by Vertical/Short Takeoff and Landing Aircraft in Competition with Automobiles and Buses, as a Function of Length of Trip and Frequency of Service

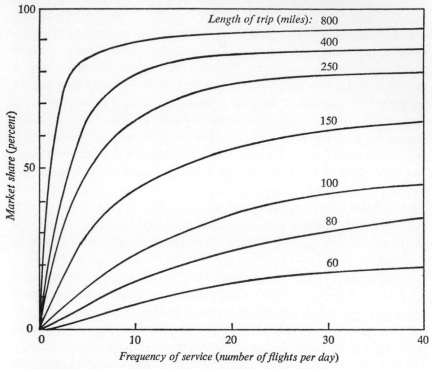

Source: Simpson and Neuve Eglise, p. 20. (Cited in note 23 to this chapter.)

appreciable share of the traffic. At a distance of 100 miles, a V/STOL service offering five flights a day would capture approximately 10 percent of the market. Increasing the V/STOL frequency to thirty flights a day—an average of more than one an hour—would increase the V/STOL market share only to 45 percent. It also appears that as distance increases or the available travel alternatives become less desirable (due perhaps to geographic barriers to surface travel), relatively few flights a day are enough to capture most of the potential market. For a trip of 400 miles (still assuming that the alternatives are to offer twenty departures a day by bus and departures by private car when the traveler wishes) a V/STOL frequency of five flights a day would capture about 70 percent of the maximum potential travel market. At distances of 800 miles, a frequency of only two trips a day would capture the same portion of the potential travel market.

Table 2-5. History of Air Service, Augusta, Maine, 1960–69

Year	Number of passengers enplaned and deplaned[a]			Number of flights per week between Augusta and Boston[b]			One-way fare, Augusta–Boston (dollars)	
	North-east Airlines	Execu-tive Airlines	Total	North-east Airlines	Execu-tive Airlines	Total	North-east Airlines	Execu-tive Airlines
1960	13,730	...	13,730	20	...	20	12.25	...
1961	11,598	...	11,598	13	...	13	13.60	...
1962	8,273	...	8,273	14	...	14	14.05	...
1963	8,502	...	8,502	14	...	14	14.05	...
1964	11,761	...	11,761	26	...	26	14.05	...
1965	14,957	...	14,957	20	...	20	14.05	...
1966	18,091	1,033[c]	19,124	26	19	45	14.05	16.00
1967	23,556	12,781	36,337	20	25	45	16.70	17.00
1968	22,758	21,113	43,871	20	27	47	17.00	18.09
1969[d]	19,855	27,180	47,035	20	27	47	19.00	20.00

Source: Systems Analysis and Research Corporation, "Proposal by Executive Airlines for Improving Scheduled Airline Service in Maine, New Hampshire, Vermont and Massachusetts" (Cambridge, Mass.: SARC, 1969; processed), pp. 17–18.
a. Includes Waterville and Augusta.
b. Southbound.
c. September–December.
d. Projected on the basis of January–June 1969.

The experience of the air taxis has reinforced the belief that frequency of service is more important than ticket price in attracting traffic in short-haul markets where good travel alternatives exist. In almost every case the air taxis have emphasized frequency as the main selling point of their service. The example of Executive Airlines in the Boston/Augusta, Maine, market is illustrative.[24] (Table 2-5 shows traffic, frequency, and fares in this market between 1960 and 1969.) Between 1960 and late 1966, Northeast Airlines, a trunkline, was the only carrier in the market. In the early 1960s Northeast cut its flight frequency by 30 percent. During the same period traffic fell by 40 percent. Between 1963 and 1965 Northeast restored its previous level of service, and traffic increased to above its former level. Executive Airlines entered the market in September 1966 using 20-seat De Havilland Twin Otters, while Northeast used 44-passenger Fairchild FH-227s.[25] Between 1965 and 1967, weekly flight frequencies increased by 125 percent, and traffic rose by 143 percent. It should be noted that North-

24. Augusta is located on the Maine Turnpike, completed in 1965, which connects it with Portland and Boston.
25. These aircraft were acquired at the beginning of 1967. Previously Northeast used DC-3s on this route.

east apparently benefited from the additional service provided by Executive, though it is not known how many persons flew one way on Northeast and the other on Executive. Note also that by 1969 Executive was attracting substantially more traffic than Northeast, in spite of the higher fares of the former.

While more frequent service improves the chances that a traveler will find a flight leaving at a convenient time, certain departure times during the day are obviously more generally desirable than others. Most airline executives agree that 8:30 a.m. and 5:30 p.m. are two such desirable times, and they schedule flights accordingly.[26] A morning flight can get a businessman to his destination in time for a full day's work. A 5:30 p.m. flight allows him to get home without having to spend the night. An attempt to measure the impact of scheduling on demand has been made by A. W. Schoennauer, who sought to quantify schedule quality by assigning a series of penalties to flights based on whether they intruded into certain times of the day.[27] The hours between 9:00 a.m. and 3:00 p.m. were designated as "prime business time"; those between midnight and 6:00 a.m. as "prime rest time." The remaining time blocks were undesignated but viewed as having some attributes of each of the adjoining designated times. The hours between 6:00 a.m. and 9:00 a.m. and the hours between 6:00 p.m. and 9:00 p.m. were designated as "prime travel time." If travel time encroached on prime business time, the penalty per half hour was three points; if it encroached on prime rest time, two points were assessed per half hour. If it fell in one of the undesignated blocks, only one point was charged.

Only city pairs in metropolitan areas having between 10,000 and 100,000 households with a disposable annual income of $10,000 or more were selected. City pairs were chosen by pairing each city of 50,000 to 100,000 qualified households with each city having 10,000 to 49,999 such households. The fourteen U.S. standard metropolitan statistical areas (SMSAs) with over 100,000 households were eliminated in order to avoid the influence of the extremes. One hundred and twelve city pairs met the multiple criteria. Schoennauer divided his sample according to whether the city pairs were more or less than 450 miles apart. He discovered that his penalties were a significant factor in explaining traffic between cities separated

26. Roger Noll (in a personal conversation) observed that the time zone differential for long-haul east-west flights creates additional prime departure times.

27. "Airline Schedules and Their Impact upon Passenger Traffic," *Transportation Research*, Vol. 3 (April 1969), pp. 69–73.

by less than 450 miles, but that they had no significant influence for cities farther apart than that.[28]

These results coincide with a priori expectations. A businessman can compensate for poor airline schedules by traveling by car. This is a solution, however, only for relatively short distances. Once the trip distance exceeds a few hundred miles, the travel time by car is so great that it pays the traveler to wait even for a flight at an inconvenient time.

The Short-haul Dilemma

This chapter has shown that while short-haul air travel is not totally insensitive to price and while certain segments of the market may indeed be quite price sensitive, the major portion of the market (which consists of business-related travel) appears to respond more to the frequency and overall quality of service than it does to direct monetary cost. Businessmen fly because by doing so they save time; but one of the major sources of time saving available to airlines—the use of faster equipment—has a limited effect on short-haul travel because of the fixed amount of time that must be spent in taxiing, landing and taking off, and climbing and descending, regardless of the aircraft used. Therefore, the best way a local service carrier can make its service more attractive in markets where good travel alternatives are available is to increase the frequency and improve the timing of its schedules. This creates a dilemma, however. A frequency of six round trips a day between two cities—one flight every two hours between 7:00 a.m. and 7:00 p.m.—which is not at all a high frequency of service, will (on the basis of a seven-day week) provide space for 1,200 passengers a day, or 437,000 passengers a year, if a 100-passenger DC-9-30 is used. The use of a Convair 580 would generate half this number of seats. If a 50 percent load factor were required for the service to be self-supporting, the two cities would have to exchange 110,000 air passengers a year to support even six round trips a day by Convairs. In 1967, however, only ten markets—Philadelphia–Pittsburgh, Philadelphia–Washington, New York– Syracuse, Albany–New York, Chicago–Milwaukee, Los Angeles–Las Vegas, Binghamton–New York, Chicago–Madison, Chicago–Peoria, and Champaign–Chicago—generated more than 100,000 passengers a year for local service carriers. The only possible way in which high frequency ser-

28. The published results do not permit the computation of elasticities, and it is not certain that given his measure of scheduling quality, such data would be useful.

vice can be offered, therefore, is with smaller aircraft. But if a 15-passenger Beech 99 turboprop is used in providing six round trips a day, a 50 percent breakeven load factor would require the city pair to generate 33,000 passengers a year, which is far fewer than the number required for the DC-9-30, but still considerably above the traffic exchanged by most local service city pairs.[29] It is clear, therefore, that while the use of smaller aircraft can expand substantially the number of city pairs for which a frequent, convenient air service can be offered, the amount of traffic between most of the smaller communities and their major centers of commerce is so low that such a service cannot be supported by the revenues generated.

29. During 1964, the locals operated in 6,703 city-pair markets; only 561 of these generated more than 10 passengers a day (or 3,650 passengers a year). *Review of the Local Air Carrier Industry*, Hearings before the Aviation Subcommittee of the Senate Committee on Commerce, 89 Cong. 2 sess. (1966), p. 30.

CHAPTER THREE

The Costs of Short-haul Air Service

THE UNIT OPERATING COSTS experienced by the local service carriers are significantly higher than the unit operating costs of the trunklines. This has led some to suggest that the small size of these carriers is responsible and to recommend a policy of mergers as a cure. This chapter will examine the reasons for the local service carriers' higher cost. It will be shown that the primary factor responsible is the low-density, short-haul nature of their routes. Consequently, a policy of mergers among local service carriers would have little beneficial effect on costs, since it would leave both of these crucial elements unaffected. While policies designed to encourage the use of aircraft that are better suited to feeder-type operations could be expected to have a significant effect on costs, it is nevertheless true that providing short-haul, low-density air service will always be relatively expensive.

Prices of Factor Services

The primary factors of production purchased by the local service carriers are labor, fuel, aircraft, and capital. In purchasing the first three of these factors the local service carriers appear to face no disadvantage relative to the trunk carriers. This is not so of the fourth factor, however. Later chapters will show how regulation has served to accentuate this difficulty—at least until recently.

Cost of Labor of Pilots and Copilots

Wages and salaries make up the largest cost item for the local service carriers, about 40 to 50 percent of total operating costs; and compensation of pilots and copilots is the largest item in the wages and salaries category

31

(about 25 percent). Pilots and copilots of domestic airlines are compensated under complex rules that reflect both federal regulations and the results of negotiation between the carriers and the unions representing the pilots—primarily the Air Line Pilots Association (ALPA).[1] The pilot wage formula has four factors: longevity pay, hourly pay, mileage pay, and gross weight pay.

Longevity pay is based on the number of years accrued by a crew member in the pilot category. During a pilot's first year of employment this is the only pay he receives. Thereafter, longevity pay drops, and the other three elements account for most of his salary. The rate of pay a pilot receives for each *hour of flight time* depends on whether the flying is done during the day or at night and on the "pegged speed" of the aircraft he is flying. The pegged speed for each type of aircraft flown by a carrier is set by negotiation between the carrier and the ALPA. While it bears some relation to the actual speed of the aircraft, Baitsell reports that it also is used sometimes to spread the productivity gains of larger, faster equipment to those pilots who fly a carrier's slower, smaller equipment.[2] *Mileage pay* is determined by multiplying flying hours (computed as described above) by the pegged speed of the aircraft being flown. Baitsell says that for some carriers all miles flown beyond a specified number are paid for at a higher rate, thus giving an advantage to pilots of higher-speed aircraft. Again, the importance of the negotiated "pegged speed" is evident. *Gross weight pay* is determined by the certified maximum gross weight of each aircraft model. (The maximum gross weight of an aircraft is the maximum weight the aircraft is allowed to carry into the air. It includes airframe, engines, fuel, and all payload.) The gross weight to be applied is also subject to negotiation, but Baitsell does not report any instance of its being used to aid any particular pilot group.

The major aims of the ALPA in negotiating pay elements have been to capture for the pilots a share of the increased productivity of larger, faster aircraft and to distribute these gains among all the pilots employed by an airline, whether they fly the more productive equipment or not. Table 3-1

1. The method of compensation is outlined in some detail in an excellent study by John M. Baitsell, *Airline Industrial Relations: Pilots and Flight Engineers* (Harvard University, Graduate School of Business Administration, Division of Research, 1966), particularly Chap. 4. Until 1951, copilots were on flat salaries, but since then their pay has been determined similarly to that of pilots. *Ibid.*, pp. 95–96.

2. *Ibid.*, pp. 89–90. Baitsell reports that one trunkline established a pegged speed of 300 miles an hour for all of its piston equipment. This pegged DC-3 speeds at a level higher than the maximum cruise speed of the aircraft, to the advantage of the DC-3 pilots.

Table 3-1. Crew Costs and Aircraft Productivity for Local Service Air Carriers, by Type and Model of Aircraft, 1968

Type and model of aircraft	Crew costs (cents per aircraft-mile)	Productivity[a] (seat-miles per hour)
Pure jet		
Douglas DC-9-30	31.2	27,019
Douglas DC-9-10	31.5	21,244
British Aircraft Corporation BAC-111-200	39.2	15,232
Turboprop		
Convair CV-580	33.3	10,382
Convair CV-600	31.2	7,240
Fairchild F-27	33.4	6,424
Fairchild Hiller FH-227	34.0	7,452
Nihon YS-11	32.2	10,560
Nord N-262	38.2	3,480
Piston		
Convair CV-340/440	38.8	6,989
Martin M-404	31.6	6,247
Douglas DC-3	37.9	2,883

Source: Civil Aeronautics Board, *Aircraft Operating Cost and Performance Report for Calendar Years 1967 and 1968* (August 1969), Vol. 3, pp. 25–29.

a. Average block-to-block speed (see note 3 to this chapter) multiplied by the number of seats per aircraft.

shows that the ALPA has been relatively successful in capturing productivity gains. It compares pilot and copilot costs and aircraft productivity for each of the aircraft with a two-man flight crew that was flown by the local service airlines in 1968. For most aircraft, whatever their productivity, pilot pay averaged between 31 and 34 cents a mile. Three of the exceptions were relatively low-productivity aircraft, the Nord 262, the DC-3, and the Convair 340/440, which may reflect the ALPA's success in spreading productivity gains to the pilots of these aircraft.

The fourth exception was a high-productivity aircraft, the BAC-111-200, which was flown only by Mohawk Airlines. The higher crew costs may reflect the severe congestion at several of the airports where Mohawk operated the aircraft. A large portion of Mohawk's BAC-111 flights either originated or terminated at Boston, New York, or Washington—all of which are noted for airport congestion. In 1968, the ratio of block-to-block[3] to airborne hours for Mohawk's BAC-111s was 1.29. This means that almost one-third of an hour was spent taxiing, awaiting clearance to

3. Block-to-block hours measure the time the aircraft is moving under its own power, from the time it first moves away from the gate until it stops at the gate at its next destination.

Table 3-2. Pilot and Copilot Expenses, Speed, and Stage Length for Selected Aircraft, Domestic Trunk and Local Service Airlines, 1968

Item	DC-9-30		FH-227	
	Domestic trunks	Local service	Domestic trunks	Local service
Pilot and copilot expense per revenue mile (cents)	37.4	31.2	44.0	34.0
Average block speed (miles per hour)	288	271	154	162
Average flight stage length (miles)	283	204	108	110

Source: Civil Aeronautics Board, *Aircraft Operating Cost and Performance Report* (August 1969), pp 18, 21, 26, 27.

take off, or awaiting gate position upon landing, for every hour actually spent airborne. The equivalent ratio for the DC-9-10 was 1.22 and for the DC-9-30, 1.25. Thus Mohawk's BAC-111 pilots spent more time on an average in unproductive ground maneuvering than did the pilots of other local service carriers.[4]

Table 3-2 shows the ALPA's success in its second aim of distributing productivity gains to all crew members regardless of the aircraft they actually fly. It compares crew costs per mile for two aircraft flown by both the trunklines and the local carriers. The aircraft were flown over roughly the same kinds of route patterns by both carrier groups, but each aircraft was a relatively productive one for the local carriers and was flown by high seniority crews; it was a low productivity aircraft for the trunklines and was flown by crews with low seniority. Per-mile crew costs were higher for the trunklines than for the local carriers for both aircraft.

This sketch of the ALPA's aims in pilot pay negotiation suggests that a local carrier acquiring high productivity aircraft must anticipate an increase in pilot and copilot expenses on its older, less productive aircraft. Indeed, DC-3 pilot and copilot costs per mile (after staying relatively constant for many years) increased sharply in the years after the local carriers acquired jets.[5] The ALPA's position on pilot compensation for less productive air-

4. Eastern Airlines has estimated that air traffic delays cost it more than $137 million during the 1967–69 period. Much of Eastern's additional cost was attributed to crew salaries that had to be paid while aircraft were waiting in queues. (Kenneth J. Stein, "Eastern Places Three-Year Cost of Traffic Delays at $137 Million," *Aviation Week and Space Technology*, Vol. 92 [April 27, 1970], pp. 30–31.)

5. Between 1966 and 1968 average crew costs per block-hour for the DC-3 rose from $36.00 to $48.09, or by 34 percent. During the same period crew costs per block-hour

craft also may be one factor behind Frontier Airlines' announcement that it would not acquire small air taxi–type planes because of "prohibitive" pilot pay scales but instead would attempt to turn over some of its thinner routes to an air taxi operator. It may explain in part also why West Coast reported pilot costs for its 6-passenger Piper Navajos of $27 per block-hour in 1967 while nonunionized air taxi operators were reporting average crew costs of $17 to $21 per block-hour for the Twin Otter, a 14- to 20-passenger turboprop, short-haul aircraft.

As will be seen in later chapters, the Civil Aeronautics Board (CAB) has often granted higher-density, competitive routes to the local carriers in the hope that this would reduce their reliance on federal subsidy. To serve such routes the carriers have acquired higher-productivity aircraft. The Board does not appear to have foreseen that this action would result in a substantial increase in a major component of operating costs on the lower-density routes and would serve to offset gains achieved by its original policy.

Cost of Other Labor

Although wages and salaries of pilots and copilots constitute the largest single labor expense item for the local carriers, the majority of airline personnel, almost 80 percent, seldom enter the air except as passengers. These are the mechanics, ticket sellers, baggage handlers, aircraft fuelers, general supervisors, and head office personnel. One would expect that such personnel would be drawn from the labor pool in the area served by each local carrier and that their wages would be at prevailing regional rates. To test this hypothesis a regression analysis was performed, with compensation per employee as the dependent variable. The measure of regional wage chosen as one independent variable was the median income for employed urban males for eight regions as reported in the 1960 Census.[6] Each carrier was assigned to the census region that most nearly corresponded to its area of operations. Admittedly a perfect fit between carriers and regions was not possible.

---

for the DC-9-10 rose from $86.09 to $88.43, or about 3 percent. Civil Aeronautics Board, *Aircraft Operating Cost and Performance Report for Calendar Years 1967 and 1968* (August 1969), Vol. 3, pp. 26, 28, and *Aircraft Operating Report . . . for Calendar Years 1965 and 1966* (September 1967), Vol. 1, pp. 23, 25.

6. U.S. Bureau of the Census, *U.S. Census of Population: 1960, General Social and Economic Characteristics, United States Summary*, Final Report, PC(1)-1C(1962), p. 289.

The regions, the states making up each, and the carriers assigned were as follows:

Northeast: Maine, New Hampshire, Vermont, Massachusetts, Rhode Island, Connecticut, New York, New Jersey, Pennsylvania (Mohawk Airlines, Allegheny Airlines)

East North Central: Ohio, Indiana, Illinois, Michigan, Wisconsin (Lake Central Airlines, North Central Airlines)

West North Central: Minnesota, Iowa, Missouri, North Dakota, South Dakota, Nebraska, Kansas (Central Airlines, Ozark Air Lines)

South Atlantic: Delaware, Maryland, District of Columbia, Virginia, West Virginia, North Carolina, South Carolina, Georgia, Florida (Piedmont Aviation)

East South Central: Kentucky, Tennessee, Alabama, Mississippi (Southern Airways)

West South Central: Arkansas, Louisiana, Oklahoma, Texas (Trans-Texas Airways)

Mountain: Montana, Idaho, Wyoming, Colorado, New Mexico, Arizona, Utah, Nevada (Frontier Airlines)

Pacific: Washington, Oregon, California, Alaska, Hawaii (Bonanza Air Lines, Pacific Air Lines, West Coast Airlines)

Another factor that presumably affects the wages paid is employee productivity. This was measured by revenue passenger-miles per employee. Other variables tested were the size of the carriers (measured by total employment), growth in traffic, and an index of the degree to which the local carriers' routes were competitive with those of the trunklines. The regressions were run on data for the years 1964 and 1965. Although a high degree of explanation was achieved, only the regional wage and productivity variables proved to be consistently significant and stable. The following equations show the results obtained for 1964 and 1965 using those two independent variables.

(1) 1965 wages (dollars) = 4,012 + 6.4 passenger-miles per employee
$$(2.6)^a$$
(thousands) + 0.35 regional wage (dollars)
$$(2.6)^a$$

$\bar{R}^2 = 0.48$, $F = 7.56$,[b] degrees of freedom = 10

(2) 1964 wages (dollars) = 4,293 + 6.0 passenger-miles per employee

(2.5)[a]

(thousands) + 0.25 regional wage (dollars)

(1.8)[c]

$\bar{R}^2 = 0.41$, $F = 5.99$,[b] degrees of freedom = 10
$\bar{R}^2 = R^2$ adjusted for degrees of freedom.
The numbers in parentheses are t-ratios.
a. Significant at 5 percent level.
b. Significant at approximately the 15 percent level.
c. Significant at 10 percent level.

One possible difficulty with these results is that they lump together all nonflying personnel. Differences in the average wage could come either from differences in factors of the sort mentioned above or from differences between carriers in the composition of the nonflying labor force. In an attempt to test this, another variable, the percentage of a carrier's maintenance that is contracted out (rather than performed "in-house"), was introduced into the equations. Mechanics make up a relatively large proportion of airline nonflying personnel, and this variable, which varies widely among the local carriers, might be expected to pick up fluctuations in the average wage resulting from variations in the composition of the labor force. There was indeed a fairly strong negative correlation between this variable and total airline employment, indicating that smaller carriers contract out much of their maintenance; but the variable was not significant in explaining intercarrier wage differentials for nonflying personnel.

A further fact that emerges is that the local service airlines generally pay average or above average wages for the region in which they operate. This is true particularly of carriers operating in the South.

The one group of workers that was omitted from the above discussion is stewardesses. An attempt was made to perform a similar analysis for this group of employees, but no variable was found that was significant in explaining stewardess wage differentials among local service carriers. Unfortunately, it was not possible to construct any proxy for the relative glamour of the different airlines or for the relative attractiveness of the various carriers' stewardess uniforms. The one factor that did emerge was that stewardesses are poorly paid relative to nonflying employees. In 1966 the average wage of nonflying personnel for the local carriers as a group was $6,952 a year, while the average wage of stewardesses was $4,885 a year. The relatively unskilled nature of the work and the short average tenure may account for this as much as does the airlines' exploitation of the glamour of flying.

Cost of Fuel

The most important factors explaining variances in fuel prices are the differences in the grades of fuel used by piston and by turbine-powered aircraft, differences in fuel tax policies by state and by grade of fuel, and regional differences in fuel prices.

The fuel used in piston aircraft is high-octane aviation gasoline, while turbine fuel is low-octane kerosene. Until 1970 there was a 2-cents-a-gallon federal tax on piston fuel but no federal tax on turbine fuel. While states generally follow the federal precedent in taxing piston fuel and not taxing turbine fuel, they vary widely in the taxes they apply. As of 1968, twenty-nine of the forty-eight contiguous states had no tax on aviation fuel of either grade, and thirty-three states did not tax jet fuel. Ten states had the same tax on both grades of fuel, and five taxed jet fuel at a lower rate. Michigan had the highest tax, 5 cents a gallon on certain grades of both aviation and jet fuel; six states had taxes of 1 cent a gallon or less.

In the fourth quarter of 1966 the average piston fuel price (including tax) for the local carriers was 19 cents a gallon; the equivalent turbine fuel price was only 11.1 cents a gallon. These prices vary widely by region. As would be expected, Trans-Texas Airways paid the lowest fuel prices—16.1 cents a gallon for piston and 8.7 cents a gallon for turbine fuel—while West Coast Airlines, a carrier operating in areas relatively remote from refineries, paid the highest fuel costs—23.3 cents a gallon for piston fuel and 12.7 cents a gallon for turbine fuel. There was no evidence that the local carriers paid higher than normal prices for the grades of fuel they used.

Cost of Aircraft

A third major input used by the local service carriers is aircraft and aircraft parts. Until recently, when they purchased their short-haul jets, the local carriers had bought most of their aircraft second hand. The exception to this was the F-27s purchased by the local carriers in the late 1950s and early 1960s. The DC-3s, Convair 240s, 340s, and 440s, and Martin 202s and 404s that formed the backbone of the local service pre-jet fleets were all purchased in the used aircraft market.

USED AIRCRAFT. It has generally been recognized that the used aircraft market approaches very closely the economist's concept of an ideal market. There are a number of dealers who specialize in buying and selling used aircraft; and maintenance requirements being what they are, any buyer is able to tell the condition of an aircraft he is interested in by checking the aircraft's log book. Furthermore, operating cost figures for each aircraft are widely known. Stephen P. Sobotka and Constance Schnabel[7] made use of these facts in devising a way of predicting the prices of used commercial aircraft. They pointed out that although the price of a new capital asset depends on its cost of production, once the asset is purchased, its price depends entirely on its value to its current or its future owners. An aircraft might cost $1 million new, but its price in the second-hand market would drop to scrap value if, once it was purchased, passengers refused to ride in it or another aircraft were produced that could perform the same service at less cost. Sobotka and Schnabel constructed a linear programming model that, given traffic forecasts for various routes, assigned aircraft to these routes based on their capacity and operating costs. For each time period the model produced a rental value for each aircraft, based on its usefulness in meeting traffic demands. These "rents" were summed and discounted, producing a "price" for each type of aircraft. The model correctly predicted that the price of used DC-7 series aircraft would quickly drop to scrap value because the task for which they were designed—long-range, high-speed flight—could be performed better by even the earliest jets. It also correctly predicted that DC-6B series aircraft, though older, would retain their value longer, since jets would not quickly displace them. More important for purposes of this study, the model correctly predicted that the prices of the used aircraft purchased by the local carriers would remain relatively constant over time due to the fact that improvements in aircraft technology were reflected primarily in larger, longer-haul aircraft, at least until the mid-1960s.

The Sobotka-Schnabel model predicted that a particular aircraft will be low in price if it is relatively inefficient; that is, for two aircraft of equal capacity and speed, the one with the higher operating cost will be priced lower. Thus aircraft that are inexpensive on the second-hand market may well be a very poor buy in the long run.[8]

7. "Linear Programming as a Device for Predicting Market Value: Prices of Used Commercial Aircraft, 1959–65," *Journal of Business*, Vol. 34 (January 1961), pp. 10–30.
8. Ideally, of course, the price of the less efficient aircraft would drop to the point where its lower price would compensate for its higher operating cost. This has indeed

NEW AIRCRAFT. In spite of many designs for a "true feeder aircraft" produced in the late 1940s, the 1950s, and the early 1960s, the only new aircraft purchased in any quantity by the local service carriers was the Fairchild F-27. Once the local carriers began to acquire jets, they were forced to turn to the new aircraft market also; until very recently there was no market for used short-haul jets. Prices in the new aircraft market are set by individual negotiation between the manufacturer and the airline, although list prices are announced, and actual sales prices do not deviate from them very widely.

Table 3-3 shows the cost of each aircraft owned by the local carriers as of March 31, 1969. Note particularly the high second-hand price of the F-27A relative to its new price and relative to the price of used Convair 240s, 340/440s, and Martin 404s, aircraft of roughly equal capacity and speed. Note also that new aircraft of equal productivity are priced approximately the same by different manufacturers, or relatively higher as productivity increases.

AIRCRAFT PARTS. While an aircraft is in production, and for several years after production ceases, the manufacturer can be counted on to have a supply of spare parts. In 1964, when local carriers were considering the advisability of converting their Convair 240s, 340s, and 440s to turboprop power rather than buying new turboprop aircraft, Convair placed advertisements in trade publications to assure carriers of the current and future availability of spare parts even though the aircraft had not been produced for several years. As aircraft become older and go out of general airline use, however, parts do rise in cost. The most striking example of this is the case of the DC-3. This aircraft was first introduced into airline service in 1936 and was considered obsolete when it began to be used by the local carriers in 1946. During World War II several thousand DC-3s were built, and a large supply of spare parts was stockpiled; after the war, production of the plane ceased. The local carriers acquired a substantial supply of parts at war surplus prices, but in the early 1950s these stocks began to be exhausted. It was then necessary for the local carriers to begin purchasing new parts, and the cost of parts rose substantially. In 1953 Frontier Airlines reported that the prices of parts for DC-3 engines had risen more than 300 percent over their 1947–50 average.

---

happened recently in the leasing market. The lease value of a DC-9-10 aircraft has fallen until it is as cheap to operate on a per-seat-mile basis as is the larger DC-9-30.

Table 3-3. Cost and Productivity of Aircraft Operated by Local Service Air Carriers, by Type and Model, March 31, 1969

Dollar amounts in thousands

Type and model of aircraft	Cost of airframes	Cost of engines	Total aircraft costs[a]	Productivity[b]
New turbojet				
Boeing B727-200	$4,729	$773	$5,569	92,026
Boeing B727-100	3,886	770	4,722	67,990
Boeing B737-200	2,693	524	3,447	64,260
Douglas DC-9-30	3,157	541	3,860	64,975
Douglas DC-9-10	2,581	549	3,289	50,310
British Aircraft Corpo-				
ration BAC-111-200	2,543	564	3,204	43,450
New turboprop				
Nihon YS-11A	1,284	222	1,723	17,520
Fairchild Hiller				
FH-227	1,117	196	1,510	15,340
Fairchild F-27J	877	180	1,190	14,112
Fairchild F-27A	747	179	1,029	14,064
Nord N-262	385	115	580	6,496
Converted turboprop				
Convair CV-580	722	216	1,090	18,126
Convair CV-600	427	226	739	14,490
Used turboprop				
Fairchild F-27A	643	95	806	14,064
New piston				
Piper PA-31	64	21	108	1,372
Used piston				
Convair CV-340/440	425	26	485	13,200
Convair CV-240	125	35	194	12,160
Martin M-404	209	36	279	11,200
Douglas DC-3	39	13	62	4,676

Sources: Civil Aeronautics Board, "Local Service Air Carriers' Unit Costs, Year Ended March 31, 1969" (processed), Attachment C, Pt. 3, p. 1; *Aviation Week and Space Technology*, Vol. 90 (March 10, 1969), pp. 149, 155, and Vol. 86 (March 6, 1967), p. 206.

a. Cost of airframes, engines, propellers, and communications equipment.

b. Productivity is measured by seat-miles per hour, computed as maximum seats times best cruise speed, or, for Piper, maximum cruise speed.

Cost of Capital

Table 3-4 shows the sources and use of funds of the local service carriers during four distinct periods of their financial history. In the first period, between 1945 and 1955, the carriers were operating under temporary cer- tificates of public convenience and necessity of three to five years' duration.

Table 3-4. Local Service Air Carriers, Changes in Sources and Uses of Funds During Significant Periods, 1945–69[a]
Millions of dollars

Source or use	1945–54	1955–60	1961–64	1965–69
Source of funds				
Depreciation	12.3	18.3	25.1	83.6
Long-term debt	1.9	41.9	26.0	451.3
Other noncurrent liabilities	...	0.2	0.3	−10.1
Deferred credits	...	0.4	2.8	−1.2
Preferred stock	0.3	−0.1	1.7	9.9
Common stock	11.0	4.8	16.9	93.3
Net income[b]	−0.8	2.3	23.5	−44.4
Other	0.9	2.9	−0.7	−37.7
Total	25.6	70.7	95.6	554.7
Use of funds				
Net working capital	1.3	−6.2	19.3	−49.9
Investments and special funds	0.6	1.9	10.5	8.0
Property and equipment	22.5	71.4	61.4	553.2
Deferred charges	1.0	3.5	1.1	41.2
Cash dividends[b]	0.2	0.1	3.3	2.2
Total	25.6	70.7	95.6	554.7
Federal subsidy[b]	136.2	203.2	264.5	247.7

Sources: Civil Aeronautics Board, *Annual Airline Statistics*, various editions; CAB, *Handbook of Airline Statistics*, various editions; CAB, *Air Carrier Financial Statistics*, Vol. 18 (December 1970).

a. Except as noted, the numbers shown represent the change in level that occurred between the beginning and the end of the period; for example, the 1955–60 data were derived by subtracting the 1954 level from the 1960 level.

b. Total for the period.

The Board was free in theory to terminate the existence of any carrier when its certificate expired. The carriers argued that the uncertainty of their continued existence made it impossible for them to float long-term debt. As Table 3-4 shows, during this period a large part of their externally generated funds came from the sale of common stock, most of which was held by their directors and management.[9]

The carriers finally prevailed upon Congress in 1955 to force the CAB to grant them permanent certificates, and during the next five years they received considerable additional help from Congress in improving their access to the capital markets. In 1957 Congress amended the Federal Bankruptcy Act to make certain of the equipment trust provisions of Chapter X of the act applicable to the aircraft and aircraft equipment of carriers.

9. This was still true as late as 1963. See Richard H. Vaughan, "A Financial Assessment of the Class Mail Subsidy Formula for the Local Service Airlines" (thesis, Stonier Graduate School of Banking, Rutgers University, 1963), p. 84.

This presumably increased the attractiveness of this source of financing by excluding any equipment so financed from bankruptcy proceedings in the event of a default. Shortly afterward Congress passed legislation authorizing the CAB to guarantee up to 90 percent of the principal and 100 percent of the interest on loans made to local service carriers for the purchase of flight equipment up to a maximum of $5 million per carrier. (This limit was raised to $10 million per carrier in 1962.) In 1958, legislation was passed exempting from taxation capital gains realized by subsidized carriers on the sale of flight equipment, provided such gains were used to purchase new flight equipment within a reasonable time. Finally, in 1959 the Federal Aviation Act was amended to facilitate the financing of aircraft engines and propellers.

These measures apparently had some effect, for during the 1955–60 period the local service carriers were able to float $42 million of long-term debt. About half of this debt, $20 million, was guaranteed by the government. Vaughan has argued, however, that even these actions by Congress did not have the effect of making the local carriers attractive to the financial community. Guaranteed loans were not particularly appealing to banks because of the red tape involved both in negotiating the loan and in securing payment in case of a default. The local carriers still had inadequate rates of return, and there were many uncertainties about subsidy payments.

In 1960 the CAB established an industry-wide "fair and reasonable" rate-of-return standard. As Table 3-5 shows, this standard provided a differential rate of return to the various elements making up a carrier's capital structure. The rate of return allowed a particular carrier depended on its actual capital structure, subject to the limits shown. The scheme provided a substantial incentive for carriers to resort to equity financing.

The unreasonableness of the extremely high return allowed on equity has been argued by Richard E. Caves, who correctly observes that if a carrier actually earned a 21.35 percent return on equity with any degree of regularity, the cost to it of floating additional equity would certainly be below this.[10] Table 3-6 shows the rates of return on equity and on total investment actually earned by the industry between 1949 and 1959. Both are extremely low and variable. Furthermore, the situation during the 1955–59 period was not appreciably better than that earlier.

The variability in the rate of return resulted in part from the method of

10. *Air Transport and Its Regulators: An Industry Study* (Harvard University Press, 1962), p. 402.

Table 3-5. Fair and Reasonable Rates of Return for Local Service Air Carriers, as Established by the Civil Aeronautics Board, 1947–72

Dates applicable	Rate of return
1947–59	Individually negotiated rates (generally 8.5 percent up to 1959, then 9.5 percent) while on "permanent" subsidy rate; 7 percent on total investment while on "temporary" subsidy rate.
1960–62	5.5 percent on debt, 21.35 percent on equity applied to carriers' actual capital structure; maximum of 12.75 percent on total investment, minimum of 9 percent; 7 percent on total investment while on "temporary" subsidy rate.
1963	Same as above, except 7.5 percent allowed on preferred stock. "Temporary" rate no longer applicable.
1964–66	5.75 percent on debt, 6.5 percent on convertible debentures, 7.5 percent on preferred stock, 16 percent on common stock. Same maximum and minimum rates.
1967–71	Same as above, except rate on common stock reduced to 14 percent.
1971	7.25 percent on debt, 20 percent on equity, which, applied to a 60/40 debt–equity ratio, yields 12.35 percent on total investment.

Sources: Richard H. Vaughan, "A Financial Assessment of the Class Mail Subsidy Formula for the Local Service Airlines" (thesis, Stonier Graduate School of Banking, Rutgers University, 1963), pp. 49–50; *Civil Aeronautics Board Reports*, Vol. 31 (May–September 1960), p. 685; Vol. 39 (September 1963–February 1964), p. 85; and Vol. 41 (August 1964–January 1965), pp. 148–50; "Board Shifts Policy on Subsidies," *Aviation Week and Space Technology*, Vol. 86 (April 10, 1967), pp. 36–37; CAB, Docket 21866-8, Domestic Passenger Fare Investigation, Phase 8 (decided April 9, 1971).

Table 3-6. Rates of Return on Equity and on Total Investment, Local Service Air Carriers, 1949–59

Percent

Year	Rate of return on equity[a]	Rate of return on total investment
1949	−18.1	−0.4
1950	−6.8	−6.6
1951	13.5	12.8
1952	−1.9	0.4
1953	−6.3	−2.2
1954	14.2	13.5
1955	7.5	7.5
1956	−4.4	−0.3
1957	−11.4	−2.6
1958	10.7	9.2
1959	0.5	5.0
Average 1949–59	−0.2	3.3

Sources: Civil Aeronautics Board, *Handbook of Airline Statistics, Calendar Years 1949–1956* (1960), pp. 117, 213; *Handbook of Airline Statistics, 1961 Edition* (1961), p. iv-7, and *1965 Edition* (1966), p. 100.
a. Does not include Braniff for the years 1952–54 or Mid Continent for the years 1951–52.

subsidy payment. A carrier remained on a "temporary" subsidy rate while negotiations on a "permanent" rate were proceeding. During this time it drew only enough subsidy to cover operating expenses and debt interest payments. Once the "final" subsidy rate was agreed upon, the CAB scrutinized the carrier's expenses, disallowed any it felt were excessive or unwarranted, and settled with the carrier, paying it a return of 7 percent on its investment for the period when it was on the "temporary" rate. At times the Board paid the carriers substantial amounts of money at the time of settlement. At other times the carriers ended up owing the Board money, even after allowing for the 7 percent rate of return. In 1961 the Board acted to change the method of subsidy payment. Under the new system, discussed in more detail in Chapter 5, a carrier knew in advance what subsidy payments it would receive, and the disallowance procedure was no longer followed.

The combination of the higher rate of return and the new subsidy system produced the intended results. Net income rose substantially during the 1961–64 period. The rate of return on equity averaged 17.4 percent, while the rate of return on total investment rose to 10.8 percent. Of equal importance was the fact that neither of these figures fluctuated greatly. Only three carriers required guarantees in order to obtain their loans, and the total value of these loans was only $8.5 million. The bulk of this amount was accounted for by a single loan of $6.5 million obtained by Bonanza Air Lines in 1964 to finance its first three DC-9s.

During negotiations for this loan another reason for the general disfavor for the loans became apparent. Bonanza originally wanted to purchase British-built BAC-111 aircraft. The Board refused to guarantee the loan. Then authority to guarantee loans was shifted to the Commerce Department, and Bonanza reapplied, this time proposing to buy U.S.-built DC-9s. The loan application was approved.

The fruit of these changes in the financial position of the local carriers was borne during the post-1965 period, when the industry was able to float almost $500 million in long-term debt to finance its acquisition of jets. But this is not to imply that these flotations were easy. The highest rating ever placed by Moody's on a local service airline public bond offering was "Ba,"[11] which was given to a Bonanza offering of May 1, 1964. All other

11. Moody's definitions are as follows:
Ba: "Bonds which are rated Ba are judged to have speculative elements; their future cannot be considered as well assured. . . . Uncertainty of position characterizes bonds in this class."
B: "Bonds which are rated B generally lack characteristics of the desirable investment.

offerings have been rated below this level, usually as "B," and the Bonanza offering itself was downgraded to "B" by Moody's in 1968. Such a poor opinion of local service airline bonds in the financial community meant that in order to sell, they had to carry relatively high interest rates and be hedged with restrictions designed to protect the purchaser. Furthermore, these offerings usually had to be "sweetened" by making them convertible into common stock.[12] During 1964, when the rate on new Aaa-rated corporate bonds was 4.40 percent, the Bonanza offering mentioned above, consisting of $3.2 million in convertible subordinated debentures (rated Ba), was priced at 5.25 percent. When the conversion feature was taken into account, the yield on the Bonanza offering actually was 6.5 percent. The company was required to establish a sinking fund and was restricted from paying dividends unless certain net income conditions were met. This latter restriction had the effect of tying up $2 million of the company's $2.8 million in retained earnings.

Furthermore, the costs of flotation have been substantially higher for low rated issues. The underwriting costs for a "Ba" rated issue in 1961 are estimated to be more than four times greater than for an issue rated "Aaa," and more than twice those for an issue rated "Baa," the next highest rating above "Ba." In effect, the flotation costs added another 0.25 percent to the interest rate on "Ba" rated securities.[13] Thus the true cost of the Bonanza offering may have been 6.75 percent, or fully 50 percent above the rate on new "Aaa" industrials. The Bonanza issue was the highest rated local service airline bond ever offered, and it came at a time when Bonanza had been averaging a 17.5 percent return on equity and 11.2 percent on its total investment. Other local airlines were not able to command such favorable rates. For example, at approximately the same time, a Lake Central Airlines public issue of convertible subordinated bonds, rated "B," was offered at 6.5 percent.

Assurance of interest and principal payments or of maintenance of other terms of the contract over any long period of time may be small."

Caa: "Bonds which are rated Caa are of poor standing. Such issues may be in default or there may be present elements of danger with respect to principal or interest." Moody's Investors Service, *Moody's Transportation Manual* (1970), p. vi.

12. Some of the increase in common stock during the 1961–69 period apparently resulted from the exercise of these conversion rights. Conversion reduces long-term debt and increases the amount of common stock but results in no increase of funds for the company.

13. See Avery B. Cohan, *Yields on Corporate Debt Directly Placed* (Columbia University Press for the National Bureau of Economic Research, 1967), p. 126.

Many local service carriers, limited in the amount of debt they could offer in the open market, turned to the banks for loans. The bank loans they obtained were generally secured by mortgages on their equipment and were made only after the carriers agreed to stringent conditions concerning the required levels of working capital and the payment of dividends. Many loans were of short maturity and at interest rates that automatically fluctuated with the prime rate.

Table 3-7, which shows the placement of the total long-term and short-term local service airline debt as of December 31, 1967, is further evidence of the generally low esteem in which the securities of these companies are held by the financial community. Of the debt at the end of 1967 identified as to holder, two-thirds was held by banks (rather than by insurance companies, trusts, pension funds, corporate and individual investors, and so on). The latter agencies held 80 percent of the identified trunkline debt, with only 20 percent being held by banks. Pension funds, trusts, and insurance companies are restricted as to the quality of bonds they can hold in their portfolios, and the failure of local service airline bonds generally to measure up to these standards has greatly limited the carriers' access to important sources of capital.

It is clear that the local carriers have had trouble in raising capital and

Table 3-7. Local Service Air Carrier Indebtedness, by Major Class of Lender, December 31, 1967

Lender	Amount of debt (millions of dollars)	Percent of total debt	Percent of identified debt
Long- and short-term debt			
Insurance companies	48.8	10.9	13.5
Banks	230.8	51.8	64.1
Airline suppliers[a]	32.5	7.3	9.0
Other identified[b]	48.2	10.8	13.4
Unidentified[c]	85.5	19.2	...
Total debt	445.8	100.0	100.0
Long-term debt	392.8	88.1	...

Sources: *Civil Aeronautics Board Reports to Congress, Fiscal Year 1968*, pp. 72–77; CAB, *Handbook of Airline Statistics, 1969 Edition* (1970), p. 299.

a. Mainly aircraft manufacturers who were financing the sale of their own planes.

b. Includes banks' holdings as trustees and/or agents, brokers, pension funds, trusts, air carriers, corporate and individual investors, and so on.

c. Under reporting requirements of the Civil Aeronautics Board, only debt issues in excess of 5 percent of a carrier's outstanding debt must be reported in detail. Of the debt reported in detail, identification is required only of those holding at least 5 percent of an issue or $500,000, whichever is smaller.

have had to pay relatively high interest rates to float their debt. In view of their past financial performance, it is somewhat surprising that they have not had even more trouble. The industry as a whole has paid only about $6 million in dividends throughout its history, the first dividend having been paid by a publicly owned local service carrier as recently as in 1964. In the past, bank loans have often been in technical default, and the current troubles of the local carriers have brought a new wave of such defaults.[14] It is surprising that an industry which at the end of 1960 had total assets of a little over $100 million could, during the next decade, float more than $500 million in debt (much of it during a period when interest rates were historically high), raise more than $100 million in equity, and, using the proceeds, transform its aircraft fleet from one composed largely of thirty-year-old, obsolete 20-passenger aircraft to one made up of 150 pure jet aircraft and 250 modern turboprops. That this financing could be accomplished at all was presumably due at least in part to the fact that during the period the government pumped $500 million in subsidy payments into the industry. In view of the high debt–equity ratios currently prevailing in the industry (7.5:1 for the industry as a whole in 1969) and the recent unfortunate experience of stockholders, it is not likely that the local service carriers will find it appreciably easier to raise funds in the near future.

The Nature of the Production Process

Some understanding of whether the production function for the local service airlines is characterized by fixed or variable proportions is no mere academic exercise, since the degree to which an air carrier that is faced with a shift in input factor prices can rearrange its use of such factors of production has an important impact on its costs. It is normally assumed that the ability of a business to respond to changes in factor prices increases as time passes after such a change. A carrier faced with an unexpected and permanent increase in piston fuel prices, for example, might be unable to make an immediate adjustment in its operations. The price increase would therefore be translated directly into an equivalent cost increase. As time progressed, however, the airline might modify its operating procedures to economize on fuel. For example, it might be justified in directing its pilots to use leaner fuel mixtures or to operate at lower cruising speeds, realizing that the former might increase engine maintenance costs, while the latter

14. See, for example, "Frontier Airlines Fails to Meet All Conditions of Its Long-Term Debts," *Wall Street Journal*, Vol. 175 (April 6, 1970), p. 13.

would raise flight-crew costs. In the longer run, a shift to more use of turboprop aircraft might be warranted, since they use a cheaper grade of fuel. That airlines can respond to changes in factor prices by economizing on the use of relatively expensive factors has been argued strongly by Straszheim.[15] He found that higher-wage firms tended to schedule their labor and aircraft somewhat more efficiently than did lower-wage firms. Evidence has been presented by others to suggest that the possibility of factor substitution exists for the local service carriers.[16]

Another factor that has an important effect on the level and composition of inputs used by an air carrier is the amount of competition it faces on its routes. The CAB restricts intercarrier price competition; thus, competition assumes nonprice forms which, while they may increase revenues, also affect costs. Inputs of advertising services, passenger food, ground services, and even aircraft services are affected by how much a particular air carrier must compete for traffic with other air carriers, rather than merely with other modes of transportation. Thus, the decision in 1966 by the CAB to allow and even promote unrestricted trunkline–local service competition has altered the production and cost function of the local service carriers.

The third major question to be answered concerning the cost function is whether it is subject to increasing, constant, or decreasing returns to scale. That is, if local service output is increased, do average costs fall, remain constant, or rise? Most authors have stated unequivocally that the local service carriers are subject to increasing returns to scale. If this is true, then increasing the scale of local service carriers by merger, for example, should result in lower unit costs. Yet mergers between local service carriers have never produced significant cost savings, and the most recent group of mergers appears to have at least contributed to substantial increases in cost.

Aircraft Operating Costs

In their classic 1940 article, Mentzer and Nourse divided air transport costs into three general classifications: "significant" or "direct" costs, "costs that change with passenger volume," and "overhead costs." They defined the first category as "those costs resulting from the flight of an air-

15. Mahlon R. Straszheim, *The International Airline Industry* (Brookings Institution, 1969), Chaps. 4 and 5, and Appendixes A and B.

16. George Eads, Marc Nerlove, and William Raduchel, "A Long-Run Cost Function for the Local Service Airline Industry: An Experiment in Non-linear Estimation," *Review of Economics and Statistics*, Vol. 51 (August 1969), pp. 258–70.

plane and those costs affected by airplane size, power, initial cost, as well as aerodynamic efficiency."[17] The equations they derived to explain the components of significant or direct costs later became the Air Transport Association Standard Method of Estimating Comparative Direct Operating Costs of Transport Airplanes, usually called the "ATA formula," and they form the basis of virtually all attempts to explain aircraft operating costs. The division of operating costs into the categories chosen by Mentzer and Nourse (which have been embedded in the CAB's data collection scheme) has been criticized as arbitrary.[18] For example, it will be shown below that "indirect costs" (those making up the latter two categories defined by Mentzer and Nourse) in fact are affected significantly by the nature of the aircraft used by a carrier. This should not be surprising. The number of stewardesses is a function of the size of the aircraft, hence passenger service expenses vary with the aircraft used. Different aircraft require different types of ground servicing, and landing fees vary according to aircraft weight; thus, aircraft and traffic servicing expense, the category of "indirect" costs that includes these two items, should also be expected to vary with aircraft type. Nevertheless, since the available data reflect the general practice of dividing costs into "direct" and "indirect" categories, this division will be used here.

The major components of significant or direct operating costs are flight crew (pilot and copilot) costs, fuel costs, aircraft maintenance expenses, and aircraft depreciation expenses. A fifth category—maintenance burden—defined as the expenses for facilities used in aircraft maintenance, is sometimes also included. Direct operating costs defined in this way make up 50 to 60 percent of total operating expenses.

Crew Costs

Flight crew costs are between 20 percent (for pure jets) and 40 percent (for DC-3s) of direct operating costs for the local service carriers. A two-man flight crew (pilot and copilot) is standard on all aircraft operated by these carriers except the Boeing 727s and 737s, on which a third pilot is re-

17. W. C. Mentzer and Hal E. Nourse, "Some Economic Aspects of Transport Airplane Performance. Part 1," *Journal of the Aeronautical Sciences*, Vol. 7 (April 1940), pp. 227–34, and ". . . Parts II and III," in the same *Journal*, Vol. 7 (May 1940), pp. 302–8.

18. Costrender [pseudonym], "ATA Formula Misleading on Costs," *Airlift*, Vol. 23 (June 1959), pp. 33–34; "Operating Costs—The Intractable Other Half," *Aeroplane*, Vol. 112 (Dec. 22, 1966), pp. 14–15.

quired.[19] The Air Line Pilots Association and the airlines have negotiated certain scheduling guarantees that assure that a flight crew member will be paid a minimum amount regardless of how much his services are used by the airline. Other agreements have been negotiated to guarantee pilots such benefits as a minimum number of days each month at their home base. The carriers must also comply with federal regulations, which put absolute upper limits on the number of hours crew members can fly each month and the number they can fly consecutively. Within these scheduling constraints, the carriers have opportunities to vary the amount of useful work they get from their crews and thus to affect their direct operating costs.

In his study of the international airline industry, Straszheim concluded that differences in crew scheduling ability explained a significant part of the differences in operating costs of the firms in his sample.[20] Results of the more limited experiments made for this study indicate that this is the case also with the local service carriers. To test this hypothesis, data for the year 1957 were used. Ten of the thirteen local carriers operated only DC-3s during that year, so the sample is small but adequate without account being taken of the complications introduced by the presence of more than one type of aircraft in a carrier's fleet. A positive correlation was found (as in Straszheim's study) between a measure of flight crew productivity (revenue-miles flown per crew member per year) and the crew member's average wage.[21] We hesitate, however, to conclude, as Straszheim does, that "higher wage firms are better flight crew schedulers."[22] Since one of the major elements in the crew pay formula is the number of miles a crew member flies, this correlation would be expected, regardless of the carrier's crew scheduling ability.

An airline is less concerned with the wages a crew member is paid than with how these wages are transformed into crew costs per mile; and the correlation between average wage per crew member and crew cost per mile

19. The airlines were seeking permission to operate the 737 with a two-man crew (as they are able to do with all other twin engine jets), and this was the source of considerable dispute with the Air Line Pilots Association. "Court Hearing Orders Piedmont's Pilots Back to Work Pending Hearing," *Aviation Week and Space Technology*, Vol. 91 (Aug. 25, 1969), p. 28.

20. *The International Airline Industry*, pp. 59, 168–70.

21. The correlation coefficient for this 1957 data was 0.22. Revenue-miles are miles flown in revenue service. This includes all flying except for personnel training, ferry flights, route extension and development, and abortive revenue flights. Crew member's average wage is total flight crew compensation divided by the number of pilots and copilots.

22. *Ibid.*, p. 247.

is far from perfect ($R = 0.41$). But, not surprisingly, an extremely strong negative correlation was found between crew cost per aircraft-mile and crew productivity.

(3) Crew costs per mile (cents)
$$= 32.52 - 0.000297 \text{ revenue-miles per crew member per year}$$
$$(8.21)\quad(3.79)^a$$

$\bar{R}^2 = R^2$ adjusted for degrees of freedom = 0.545, $F = 13.99^b$
The numbers in parentheses are t-ratios.
a. Significant at 1 percent level.
b. Significant at 25 percent level.

The equation predicts that Bonanza, the "worst" crew scheduler in 1957, would have had crew costs per aircraft-mile approximately 25 percent lower if it had achieved the same level of crew utilization as did Trans-Texas, the "best" scheduler. This would have represented an annual saving of more than $150,000, an amount equivalent to 4 percent of Bonanza's 1957 operating costs and 11 percent of its subsidy.

Why do firms differ in the effectiveness with which they utilize flight crews? Straszheim attributes much of the difference to variations in the quality of airline management. To be sure, management quality probably does vary, but it is crucial to Straszheim's conclusion that the opportunities for pilot utilization are approximately constant across firms or that correction has been made for systematic differences in scheduling opportunities. We agree with Straszheim that the most obvious correction would be for differences in route structure and, like him, are puzzled that such factors as flight stage length and route density do not prove to be significant explanatory variables.[23] A carrier operating routes of relatively short stage length would be expected to have its pilots on the ground a greater proportion of the time than would a carrier with routes of longer stages. Higher route density should mean more frequent flights and relatively fewer reserve crew members needed. A priori, one would expect increases in these variables to reduce crew costs per aircraft-mile, but neither proved to be statistically significant. Two possible explanations come to mind. Although there was considerable percentage variance in the average stage length for the local carriers for the sample year used (Lake Central, the lowest, 68 miles; Bonanza, the highest, 112 miles), the average stage for the sample as a whole was so low (83 miles) that pilot utilization by all carriers may have suffered about equally. Furthermore, the two parameters used may

23. Route density is a measure of the number of passengers flying a particular route. The variable used here was the number of enplaned passengers (total passengers boarded) per route-mile.

not have adequately characterized a carrier's route structure as far as pilot scheduling ability is concerned. For example, two carriers with equal stage length and route density might have route structures differing in the proportion of "stub-end" and "closed-loop" segments. The crew scheduling requirements negotiated by the ALPA might be expected to require the carrier with more "stub-end" segments to have extra crews in order to meet the requirement of a minimum number of away-from-base rest periods.[24]

Therefore, while differences in crew scheduling ability do have an important impact on crew costs, a reading of Baitsell's description of the procedures by which crew assignments are made[25] convinces one that to summarize such differences in a few parameters is not possible.

Fuel and Oil Costs

Fuel and oil costs make up between 15 and 25 percent of direct operating costs. They depend on the price of fuel and fuel usage. The former has been discussed above; the latter is determined primarily by the types of aircraft and the route structure over which they are used. Equations (4) and (5) below illustrate this. The dependent variables were gallons of piston fuel and turbine fuel used. Independent variables were number of aircraft-miles flown and average flight stage length for aircraft of a particular class. Piston engine aircraft were divided into two classes: DC-3s and larger piston aircraft (Convair 240s, 340s, and 440s and Martin 202s and 404s). Turbine-powered aircraft were divided into turboprops (excluding the Nord 262) and pure jets. The data used consisted of quarterly observations by carrier. Piston fuel data were available for twelve carriers over a period of thirty-six quarters (I, 1958 to IV, 1966), and turbine fuel data were available for nine carriers over seven quarters (II, 1965 to IV, 1966). The equations reveal that turbine aircraft burn considerably more fuel than do piston aircraft. The larger piston aircraft and the turboprops are of roughly the same size, and in some cases the turboprops are conversions of former piston aircraft. The turboprops burn 1.62 gallons of fuel per mile; the larger pistons 1.22 gallons per mile. This increased fuel usage, however, does not overcome the advantage that the turboprops have of burning cheaper fuel.

24. This aspect of the routes of Northwest Airlines recently was suggested as a possible reason for that carrier's low crew costs. It was observed that Northwest's routes constitute a circle running from Miami and New York to Chicago, Seattle, Alaska, and Japan. William H. Gregory, "U.S. Trunks React to Cost Rise," *Aviation Week and Space Technology*, Vol. 92 (June 8, 1970), p. 27.

25. Baitsell, *Airline Industrial Relations*, pp. 112–56.

For example, in 1966 the Convair 240 had fuel and oil costs of 22.7 cents a mile (119 mile average stage length); the Convair 600, the turboprop conversion of the Convair 240, had fuel costs of 17.7 cents a mile (122 mile average stage length), almost 22 percent lower.

The equations also reveal that the length of hop has an effect on aircraft fuel consumption. A carrier flying its fleet of DC-3s one million miles per quarter (approximately the average usage) would use 737,000 gallons of fuel if these miles were flown over an average stage length of 80 miles (approximately the DC-3 average) and 721,000 gallons if flown over a 200-mile average stage length. This result is to be expected. Activities associated with landing and takeoff consume a disproportionate amount of fuel relative to the total elapsed time of the trip; and, furthermore, a fixed amount of fuel is used in these activities regardless of how far the aircraft is going to fly. The only offsetting factor is that cruising altitude is lower on shorter flights, so fuel spent in climbing is relatively less.

The final fact that these equations reveal is that there are some differences among firms in their use of fuel that is unaccounted for by the aircraft-mile and stage-length variables, though their significance is not great. These interfirm differences may be a reflection of differences in congestion, climate, passenger load, and other such operational factors.

(4)   Gallons of piston fuel (per quarter) = 97,870 + 0.65 DC-3 miles

$$(51.10)^a$$

+ 1.22 larger piston miles − 135.66 DC-3 stage length
  $(162.44)^a$ (1.45)

+ 89.20 larger piston stage length + 74,716 Allegheny
  (0.98) $(3.21)^a$

− 8,222 Central − 44,964 Frontier + 686 Lake Central
  (0.39) $(1.85)^b$ (0.03)

− 70,587 Mohawk + 65,574 North Central + 69,891 Ozark
  $(3.00)^a$ $(2.00)^c$ $(2.91)^a$

− 60,509 Pacific + 71,341 Piedmont + 49,400 Southern
  $(2.69)^a$ $(3.39)^a$ $(2.22)^c$

− 123,610 Trans-Texas.
  $(5.11)^a$

$\bar{R}^2 = 0.99$, $F = 5,267$,[a] F (firm constants as a group) = 0.90[d]
The numbers in parentheses are t-ratios.
a. Significant at 1 percent level.
b. Significant at 10 percent level
c. Significant at 5 percent level.
d. Significant at 75 percent level.

(5) Gallons of turbine fuel (per quarter)
$$= -383,800 + 1.62 \text{ turboprop-miles}$$
$$(46.43)^a$$

$+ 3.39$ jet-miles $- 675.23$ turboprop stage length
$(38.22)^a$ $(1.78)^b$

$- 71.99$ jet stage length $+ 592,710$ Allegheny $+ 416,450$ Central
$(3.06)^a$ $(7.64)^a$ $(5.00)^a$

$+ 14,737$ Frontier $+ 370,490$ Mohawk $+ 230,650$ Ozark
(0.17) $(2.97)^a$ $(2.90)^a$

$+ 359,140$ Pacific $+ 202,460$ Piedmont $+ 386,450$ Trans-Texas.
$(4.62)^a$ $(2.64)^c$ $(4.42)^a$

$\bar{R}^2 = 0.99$, $F = 773$,[a] F (firm constants as a group) $= 2.72$[c]
The numbers in parentheses are t-ratios.
a. Significant at 1 percent level.
b. Significant at 10 percent level.
c. Significant at 5 percent level.

Depreciation and Maintenance and Rental Expenses

Depreciation expenses are charges made against revenues to account for either physical or economic obsolescence of a capital good. Maintenance expenses are expenses undertaken to protect or restore the productivity of a capital good. The former account comprises from 2 percent (for the DC-3) to 26 percent (for the DC-9-30) of total operating costs. The latter comprises from 20 percent (for the DC-9-30) to almost 50 percent (for the Convair 240) of total costs if overhead costs related to aircraft maintenance (usually termed "maintenance burden") are included (from 14 percent to 37 percent, respectively, if they are excluded).

The policies adopted by the local service carriers concerning depreciation of their principal asset—flight equipment—are of obvious concern to the Civil Aeronautics Board. They affect both the level of subsidy payments and the availability of investable funds for the carriers. The current CAB policy is to prescribe a straight line depreciation policy, with the useful lives and residual values that prevailed in 1969 shown in Table 3-8. It is not clear that this policy is justifiable economically. The fact that most carriers have managed to make significant capital gains on the sale of their used aircraft—aircraft that had been used when they bought them in the first place—suggests that economic obsolescence of these aircraft has not been serious. As was noted above, Sobotka and Schnabel have shown that

Table 3-8. Useful Service Lives and Residual Values Prescribed by the Civil Aeronautics Board for Local Service Carrier Aircraft, 1969

Type of aircraft	Service life (years)	Residual value (percent)
Douglas DC-3	3	10
All other piston-powered	7	15
Turboprop[a]	10	15
Turbojet	12	15

Source: Civil Aeronautics Board, "Local Service Air Carriers' Unit Costs, Year ended March 31, 1969" (processed), p. 13.

a. Turboprop conversions of piston aircraft are to be amortized as turboprop aircraft.

the price of a used aircraft can be quite accurately predicted as the sum of a discounted stream of anticipated future net earnings.[26] Since this value has increased over the years for most of the aircraft flown by the local carriers, it seems hard to argue that economic obsolescence has been great and that depreciation should be taken on these grounds.

The standards for maintenance of flight equipment are a subject of federal regulation. Frequent inspections and periodic complete overhauls are performed on all flight equipment. The effect of this on aircraft life is shown by the case of the DC-3. This aircraft first entered airline service in 1936. The production of DC-3s was discontinued at the end of World War II. After thirty-five years of service there is no sign that any DC-3s will have to be retired because of physical deterioration. Because of this sort of maintenance, there appears to be no reason to assume that depreciation charges computed by the local service carriers reflect physical wear and tear.[27]

In light of these facts, a better assumption for aircraft depreciation would be that the capital asset is completely restored each period and that maintenance expenses associated with the restoration reflect depreciation.

26. "Linear Programming as a Device for Predicting Market Value."
27. The Board recently said: "Aircraft do not deteriorate in a physical sense. Under normal maintenance they can be kept in an operational state for indefinite periods of time. Thus, depreciation is essentially caused by the loss in market value of the aircraft attributable to technological obsolescence factors." ("CAB Proposes Depreciation Revisions," *Aviation Week and Space Technology*, Vol. 93 [Aug. 17, 1970], p. 22.) Carriers do have the option of capitalizing expenses associated with major airframe and engine overhauls and amortizing these expenses over the life of the overhaul. To the extent that stated depreciation figures reflect such charges, they do represent physical depreciation; but there is little evidence, except for the DC-3, which entered the local carriers' fleets many years ago and which has been completely written off, that depreciation charges are primarily of such a type.

This assumption was adopted in a recent cost study.[28] However, in view of the depreciation policies prescribed by the Board, it is obvious that *reported* depreciation expenses per aircraft-mile vary inversely with aircraft utilization and directly with aircraft price.

Aircraft maintenance expenses depend primarily on the type of aircraft, the pattern of its use, and its age. Most airframe and engine components are maintained on a time-in-use basis, which is dependent on the rate of unscheduled removal of the component. If operating evidence indicates that a component has a low rate of unscheduled removal, its time between overhaul (TBO) is increased. For example, when the Rolls-Royce Dart turboprop engine first entered service on the Viscount airline in 1955, it had a TBO of 1,050 hours. The TBO on the Dart was gradually increased until in 1968 it was 6,000 hours.[29] Such a change has a significant impact on aircraft operating expenses. In 1967 a Dart overhaul cost about $18,000. At a TBO of 1,050 hours and an average flying speed of 200 miles an hour, overhaul costs would be $17 an hour, or 8.6 cents a mile. Increasing the TBO to 6,000 hours lowered overhaul costs to $3 an hour, or 1.5 cents a mile. Furthermore, a high TBO means that an airline can carry fewer spare engines. At a cost of $80,000 to $100,000 per engine, this is not inconsequential.

Time between overhaul is based on the total number of hours an engine is running. Since the time required for taxi, takeoff, climb, descent, and landing is virtually independent of the distance flown, engine maintenance costs per aircraft-mile flown should decline sharply with the increase of stage length. Airframe maintenance costs also should decline substantially with increases in average stage length. Many airframe components, such as landing gears and flaps, are cycled only twice during a normal flight—once for landing and once for takeoff. Furthermore, aircraft on short flights do not generally climb as high as those on long flights and do not have the option of circumventing small areas of bad weather. Therefore, central surfaces and airframe structural members are under greater stress.

The age of an aircraft has a twofold effect on maintenance expenses. When an aircraft first enters a carrier's fleet, it takes some time to work out any "bugs." As more experience is obtained, time between overhaul for components becomes longer. However, the maximum time between over-

28. Eads and others, "A Long-Run Cost Function for the Local Service Airline Industry," pp. 258–70.
29. *Flight Magazine*, Vol. 57 (June 1968), p. 142.

haul eventually is reached, and usage beyond that point begins to take its toll on an aircraft, requiring the replacement of more and more parts. Finally, as an aircraft becomes very old, obtaining parts for it may become more expensive. Thus, maintenance expenses per aircraft-mile would be expected to be at first a decreasing, and then an increasing, function of age.

Total Direct Operating Expenses

The above discussion of the major components of direct operating costs suggests that these costs should vary both by aircraft type and by stage length.

Table 3-9 presents direct operating cost data by stage length, calculated by the ATA formula for a representative sample of the aircraft operated by the local service carriers: the DC-3, the Convair 340/440 (representing the larger piston-engine aircraft), the Fairchild F-27 and Convair CV-580 (rep-

Table 3-9. Direct Operating Costs per Aircraft-mile and Seat-mile at Various Stage Lengths, Selected Aircraft, Mid-1960s
Cents

	Stage length (miles)						
Aircraft	50	80	100	200	300	400	500
	Cost per aircraft-mile						
Douglas DC-3	73	70	68	63	60	58	56
Convair CV-340/440	n.a.	133	124	102	95	93	n.a.
Fairchild F-27	128	115	112	96	87	80	75
Convair CV-580	143	132	124	105	93	85	79
Douglas DC-9-30	208	190	181	153	137	125	117
De Havilland Twin Otter	63	55	53	48	47	46	45
	Cost per seat-mile[a]						
Douglas DC-3	3.04	2.90	2.83	2.63	2.50	2.42	2.33
Convair CV-340/440	n.a.	3.02	2.82	2.32	2.16	2.11	n.a.
Fairchild F-27	3.20	2.88	2.80	2.40	2.18	2.00	1.88
Convair CV-580	2.65	2.44	2.30	1.94	1.72	1.57	1.46
Douglas DC-9-30	2.08	1.90	1.81	1.53	1.37	1.25	1.17
De Havilland Twin Otter	3.15	2.75	2.65	2.67	2.94	3.07	3.21

Sources: CV-340/440: adapted from Systems Analysis and Research Corporation, "Economic Analysis of the Short-Haul Transport" (Cambridge, Mass.: SARC, 1964; processed), p. 50. Twin Otter: basic data were provided by De Havilland Aircraft of Canada, Limited. All other aircraft: *Review of the Local Air Carrier Industry*, Hearings before the Aviation Subcommittee of the Senate Committee on Commerce, 89 Cong. 2 sess. (1966), pp. 136, 159.
n.a. Not available.
a. Based on number of seats per aircraft as follows: DC-3, 24; CV-340/440, 44; F-27, 40; CV-580, 54; DC-9-30, 100; Twin Otter: for stage lengths up to 100 miles, 20; 200 miles, 18; 300 miles, 16; 400 miles, 15; 500 miles, 14.

resenting the turboprops), and the DC-9-30 (representing the pure jets). Also shown are cost data for the De Havilland Twin Otter, which is not flown by the local carriers but which has been proposed as a replacement for the DC-3. Because the data for these six aircraft are not from the same source, Table 3-9 should be taken as reflecting only the approximate relationship of direct operating costs among the types of aircraft shown for representative stage lengths.

It is clear that direct operating costs increase with increases in aircraft capacity, but they increase less than proportionally. Consequently, for a given stage length a larger aircraft almost certainly will have a lower cost per seat-mile but a higher cost per aircraft-mile than will a smaller aircraft. Table 3-9 also shows that costs tend to fall as stage length increases and that this fall is most rapid at the lower end of the range. Thus direct operating costs per aircraft-mile for the DC-9-30 fall by 15 percent as stage length increases from 100 to 200 miles, but by only 6 percent as stage length rises from 400 to 500 miles. Furthermore, except for the Twin Otter, all aircraft show a decline in costs per seat-mile as stage length increases to 500 miles. For the Twin Otter, however, seat-mile costs are lowest at about a 150-mile stage length. If it must operate at stage lengths beyond 150 miles, it must carry fewer passengers. This reflects the fact that of all the aircraft shown, only the Twin Otter was designed for short-haul purposes. The others have been adapted to this use. The DC-3, Convair, and DC-9 all were designed to trunkline specifications for trunkline routes. The F-27 was designed for local service operations, but primarily for the longer routes of these carriers.

Indirect Operating Costs

Indirect operating costs make up roughly 45 percent of total operating costs. The four major indirect cost categories are passenger service expense, aircraft and traffic servicing expense, promotion and sales expense, and general and administrative expense. Table 3-10 shows indirect costs, on both a percentage and a per–enplaned-passenger basis, for each of these categories and for major subcategories.

It is in the area of indirect costs that the local carriers are said to suffer most from their small size relative to the trunklines. A fairly detailed study was therefore made of the factors affecting each of the major cost subcategories so that the question of economies of scale could be more readily

Table 3-10. Percentage Distribution of Components of Indirect Operating Expense, and Cost per Passenger, Local Service Air Carriers, 1962–66 Average

Expense component	Percent of indirect operating expense	Cost per enplaned passenger (dollars)
Passenger service expense	11.0	1.04
Cabin crew salaries	4.5	0.43
Passenger food	1.9	0.18
Traffic liability insurance	1.2	0.11
Personnel expenses	1.5	0.14
Miscellaneous other expenses	1.9	0.18
Aircraft and traffic servicing expense	56.0	5.31
General aircraft and traffic handling personnel	20.2	1.92
Salaries of passenger handling personnel	9.5	0.90
Communications purchased	3.9	0.37
Landing fees	3.9	0.37
Other services, purchased outside	3.4	0.32
Rentals	3.4	0.32
Aircraft control personnel	2.2	0.21
Cargo handling personnel	1.6	0.15
Miscellaneous other expenses	7.9	0.75
General and administrative expense	13.0	1.23
Record keeping and statistical personnel	3.2	0.30
General management personnel	2.0	0.19
Taxes other than payroll	1.2	0.11
Rentals	1.0	0.09
Other personnel expenses	0.8	0.08
Miscellaneous other expenses	4.8	0.46
Promotion and sales expense	20.0	1.90
Passenger handling personnel	5.4	0.51
Advertising	5.2	0.49
Commissions	2.0	0.19
Communications purchased	1.6	0.15
Miscellaneous other expenses	5.9	0.56
Total indirect operating expenses	100.0	9.49
Percent of total operating expenses	44.0	...

Sources: CAB, *Handbook of Airline Statistics, 1967 Edition* (1968), pp. 135, 225; N. K. Taneja and R. W. Simpson, "A Multi-Regression Analysis of Airline Indirect Operating Costs," FTL Report R-67-2 (Massachusetts Institute of Technology, Flight Transportation Laboratory, June 1968; processed).

addressed.[30] Annual firm data were used for the years 1962–66. Individual firm constant terms were used to adjust for firm effects. In three of the four cases these individual firm constants proved to be significant as a group at the 1 percent level, indicating the presence of important firm effects.

Passenger Service Expenses

Passenger service expenses are defined by the CAB as "costs of activities contributing to the comfort, safety, and convenience of passengers while in flight and when flights are interrupted. Includes salaries and expenses of cabin attendants and passenger food expense."[31] During the 1962–66 period, cabin crew (stewardess) salaries made up almost half of the expenses in this category. This is a reflection of the short-haul, noncompetitive nature of the majority of the local service routes at that time. During the same period, food expenses were the largest passenger service expense for the longer-haul, more competitive trunklines (8.2 percent of indirect operating costs, $1.38 per passenger). Local service aircraft (with the exception of the jets) have been operated with a single stewardess. In early 1970, however, the FAA instituted a rule requiring all aircraft with a capacity of between 44 seats and 100 seats to have two stewardesses. This was protested strongly by the local service carriers. North Central, which operated its turboprop Convair 580s with 48 seats, estimated that to put a second stewardess on each of its thirty-four Convair 580s would cost over $1 million in the first year.[32] In response to the pleas of the locals, the FAA issued a "temporary" exemption (until December 31, 1970) which permitted operation with a single cabin attendant for a maximum of 50 passengers. While this ruling satisfied North Central and Ozark Air Lines, which operated its FH-227s with 46 seats, it required Allegheny Airlines and Frontier Airlines, each of which operated its Convair 580s with 53 seats, to block off 3 seats from sale.

Equation (6) explains passenger service expense by carrier as a function

30. While the impetus for this work was provided by the study by N. K. Taneja and R. W. Simpson, "A Multi-Regression Analysis of Airline Indirect Operating Costs," FTL Report R-67-2 (Massachusetts Institute of Technology, Flight Transportation Laboratory, June 1968; processed), the results here were derived independently of theirs.

31. CAB, *Handbook of Airline Statistics, 1967 Edition*, p. 538.

32. North Central Airlines estimated that the revenue loss from eliminating the four seats would be $100,000 per year. "FAA Eases New Attendant Rule Temporarily for Eight Airlines," *Aviation Week and Space Technology*, Vol. 92 (May 4, 1970), p. 36.

of the number of jet and nonjet aircraft-miles flown and the wages of stewardesses.

(6)   Passenger service expenses (dollars)

$$= 308{,}900 + 0.450 \times 10^{-8} \text{ (nonjet aircraft-miles)}^2$$
(15.72)[a]

$$+ \text{ 0.198 jet aircraft-miles} + 0.00822 \text{ (stewardess wages [dollars])}^2$$
(10.44)[a]   (2.267)[b]

$$- \text{ 2,802 Allegheny} - 165{,}800 \text{ Bonanza} - 109{,}800 \text{ Central}$$
(0.04)   (3.10)[a]   (1.96)[b]

$$- \text{ 172,800 Frontier} + 31{,}890 \text{ Lake Central} + 67{,}120 \text{ Mohawk}$$
(2.78)[a]   (0.61)   (1.03)

$$+ \text{ 26,220 North Central} - 67{,}460 \text{ Ozark} - 166{,}200 \text{ Pacific}$$
(0.37)   (1.18)   (3.15)[a]

$$- \text{ 57,970 Piedmont} - 138{,}800 \text{ Southern} - 140{,}800 \text{ Trans-Texas.}$$
(0.98)   (2.58)[a]   (2.32)[b]

$\bar{R}^2 = 0.9588$, $F = 101.87$,[a] F (firm constants as a group) = 1.49.[c]
The numbers in parentheses are t-ratios.
a. Significant at 1 percent level.
b. Significant at 5 percent level.
c. Significant at 25 percent level.

The coefficients and elasticities evaluated at sample means (corrected for zero observations if necessary) are:

	Coefficient	Elasticity
Nonjet aircraft-miles	$0.0925	0.982
Jet aircraft-miles	0.1984	0.234
Stewardess wages	0.0742	0.347

To aid in interpretation, equation (6) also shows estimates of each coefficient and its associated elasticity computed at the sample means. Passenger service costs per mile for jet aircraft are shown to be more than twice those for nonjet aircraft. This is the result of two factors: (1) the jets with their higher seating capacity must carry more stewardesses; and (2) the jets generally are flown over longer and more competitive routes; hence, food expenses are higher.

Passenger amenities are one of an airline's major competitive weapons. Thus one would expect increased competition to have an important effect on passenger service costs. There is strong evidence to suggest that this is indeed the case.[33] Between 1960 and 1965, passenger service expense for

33. Allegheny, which in 1965, before the onset of significant direct trunk–local service competition, was spending approximately 9 cents per passenger on food, was by 1970

the local carriers as a group fell from $1.28 to $1.09 per passenger. This was a reflection of the increasing passenger loads during this period. Between 1965 and 1969, expenses per passenger rose to $1.67. While inflation was blamed for the increase, it was not the only factor. If one is willing to assume that the trunklines were subject to similar inflationary pressures, one can correct for inflation by expressing passenger service expense per passenger for the local carriers as a percentage of the equivalent trunkline figure. Between 1960 and 1965, local service per-passenger expenses fell from 38 percent to 29 percent of trunk per-passenger expenses. During the 1965–69 period, however, they rose to 35 percent of the trunkline figure. Furthermore, carriers that were awarded important competitive routes saw their costs in this area rise even further. The per-passenger expenditure for the three airlines that became Air West in 1968 rose from 26 percent to 38 percent of trunkline levels between 1965 and 1969. After falling from 32 percent in 1960, Allegheny's rose from 25 percent in 1965 to 36 percent in 1969; Frontier's rose from 38 percent to 50 percent, and Piedmont Aviation's rose from 28 percent to 40 percent. From all indications, by 1970 the locals were matching the trunklines in the level of their passenger amenities where they competed with the trunklines.

Aircraft and Traffic Servicing Expenses

Aircraft and traffic servicing expenses consist of "compensation of ground personnel and other expenses incurred on the ground to protect and control the in-flight movement of aircraft, schedule and prepare aircraft operational crews for flight assignment, handle and service aircraft while in line operation, and service and handle traffic on the ground after issuance of documents establishing the air carrier's responsibility to provide air transportation [that is, tickets] and in-flight expenses of handling and protecting all nonpassenger traffic including passenger baggage."[34] Such expenses accounted for more than half of local service indirect operating costs during the period 1962–66. Equation (7) shows an analysis of this class of "indirect" expenses. As would be expected, the number of departures made per station and the number of passengers handled per sta-

---

boasting that the passenger amenities on its jet custom class coach flights (which made up 42 percent of its 1969 aircraft-miles) were equal to those on trunkline flights. Food was said to include "steak for all" if "there's steak for one" (*New York Times*, March 9, 1970, p. 52).

34. CAB, *Handbook of Airline Statistics, 1967 Edition*, p. 535.

tion, together with the average wage paid to nonflying personnel, provide an extremely good explanation of these costs. Furthermore, these costs are found to vary systematically by aircraft type. Each DC-3 departure creates $32.20 in aircraft and traffic servicing expenses, while each jet departure creates almost twice as much, $55.00. (In the equation, DC-3 departures include Nord 262 departures; wages are average annual compensation of personnel excluding pilots, copilots, and stewardesses.)

(7) Aircraft and servicing expenses (dollars)

$$= -2,712,000 + 32.2 \text{ DC-3 departures}$$
$$(7.37)^a$$

$+ 45.2$ larger piston departures $+ 52.3$ turboprop departures
$(12.66)^a$ $\qquad\qquad\qquad\qquad (13.14)^a$

$+ 55.0$ jet departures $+ 0.609 \times 10^{-9}$ (passengers per station)^2
$(4.02)^a$ $\qquad\qquad\qquad (4.16)^a$

$+ 394.6$ wages $+ 851,500$ Allegheny $- 610,700$ Bonanza
$(3.75)^a$ $\qquad (3.73)^a$ $\qquad\qquad (2.56)^b$

$+ 588,400$ Central $+ 459,300$ Frontier $+ 379,900$ Lake Central
$(3.63)^a$ $\qquad\qquad (2.41)^b$ $\qquad\qquad (2.11)^b$

$+ 334,100$ Mohawk $+ 962,900$ North Central $+ 445,000$ Ozark
(1.14) $\qquad\qquad (2.34)^b$ $\qquad\qquad\qquad (1.84)^c$

$- 129,700$ Pacific $- 512,900$ Piedmont $+ 622,900$ Southern
(0.74) $\qquad\qquad (1.95)^b$ $\qquad\qquad (3.01)^a$

$+ 338,700$ Trans-Texas.
(1.66)

$\bar{R}^2 = 0.9887$, $F = 316.92$,^{a} F (firm constants as a group) $= 4.20$.^{a}
The numbers in parentheses are t-ratios.
a. Significant at 1 percent level.
b. Significant at 5 percent level.
c. Significant at 10 percent level.

The coefficients and elasticities evaluated at sample means (corrected for zero observations if necessary) are:

	Coefficient	Elasticity
DC-3 departures	$32.20	0.37
Larger piston departures	45.20	0.53
Turboprop departures	52.30	0.38
Jet departures	55.00	0.07
Passengers per station	26.78	0.13
Wages	394.60	0.53

The effect of competition on aircraft and traffic servicing expenses is less direct than its effect on passenger servicing expenses. If competitive pressures lead a carrier to use a larger aircraft than traffic requires on a route, aircraft and traffic servicing expenses will rise. As equation (7) shows, this impact is largest when a large piston or turboprop aircraft is used instead of a DC-3. Furthermore, as carriers are granted access to more large cities, they often must offer the same level of ground services as trunks do, just because of the way the airports are organized. They must pay their share of the costs of departure lounges, aircraft boarding ramps, and such, and must bear a share of the general cost of operating the terminal. At some points they must pay for the construction of satellite terminals or arrange to share an existing satellite terminal.

Offsetting these influences that tend to increase costs is the relatively small cost-reducing effect that increases in departures and in numbers of passengers per station have on aircraft and traffic servicing expenses.[35] Between 1960 and 1965, aircraft and traffic servicing expenses on a per-passenger basis declined from 98 percent of trunkline levels to 81 percent. The decline in DC-3 utilization from 66 percent of local service aircraft-miles in 1960 to 24 percent in 1965 served to raise costs. This was more than offset by an increase in the number of passengers per station per year from 9,500 in 1960 to 23,000 in 1965. During the 1965 to 1969 period, per-passenger aircraft and traffic service expenses for the locals continued to decline relative to those of the trunks (although they were at a far lower level), reaching 76 percent of the trunkline level in 1969. During this period the DC-3 was eliminated entirely from scheduled operations, but traffic density continued to grow, reaching 45,000 per station per year by the end of 1969.

Table 3-11 provides a further analysis of these costs during the period and helps explain the decline. It shows that the decline has been greatest and continued most steadily among carriers which originally had the lowest average station density and which have increased this density the most. The expectation for the future, therefore, would seem to be that per-passenger aircraft and traffic servicing costs should not decline relative to trunkline levels nearly as rapidly as they did during the early 1960s. The only exception to this might be carriers, such as Frontier and Southern

35. The average annual number of passengers per station, per carrier during the 1962–66 period was 21,986 (60.2 per station per day). The elasticity based on Allegheny's 1966 station density of 52,077 passengers per station per year (142.7 per station per day) was calculated at 0.317, still substantially below unity.

Table 3-11. Station Density and Local Service Aircraft and Traffic Servicing Costs Relative to Trunkline Costs, by Carrier, 1960, 1965, 1969

	1960		1965		1969	
Carrier[a]	Density[b]	Relative cost[c]	Density[b]	Relative cost[c]	Density[b]	Relative cost[c]
Air West	11.1	83	21.6	73	39.7	84
Allegheny Airlines	10.3	83	26.4	83	69.6	73
Frontier Airlines	5.2	141	12.7	101	27.6	82
Mohawk Airlines	18.9	79	52.8	68	69.7	69
North Central Airlines	12.3	96	23.4	81	47.7	70
Ozark Air Lines	10.0	95	25.3	76	45.9	74
Piedmont Aviation	9.6	102	30.1	74	44.7	75
Southern Airways	5.0	130	17.3	89	28.6	85
Trans-Texas Airways	7.2	114	20.2	90	41.8	74
Local average	9.6	98	23.2	81	44.7	76

Sources: Civil Aeronautics Board, *Handbook of Airline Statistics, 1969 Edition;* CAB, *Air Carrier Financial Statistics* (December 1970); and CAB, *Air Carrier Traffic Statistics,* Vol. 16 (December 1970); *Flight Magazine,* Vols. 50, 55, 59 (June 1961, 1966, 1970).

a. The carrier names shown are the official names in 1969. Acquisitions, mergers, and name changes between 1960 and 1969 are reflected in the data for all years, as follows: Air West includes Bonanza, Pacific, and West Coast; Allegheny includes Lake Central; Frontier includes Central; and Texas International includes Trans-Texas.

b. Average number of passengers per station per year in thousands.

c. Per passenger aircraft and traffic servicing expense for local carrier as percent of equivalent figure for trunkline.

Airways, which even in 1969 had station densities that were substantially below the average.

Promotion and Sales Expenses

Promotion and sales expense includes "costs incurred in promoting the use of air transportation generally and creating a public preference for the services of particular air carriers. [It] includes the functions of selling, advertising and publicity, space reservations, and developing tariffs and flight schedules for publication."[36] Since the functions of space reservations and ticketing are included in this category, one would expect these expenses to be sensitive to traffic volume. There are, however, certain fixed costs involved in maintaining counter space, preparing timetables and schedules, advertising in newspapers, and so on, which, particularly at smaller stations, should not increase significantly with increased traffic. Equation (8) shows that promotion and sales expenses do depend on station density (as measured by the average number of passengers per station), at least over

36. CAB, *Handbook of Airline Statistics, 1967 Edition,* p. 538.

the range in which the carriers were operating during the 1962–66 period, but that increases in station density result in substantially less than proportional increases in promotion and sales costs.

(8) Promotion and sales expenses (dollars)
$$= 7{,}482{,}000 + 0.1593 \times 10^{-9} \text{ (passengers per station)}^2$$
$$(2.290)^a$$
$+ 0.129$ non-DC-3 aircraft miles $- 2{,}295$ wages $+ 0.1884$ (wages)^2
$(10.90)^b$ $(2.97)^b$ $(3.07)^b$
$+ 121{,}300$ Allegheny $- 152{,}600$ Bonanza $+ 11{,}350$ Central
(1.07) $(1.73)^c$ (0.14)
$+ 21{,}800$ Frontier $+ 202{,}800$ Lake Central $+ 540{,}700$ Mohawk
(0.25) $(2.48)^a$ $(3.66)^b$
$+ 770{,}900$ North Central $+ 236{,}200$ Ozark $- 3{,}050$ Pacific
$(8.67)^b$ $(2.71)^b$ (0.39)
$- 696{,}700$ Piedmont $- 8{,}060$ Southern $- 247{,}400$ Trans-Texas.
$(5.48)^b$ (0.10) $(2.89)^b$

$\bar{R}^2 = 0.9749$, $F = 159.17$,[a] F (firm constants as a group) $= 12.43$.[a]
The numbers in parentheses are t-ratios.
a. Significant at 5 percent level.
b. Significant at 1 percent level.
c. Significant at 10 percent level.

The coefficients and elasticities evaluated at sample means (corrected for zero observations where necessary) are:

	Coefficient	Elasticity
Passengers per station	$ 70.0	0.092
Non-DC-3 aircraft-miles	128.9	0.572
Wages	92.0	0.349

While it was not found possible to obtain a direct measure of the effect of competition on promotion and sales expense for the local carriers, certain indirect evidence exists to support the hypothesis of a significant and strongly positive relationship. Promotion and sales expenses per passenger for the locals fell, both absolutely and in relation to trunkline levels, between 1960 and 1965 and rose between 1965 and 1969. As Table 3-12 shows, except in the case of Mohawk Airlines and Texas International Airlines, most of this increase occurred in 1969—the first full year in which the impact of competitive route awards and full-scale jet operations was felt.[37]

37. Mohawk began large-scale jet operations before most other local carriers, and its routes already were competitive prior to 1968. In 1967 only 15 percent of local service revenue-miles were flown by jets. By 1969 this figure had reached 49 percent.

Table 3-12. Promotion and Sales Expense per Originating Passenger, Local Service Air Carriers as a Percent of That of Trunklines, 1960, 1965, 1968, 1969

Carrier[a]	1960	1965	1968	1969
Air West	52	46	47	59
Allegheny Airlines	47	38	39	43
Frontier Airlines	53	49	54	67
Mohawk Airlines	45	41	46	44
North Central Airlines	33	38	33	36
Ozark Air Lines	29	32	35	45
Piedmont Aviation	32	27	31	34
Southern Airways	51	34	35	39
Texas International Airlines	56	34	30	31
All locals	44	38	40	45
Expenditures per passenger				
Local	$2.08	$1.91	$2.10	$2.52
Trunk	$4.76	$4.98	$5.31	$5.64

Sources: Civil Aeronautics Board, *Handbook of Airline Statistics, 1967 Edition;* CAB, *Air Carrier Financial Statistics,* Vol. 17 (December 1969); CAB, *Air Carrier Traffic Statistics,* Vol. 15 (December 1969).

a. The carrier names shown are the official names in 1969. Acquisitions, mergers, and name changes between 1960 and 1969 are reflected in the data for all years, as follows: Air West includes Bonanza, Pacific, and West Coast; Allegheny includes Lake Central; Frontier includes Central; and Texas International includes Trans-Texas.

The case of Ozark provides an illustration. This carrier spent $574,000 in 1965 on all forms of advertising and publicity. However, in 1969 it announced that it was spending more than $800,000 just to promote its new "by-pass" service linking Peoria, Illinois, with New York City and Washington, D.C.[38] More direct evidence on the impact of competition on advertising expenses can be obtained from the experience of the trunklines in the late 1950s. According to a study made in 1959 by United Research, approximately half of all trunkline passengers in 1955 traveled over noncompetitive routes.[39] (Routes were listed as noncompetitive if a single airline carried over 90 percent of all passengers flying on the route.) The CAB made substantial trunkline route awards during the mid-1950s, particularly favoring the smaller, "weaker" trunklines. By 1957 over 60 percent of trunkline passengers were traveling on competitive routes. If changes in competition normalized by the 1955 level are regressed on changes in advertising expenditures per passenger (again normalized), 94 percent of the

38. "Regional Makes It to the Big Town," *Business Week,* No. 2069 (April 26, 1969), pp. 102, 106.

39. United Research Incorporated, "Federal Regulation of the Domestic Air Transport Industry," Prepared for the U.S. Department of Commerce (Cambridge, Mass.: United Research, 1959; processed), p. 39.

variance in the latter variable can be explained. An increase of 1 percentage point in the normalized competition variable was accompanied by a 2.5 percentage point increase in advertising expenditures per passenger. Increased competition indeed had a substantial effect on trunkline advertising expenditures in the late 1950s, and it is apparently having an equally strong effect on local service advertising expenditures in the early 1970s.

General and Administrative Expenses

General and administrative expenses are "expenses of a general corporate nature and expenses incurred in performing activities which contributed to more than a single operating function such as general financial accounting activities, purchasing activities, representation at law, and other general operational administration not directly applicable to a particular function."[40]

In 1960 general and administrative expenses of the locals amounted to $1.48 per passenger. This was 90 percent of the average trunkline per-passenger expense. By 1965 it had fallen to $1.21—only 72 percent of trunkline per-passenger expenditures. In the ensuing four years, per-passenger spending rose to $1.48—73 percent of the trunkline level.[41] As is to be expected with an overhead cost category, increases in traffic (measured in aircraft-miles) produce somewhat less than proportional increases in general and administrative expenses (see Equation 9).

It was somewhat surprising to find the strong indication that this impact varied depending on the aircraft used to fly these miles. Each additional DC-3 mile flown was associated with a 3.4 cent increase in these expenses, while each additional jet-mile flown was associated with a 17.2 cent increase. Unlike the case of aircraft and traffic servicing expense or passenger servicing expense, technological factors alone do not explain this difference. In part it may be a reflection of the effect of competition on general and administrative expenses, with larger aircraft being a proxy for competition. Perhaps the answer is simply that an airline flying jets is more complex to administer than an airline flying DC-3s.

40. CAB, *Handbook of Airline Statistics, 1967 Edition*, p. 537.
41. This latter figure is distorted to some degree by the expenditures of Air West, whose costs per passenger in 1969 were $2.47 (22 percent above the next highest carrier) and which during the year was suffering severe managerial difficulties. Omitting Air West, the per-passenger expenditure in 1969 was $1.35—67 percent of the trunkline level.

(9)   General and administrative expenses (dollars)
$$= 3{,}965{,}000 + 0.0338 \text{ DC-3 aircraft-miles}$$
$$(2.52)^a$$
$$+ 0.0732 \text{ large piston aircraft-miles} + 0.0713 \text{ turboprop aircraft-miles}$$
$$(8.74)^b \qquad\qquad\qquad\qquad (8.34)^b$$
$$+ 0.172 \text{ jet aircraft-miles} - 1{,}248 \text{ wages} + 0.111 \text{ (wages)}^2$$
$$(7.80)^b \qquad\qquad (2.28)^a \qquad\quad (2.56)^b$$
$$- 113{,}410 \text{ Allegheny} - 83{,}430 \text{ Bonanza} - 168{,}240 \text{ Central}$$
$$(1.34) \qquad\qquad\quad (1.47) \qquad\qquad (2.77)^b$$
$$- 108{,}450 \text{ Frontier} - 105{,}360 \text{ Lake Central} + 55{,}000 \text{ Mohawk}$$
$$(1.56) \qquad\qquad (1.73)^c \qquad\qquad\quad (0.62)$$
$$- 80{,}250 \text{ North Central} - 131{,}380 \text{ Ozark} - 30{,}880 \text{ Pacific}$$
$$(0.79) \qquad\qquad\qquad (1.74)^c \qquad\quad (0.53)$$
$$- 521{,}690 \text{ Piedmont} - 187{,}460 \text{ Southern} - 153{,}540 \text{ Trans-Texas.}$$
$$(6.07)^b \qquad\qquad (2.70)^b \qquad\qquad (1.91)^c$$

$\bar{R}^2 = 0.9571$, $F = 81.68$,[a] F (firm constants as a group) = 4.278[a]
F (separate aircraft-miles as a group) = 12.49[b]
The numbers in parentheses are t-ratios.
a. Significant at 5 percent level.
b. Significant at 1 percent level.
c. Significant at 10 percent level.

The coefficients and elasticities evaluated at sample means (corrected for zero observations if necessary) are:

	Coefficient	Elasticity
DC-3 aircraft-miles	$ 0.034	0.143
Large piston aircraft-miles	0.073	0.414
Turboprop aircraft-miles	0.071	0.288
Jet aircraft-miles	0.172	0.186
Wages	158.20	0.949

Non-operating Costs

The main category of non-operating costs is interest expense. It has been seen above that securing access to capital has been a major problem for the local service carriers and that they have had to pay relatively high interest rates and accept limitations on their freedom of operations. Table 3-13 shows total debt (long-term debt plus notes payable), interest expense, the latter as a percent of the former, and the ratio of interest expense to operating profit (operating revenues, including subsidy, minus operating ex-

Table 3-13. Debt and Interest Expense, Local Service Air Carriers, 1950–70
Dollar amounts in thousands

Year	Total debt[a]	Interest expense	Interest expense as percent of debt	Ratio of interest expense to operating profit or loss[b]
1950	$3,861	$133	3.4	0.22
1951	3,943	169	4.3	0.22
1952	6,128	251	4.1	n.a.
1953	5,157	360	7.0	n.a.
1954	3,816	228	6.0	0.14
1955	6,448	245	3.8	0.34
1956	11,257	431	3.8	n.a.
1957	13,276	671	5.1	n.a.
1958	22,889	827	3.6	0.50
1959	39,043	1,887	4.8	2.97
1960	53,957	2,872	5.3	1.32
1961	61,095	3,277	5.4	0.35
1962	63,532	3,748	5.9	0.28
1963	70,955	3,905	5.5	0.33
1964	77,212	4,160	5.4	0.25
1965	126,527	5,189	4.1	0.22
1966	245,759	7,796	3.2	0.33
1967	445,757	17,697	4.0	25.61
1968	590,882	30,637	5.2	n.a.
1969	605,521	41,495	6.9	n.a.
1970	598,282	44,382	7.4	n.a.

Sources: CAB, *Handbook of Airline Statistics, Calendar Years 1949–1956*, pp. 117, 213; *Handbook of Airline Statistics, 1967 Edition*, pp. 225, 315, and *1969 Edition*, pp. 205, 299; CAB, *Air Carrier Financial Statistics* (December 1970), pp. 3, 37.
n.a. Not applicable since a loss was incurred during the year, producing a negative number.
a. Long-term debt plus notes payable.
b. Includes U.S. mail and subsidy revenue.

penses). The figure for interest expense as a percent of total debt in no way represents the "cost of capital" to the local carriers but is merely the average interest paid. It is affected by the term structure of the debt as well as by market interest rates. (Note the rise of this figure during times of generally tight money and in particular its extremely sharp rise after 1967.) The ratio of interest expense to operating profit, sometimes called the "times-interest ratio," reflects the amount of maneuvering room open to management. The wide fluctuations of this ratio during the 1950s and frequent occurrences of negative values are yet another reason why investors considered the securities of local service carriers to be risky. The granting of permanent certificates to the locals in 1955 and the passage of guaranteed loan legislation in 1957, although they may have enabled the locals to float long-term debt, did not in themselves improve the debt-carrying ability of the local carriers. The improvement in stability of this ratio during the early 1960s was a direct result of the class rate subsidy system and the improved rate of return allowed. The sharp increase in 1967 and the negative values that followed in 1968, 1969, and 1970, reflect the profit deterioration experienced at the end of the 1960s.

Returns to Scale

It has generally been assumed by economists that the local service airlines suffer a cost disadvantage due to their small size, although estimates vary as to its importance. Caves showed a plot of average cost per available ton-mile versus available ton-miles, based on 1958 data. Trunkline costs generally were about 30 cents per available ton-mile, while local service costs ranged from about 45 cents to slightly above 60 cents, roughly 50 to 100 percent above trunkline levels. The line plotted through these points became horizontal at approximately 100 million available ton-miles per year, implying that carriers reaching this level of traffic would reap virtually all available economies of scale.[42] In 1958 the largest local carrier was one-fourth that size, while the average local service carrier generated only 14 million available ton-miles. By 1969, as a result of growth and merger, the smallest local carrier generated 104 million available ton-miles, and the average carrier generated twice that. Yet in 1969 average per ton-mile costs for the local carriers were still 50 to 100 percent above the trunkline average of 21 cents per available ton-mile. Mere growth in size had not served to overcome the cost disadvantage of the local carriers.

Growth in the scale of operations of a local service carrier can occur in at least three ways:

1. The basic route structure can be held constant, and traffic can grow. This increases passengers per station and departures per station. As traffic reaches higher levels, larger aircraft can be justified. At some point, traffic may warrant nonstop flights between major cities, thus increasing average stage length and aircraft utilization.

2. Routes can be expanded to larger cities, and smaller traffic points can be dropped. The impact on the number of passengers per station and departures per station is similar to that implied by growth pattern (1) above, although larger aircraft are more easily justified and the increase in average stage length is relatively greater in this case.

42. Caves, *Air Transport and Its Regulators*, p. 59.

3. Contiguous local service carriers can merge, or routes can be expanded to cities equivalent in traffic-generating potential to those already being served. In the absence of any subsequent route adjustments by the CAB, passengers per station, departures per station, aircraft size, stage length, and aircraft utilization are essentially unchanged by this pattern of growth.

Based on the results of this chapter, the first two growth patterns described would be expected to result in significant decreases in average operating costs—the second more than the first. The indirect operating cost equations estimated above reveal that increases in station density and departures per station lead to significantly less than proportional increases in costs, though this advantage is offset to some degree by the substitution of larger for smaller aircraft. The use of larger aircraft reduces the average seat-mile operating cost, as does an increase in stage length and equipment utilization. The second growth pattern, by eliminating low-density stations and by increasing average stage length and station density even more than the first, should mean larger reductions in average costs. Finally, the third pattern promises very limited reductions in average costs, except perhaps in the category of general and administrative expenses.

Table 3-14 shows the growth of the local service carriers between 1958 and 1969. Available ton-miles increased ten-fold. Aircraft-miles flown increased only slightly more than three times, but the average seating capacity of the aircraft flown more than doubled. On the other hand, average utilization was almost static, and the average length of hop, although it rose by 73 percent, was only 36 percent of the 1969 trunkline figure (about the same as in 1958).

It is clear that the growth pattern that best describes the local carriers is

Table 3-14. Growth in Available Ton-miles, Aircraft-miles, and Related Factors, Local Service Air Carriers, 1958–69

Factor	1958	1969	1969 as per-cent of 1958
Available ton-miles (thousands)	182,205	1,857,521	1,020
Aircraft revenue-miles (thousands)	72,253	231,151	320
Average available seats	24.8	64.9	262
Average length of hop (miles)	84	145	173
Average daily aircraft utilization (hours)	5.55	6.11	110
Number of departures per station annually	2,203	2,884	131

Sources: CAB, *Handbook of Airline Statistics, 1969 Edition*, pp. 14, 57, 59, 61; *Flight Magazine*, Vol. 48 (June 1959), pp. 56, 62–63; and Vol. 59 (June 1970), p. 47.

the second one. The low-traffic stations have not grown in step with high-traffic ones, and many have been eliminated (though many are still being served). The CAB has given the locals access to denser markets. It also has removed certain route restrictions, thus allowing increases in average stage length. And average cost per available ton-mile has declined, though it remains considerably above trunkline levels.

The one countervailing factor has been the increase in competition that has resulted from these route awards. It has been argued above that competition affects costs both in direct ways (such as increased advertising expenses, passenger service expenses, and aircraft and traffic servicing expenses) and in indirect ways (such as increased salaries for pilots flying smaller aircraft on noncompetitive routes as a result of the acquisition of larger, more productive aircraft for use on competitive routes). This increase in competition has had the effect of reversing the trend in the improvement of local service average costs relative to those of trunklines that was evident during the early 1960s.

The local service carriers do suffer a cost disadvantage because of the scale of their operations, but this is inherent in the nature of their business and cannot be solved by mergers. Short-haul, low-density air service is expensive to provide. It is considerably more expensive to provide with large aircraft than with small. Furthermore, attempts to strengthen local carrier routes by allowing the local carriers to compete directly with trunklines may have an adverse effect on the costs of operation on noncompetitive routes, especially if the local carriers are induced by this policy to use aircraft that are too large for the latter routes. The post-1965 reversal of the 1960–65 declines in local service per-passenger costs relative to trunkline costs in two of the four indirect cost categories, and the slowing of the trend in the other two in spite of continued and even accelerated growth during the latter period is evidence that the effects of increased competition can more than offset declines in cost due to scale effects. In short, the only way to remove the cost disadvantage of local service carriers is to turn them into trunkline carriers—to drop their short-haul, low-density routes.[43] Doing this, however, would remove the rationale for their existence as a separate carrier group and also remove the justification for their support through government subsidy, although it might at the same time end the need for such support.

43. Both Caves (*Air Transport and Its Regulation*), p. 87, and Straszheim (*The International Airline Industry*), p. 104, recognize this fact.

CHAPTER FOUR

The Local Service "Experiment"

THE GROWTH OF THE "avalanche of pressures generated by chambers of commerce, lower levels of government, prospective local service operators, and other components of the feeder movement"[1] led the Civil Aeronautics Board (CAB) to announce on March 22, 1943, its intention to investigate the feasibility of feeder air service. At this time the Board had applications covering 16,771 miles of feeder routes and 44,966 miles of airmail "pick-up" routes,[2] but there was a continuing lack of enthusiasm on the part of CAB and Post Office Department authorities for such service.

The subsequent Investigation of Local, Feeder, and Pick-Up Air Service did not increase their enthusiasm. The findings of both the examiners and the Board on the costs of providing the service were not encouraging. Nevertheless, the Board decided to establish feeder service on an experimental basis, stating:

Since the challenge exists, and the investigation has disclosed an eagerness on the part of the proponents of such a service to take up the challenge, and since the experiment may well result in public benefit beyond present expectations, the responsibility imposed upon us to encourage the development of an air transportation system properly adapted to the present and future needs of the commerce of the United States, the Postal Service, and the national defense, and to encourage the development of civil aeronautics generally, justifies us, within reasonable bounds, in translating into results of experience what are now plans and estimates.[3]

1. See Donald Solar, "The Federal Interest in Local Air Service: A Study in the Evolution of Economic Policy" (Ph.D. thesis, Columbia University, 1963), Chap. 3. The quotation is from pp. 29–30.
2. Pick-up service involves the use of a hook attached to an aircraft to pick up mail without the need to land the aircraft. All American Aviation, the predecessor of Allegheny Airlines, operated such a service for several years in Pennsylvania, West Virginia, and Ohio.
3. *Civil Aeronautics Board Reports*, Vol. 6 (July 1944–May 1946), p. 3.

Once having decided to establish a local, or feeder, service, the Board was faced with the task of deciding whether to accomplish this expansion by using the existing sixteen trunk carriers or by creating a new special class of carriers. The examiners listed five advantages cited by the existing carriers in their favor:

(a) The additional overhead expense involved in extending the routes of existing carriers would be less than the overhead expenses incurred by a separate enterprise;

(b) The existing carriers, at least in some instances, would be able to operate a local route which might be unprofitable in itself by absorbing such losses with profit from long-haul services. . . . Revenue from a passenger pick-up at a "local" point and continuing beyond a terminal of a local route would be available for the entire journey to the existing carrier, whereas only that part for the local transportation would be available to a local operator;

(c) Greater utilization of equipment would be possible;

(d) The experience of existing carriers would be available for the air transportation needs of the small cities;

(e) The quality of service in general would be higher if existing air carriers provided it. In this connection specific reference was usually made to the larger and more comfortable equipment that would be used, and the fact that day and night, all-weather service would be provided, as contrasted with the proposals of some new carriers to use smaller equipment and, at least at the outset, to limit operations to a contact [pick-up] basis.[4]

However, the examiners recommended that in most cases new carriers should be used. They had examined the traffic data for the 88 cities with populations of less than 50,000 that received air service as of September 1940 and found that the 18 of these whose population was below 10,000 had generated an average of only 4.03 arriving and departing passengers per day. The 31 cities in the 10,000–20,000 population bracket had averaged 5.7 passengers a day, while the 39 cities with populations of 20,000 to 50,000 averaged 13.4 a day.[5] One of the more modest proposals before the Board in 1943 envisioned the expansion of service to 129 additional airports. This would have placed all cities of 25,000 or more within fifteen miles of scheduled air transportation.[6] If these cities generated no more traffic than had been generated at those cited above, this expansion would have been tremendously costly to the government in terms of additional subsidy required. Expansion of air service to all urban points (incorporated areas with a population of more than 2,500), which one of the proposals

4. *Ibid.*, pp. 29–30.
5. *Ibid.*, pp. 13, 46. The examiners concluded that the lack of patronage was not the result of poor service provided by the airlines.
6. *Ibid.*, p. 29.

called for, would have cost the government an estimated $150 million in mail payments per year.[7]

The examiners realized that if any appreciable expansion of air service was to have a chance of success at a reasonable cost to the government, it would be necessary for the operators of such service to achieve substantial savings in operating costs over the cost levels that the trunklines had been able to reach to that date. They therefore cited the reasons given for using existing trunklines as, in reality, reasons for creating new carriers:

Most of the presently operating air carriers also urge as a reason for putting small cities on existing routes the fact that the services will be provided with the type of equipment used on the long-haul routes. . . . The various proposals described in that part of this report relating to the proposals of new carriers . . . have the common characteristic of emphasizing economy and less luxurious standards of service. This characteristic must be constantly emphasized, and the more progress that is made in this direction the more prospects for air service will be created. Any substantial economy of operation will have to result from departures from the existing type of service. It is reasonable to assume that necessarily different standards of operation can best be developed by new carriers, organized for such a purpose.[8]

The Board concurred with the examiners' recommendations. In the route cases that established the feeder system, it generally adhered to a policy of granting the routes to newly created carriers. In the Florida Case, for example, National Airlines applied for feeder routes, claiming that it would achieve substantial cost savings by eliminating ground personnel and using the copilot to handle mail and sell tickets.[9] The Board rejected National's application and awarded the route in question to Orlando Airlines, a newly created feeder carrier (the predecessor of Florida Airways).[10]

Donald Solar notes that several trunkline carriers, believing that feeder carriers would not remain confined to their low-density, short-haul routes, applied for feeder routes to forestall the establishment of future competitors.[11] The Board was properly skeptical of the sort of service that these

7. *Ibid.*, p. 49. In fiscal year 1943 the domestic trunklines received $5 million in subsidy. During the peak year of subsidization—1942—the subsidy amounted to $14 million (*Civil Aeronautics Board Reports to Congress, Fiscal Year 1968*, p. 138).

8. *Civil Aeronautics Board Reports*, Vol. 6 (July 1944–May 1946), pp. 52–53.

9. *Ibid.*, p. 782.

10. The major exception to this policy occurred in 1947 in the Great Lakes Area Case, in which Transcontinental and Western Air was awarded feeder routes in Indiana and Ohio as an "experiment." (*Civil Aeronautics Board Reports*, Vol. 8 [April–December 1947], p. 392.) Sometime later these routes were taken from TWA and given to Lake Central Airlines, a feeder carrier.

11. "The Federal Interest in Local Air Service," pp. 28–29. Solar quotes the president of United Air Lines as asking, "How long would it be before a feeder company becomes a trunk-line?" (p. 29).

carriers might offer to smaller cities if indeed they were granted feeder routes. In other cases the trunklines admitted that they planned to operate the feeder routes for which they were applying primarily to generate long-haul traffic for their particular systems, rather than try to develop the routes to their full potential.[12] The use of specialist feeder carriers thus freed the CAB from having to choose among trunkline applicants, each of which was anxious to capture any traffic that the feeder systems might generate.

Swaine has suggested yet another reason why the Board chose to create a new class of carriers rather than use the existing ones.[13] By the mid-1940s the existing carriers were well on their way to achieving subsidy-free operation. It was obvious that the proposed new services would require extensive subsidization for an indefinite period and would mean certain financial risks for the participants. If existing carriers were used and if the "local service experiment" failed, it might pull some of the weaker "grandfather carriers" down with it. If failure was possible, far better for it to affect only a few small carriers serving minor routes rather than major carriers which also provided the nation's long-haul air transportation. The Board seemingly recognized this when it stated:

We must not lose sight of the fact that Congress in enacting the Civil Aeronautics Act of 1938 laid down with great care the guides to the objective of an economically and technically sound air transportation system. This Act contemplated, and actually resulted in, the payment of substantial sums of money out of the Federal Treasury to encourage the attainment of this objective. These payments represent, in effect, an investment by the Government, for the common welfare, in our present air transportation system. Needless to say we have an obligation to avoid the adoption of any ill-considered policy with respect to a general expansion of air services that would endanger the results thus far achieved under the enlightened national policy established by that Act.[14]

Having made the decision to create a new class of feeder carriers, the Board was still faced with the task of deciding which of the many new applicants to choose. There were several applicants for almost every route. Most had previous aviation experience. Some had operated cargo or intrastate passenger services. Still others had operated flying schools or maintained other fixed base operations.

The backgrounds of the companies that received local service certificates

12. *Civil Aeronautics Board Reports*, Vol. 6 (July 1944–May 1946), p. 786.
13. Howard Ralph Swaine, "Subsidization of Local Air Services" (Ph.D. thesis, University of California, Los Angeles, 1965), pp. 37–46.
14. *Civil Aeronautics Board Reports*, Vol. 6 (July 1944–May 1946), p. 3.

bear a close relation to the backgrounds of the companies that more recently have entered the third-level carrier business. In some cases, the same people are involved. For example:

The decline of local airline service in Wisconsin is especially ironic. North Central Airlines, one of the principal local service airlines in the country today, was born in Clintonville, Wisconsin, in 1945 because a small group of enlightened community leaders there foresaw the need for airline service. Eventually they were required to divest themselves of control of this company.

Now the airline born in Clintonville has become too big to serve this community and others like it [Clintonville was dropped by North Central in 1966], and the businessmen of Clintonville are starting all over again. They are considering buying a twin-engine Beechcraft and converting it for use as [a] nine-passenger commercial carrier. [North Central Airlines started with 10-passenger Lockheed L-10s.] . . . Twenty years after they pioneered in local service aviation, they are right back again where they started.[15]

This service was in fact set up and was operating in June 1968.

The Board announced early that it would favor residents of the area to be served, arguing that they would provide "maximum development of the traffic potential."[16] The precise definition of "residents of the area to be served" created some controversy within the Board, however, provoking at least one dissent concerning carrier choice.[17]

Even having adopted this principle, the Board still found itself confronted with more than one qualified carrier for a route. In such cases, it often adopted somewhat capricious reasoning in arriving at its final choice. In the West Coast Case, the Board selected Southwest Airways over Coast Aviation for a Los Angeles–San Francisco route (with intermediate stops) partly because of "the broader experience of the Southwest management," but also partly because, while Coast Aviation had proposed "a conventional type of service contemplating traffic stops at the various points to be served," Southwest had "presented a plan of operation for the conduct of a combination passenger and pick-up service utilizing a passenger plane equipped with a pick-up device."[18] However, in the New England Case[19] the Board apparently was not impressed by All American Aviation's proposal to operate a joint passenger–pick-up service, using a pick-up device.

15. See *Review of the Local Air Carrier Industry*, Hearings before the Aviation Subcommittee of the Senate Committee on Commerce, 89 Cong. 2 sess. (1966), p. 318.

16. *Civil Aeronautics Board Reports*, Vol. 6 (July 1944–May 1946), pp. 789–90.

17. *Ibid.*, pp. 791–93.

18. *Ibid.*, pp. 997–98. Southwest was not allowed to operate such a service. It was required to stop at every point on its route even if no passengers or mail were to be dropped or picked up. Presumably Southwest's innovative attitude was what the Board liked.

19. *Civil Aeronautics Board Reports*, Vol. 7 (June 1946–March 1947), p. 40.

Table 4-1. Population and Number of Potential Points for Air Service in the United States, and Number of Cities Certificated for Service by "Grandfather" Carriers, by Population Grouping, 1943

Population grouping (thousands)	Number of points	Population (thousands)	Number of cities certificated[a]	Population of certificated cities (thousands)
Urban				
1,000 or more	5	15,911	5	15,911
500–1,000	9	6,457	9	6,457
250–500	23	7,828	22	7,526
100–250	55	7,793	40	5,970
50–100	107	7,344	48	3,428
25–50	213	7,417	56	1,956
10–25	665	9,967	61	966
5–10	965	6,682	23	169
2–5	1,422	5,026	12	44
Total urban areas	3,464	74,424	276	42,428
Nonurban				
Under 2,500	13,288	9,343	3	5
Unincorporated	...	47,903	9	32
Total	16,752	131,669	288	42,465

Source: *Civil Aeronautics Board Reports*, Vol. 6 (July 1944–May 1946), p. 11. Figures are rounded and may not add to totals.

a. The "grandfather provision" of the Civil Aeronautics Act of 1938 gave automatic certification to the nineteen domestic air carriers that had previously been in continuous operation. Of 288 points certificated, 112 were not receiving service as of August 31, 1943. Some of the suspensions were because of war, but about fifty points were suspended because of inadequate airport facilities. Some of the points had never received service.

Choice of Cities and Routes

The United States already had an air transport network that provided a large proportion of the population with access to scheduled air service. As of 1943, 57 percent of the urban population (an "urban area" being defined as an incorporated area with a population of more than 2,500) lived in cities where scheduled air service was already certificated (see Table 4-1). About 75 percent of the urban areas not certificated lay within fifty miles of a point that was certificated; 40 percent of such cities lay within twenty-five miles (see Table 4-2).[20]

Since the Board itself was aware of the low traffic potential of the remaining smaller cities and towns, it is somewhat surprising that it adopted

20. Of the 288 cities certificated in 1943, 112 were not receiving service. Some suspensions were due to World War II; about fifty were due to inadequate airport facilities. Others had never received service even though they were certificated.

Table 4-2. Air Service Status of Cities in the United States, by Distance from Scheduled Service and by Population Class, 1946

Air service status and distance from scheduled service	Population class						
	2,500– 5,000	5,001– 10,000	10,001– 25,000	25,001– 50,000	50,001– 100,000	100,001– 250,000	250,001 and over
Cities not receiving service	1,412	937	597	147	54	12	1
50 miles or less from air-served city	1,027	732	498	128	50	12	1
51–100 miles from air-served city	356	193	92	19	4	0	0
100 miles and over from air-served city	29	12	7	0	0	0	0
Cities receiving service	10	28	68	66	53	43	36
Total cities	1,422	965	665	213	107	55	37

Source: United Research Incorporated, "Federal Regulation of the Domestic Air Transport Industry," Prepared for the U.S. Department of Commerce (United Research, 1959; processed), Table B-7; *Civil Aeronautics Board Reports*, Vol. 6 (July 1944–May 1946), p. 11.

no standards to determine which cities should receive air service. In the first of the area cases (Service in the Rocky Mountain States Area), it did lay down some "guiding principles," which it intended to apply on a case-by-case basis in the future:

In determining whether the public convenience and necessity require a proposed local-feeder service, the Board will consider, among other things, the importance to our nation of linking smaller communities with air service where there is the best prospect of its financial success, as well as, of course, the question of whether the communities involved will benefit by substantial improvement over the existing surface transportation facilities. Considerations entering into such a determination include the distance of a community from its normal metropolitan trading center; the time presently required to travel the distance by existing surface transportation as compared with the estimated time required for accomplishing the trip by air, including the travel time to and from the airports to be used by the service; and the frequency of existing transportation schedules as compared with that proposed or practicable for the air transport service. Distance between communities will not always be the determining factor. Thus, conditions of intervening mountainous terrain may result in the isolation of communities which can best be overcome by the inherent advantages of air transportation.[21]

But it soon became apparent that these "guiding principles" would not be adhered to. For example, in the West Coast Case[22] the Board decided to authorize additional air service between Los Angeles and San Francisco,

21. *Civil Aeronautics Board Reports*, Vol. 6 (July 1944–May 1946), p. 731.
22. *Ibid.*, pp. 961–1039.

which are 327 air-miles apart. At the time of the case, air service was already authorized between these two cities, both on a nonstop basis and with intermediate stops at Monterey (84 miles south of San Francisco) and Santa Barbara (90 miles north and west of Los Angeles); Monterey and Santa Barbara are about 190 miles apart. The new route, awarded to Southwest, included eight intermediate stops: Oxnard-Ventura, Santa Barbara, Santa Maria, San Luis Obispo, Coalinga, Monterey, Santa Cruz, and San Jose. It was 401 miles in length (some 25 percent longer than the direct Los Angeles–San Francisco distance) and had an average length of hop of only 50 miles. (In June 1948 Southwest was offering three flights a day over the entire route, one flight a day stopping everywhere except at Coalinga and San Luis Obispo, and one flight a day covering only the San Francisco–Monterey segment.) The choice of cities to be served seems to have been based on their population and distance from existing air service. Tradeoffs were made between these two factors. Coalinga was granted air service, even though it had a population of only 5,000, because it was 65 miles from Visalia, the nearest city with scheduled air service. No effort was made to estimate potential patronage or to determine to what extent the new service at the frequencies proposed actually represented an improvement over existing means of transportation. For example, in refusing to allow additional air service in the Central Valley of California, the Board had cited the "excellent" surface transportation facilities already available. The San Joaquin Valley Line of the Southern Pacific railroad ran through the valley, providing up to five round trips a day between most valley points and Los Angeles.[23] But all of the cities on Southwest's new route, except Coalinga and Santa Maria, were on the Southern Pacific's Coast Line and were served by up to six trains a day in each direction.[24] Santa Maria was on a branch of this line, and Coalinga was on a branch of the San Joaquin Valley Line. Most of the cities were located on U.S. 101, a highway that, while not up to the quality of U.S. 99, was still an excellent all-weather highway. In fact, the only city that was "isolated" to any degree was Coalinga.[25]

23. National Railway Publication Co., *The Official Guide of the Railways and Steam Navigation Lines of the United States* (December 1947), p. 890.

24. *Ibid.*, p. 887.

25. During the month of March 1949 Coalinga generated sixty-nine arriving and departing passengers—an average of slightly more than two a day. (Civil Aeronautics Board, *Airline Traffic Survey, March 1949*, Vol. 1, p. 261.) In June 1948, it was receiving three flights in each direction each day. By July 1949, service to Coalinga had been suspended. (American Aviation Associates, *Air Traffic Guide* [June 1948], p. 145, and American Aviation Publication, Official Airline Guide [July 1949], p. 203.)

In this same case the Board authorized United to add Salinas as an intermediate

In the New England Case the Board authorized E. W. Wiggins Airways to provide service to several cities in Massachusetts, Rhode Island, Connecticut, and Vermont, even after noting that there were already generally excellent transportation facilities throughout the region.[26] The frequency of service Wiggins proposed to offer was two trips each day in each direction. The Board decided to authorize the carrier to operate a route connecting Boston, Massachusetts, and Albany, New York, with intermediate stops at Lowell, Fitchburg, Athol-Orange, Greenfield, and Adams-North Adams, and another route connecting the same two terminals with intermediate stops at Framingham, Worcester, Southbridge, Springfield, Northampton, and Pittsfield—all in Massachusetts. The former route was served by the Boston and Maine Railroad, which offered an average of five passenger trains daily in each direction. The southern route paralleled the Boston and Albany division of the New York Central Railroad, which offered approximately ten trains each day in each direction.[27] Concerning the modes of ground transportation in the area the Board said: "The pattern of bus service is much more comprehensive than the rail service. Service by bus is available to and from practically every community in the area, and to go into further detail would merely result in an itemization of the various highways which honeycomb the area."[28]

In deciding what pattern of air service to authorize, the Board relied heavily on the concept of "community of interest," usually estimated by the amount of business transacted between two communities and the number of travelers and pounds of mail exchanged. For example, in the New England Case, mentioned above, the Board authorized a route between Boston and Providence that included both Brockton, with a population of 60,000, lying twenty miles south of Boston and thirty miles from Providence, and Taunton with 37,000, sixteen miles east of Providence and thirty-seven miles south of Boston, after concluding that "their principal community of interest is with Boston, but Providence is also an important

---

point on its Los Angeles–San Francisco route, even though it was only sixteen miles from Monterey, a city already served by United. The Board admitted that its actions were unusual but justified them by stating that "[Salinas] is the largest lettuce-shipping point in the world and attention has recently been directed to the shipments of this commodity by air from this section to all parts of the country" (*Civil Aeronautics Board Reports*, Vol. 6 [July 1944–May 1946], p. 985). The Board did not say why lettuce could not be trucked sixteen miles to Monterey for air shipment. In any event, no substantial amounts of lettuce have ever been shipped by air.

26. *Civil Aeronautics Board Reports*, Vol. 7 (December 1946–March 1947), p. 27.
27. *Ibid.*, pp. 37–38, 62–63.
28. *Ibid.*, p. 30.

trading center for Taunton." The Board refused to authorize air service between Taunton, Brockton, and New York because "their community of interest with New York is considerably less than other cities in the area, and it appears that air service of a local character which would provide access to Boston and Providence would meet the needs of these cities to a greater extent than by including them as an intermediate point on a trunk-line between New York and Boston."[29]

In applying such criteria to decide which cities should be served and with which other cities they should be connected, the Board seemed not to realize the possibility that a high "community of interest" reflected in part the existence of good transportation and communication facilities between cities, as in the case of the Boston–Albany routes referred to above. Consequently, by choosing routes and cities to be served on this basis, the Board was maximizing the amount of competition the feeder air carriers would face from existing modes of transportation. Ideally, the carriers would have been given a high degree of flexibility in establishing routes, stations served, and schedules. In this way the feeder carriers could have attracted traffic by seeking out and exploiting situations in which air service provided some clear advantage over existing transportation. However, given the Board's inability or unwillingness to establish definite standards by which to judge the success of its "experiment," this flexibility could not be allowed, for it would have imposed a virtually limitless financial obligation on the Board. (The ability to experiment with the services offered is one of the major advantages the unsubsidized third-level air carriers have had.) Consequently, the CAB was forced to choose cities and routes to be served on the basis of whatever sketchy information it could obtain and in an atmosphere of strong political pressures.

Finally, much to the dismay of some of its members, the Board did not award just a few routes and then evaluate the results before going any further.[30] It proceeded instead to authorize a nationwide system of feeder routes. By 1950, certificates of public convenience and necessity had been granted to seventeen feeder airlines with sixteen of them in operation, in comparison with one in operation in 1945. Nine had started operations in 1947, and seven started in 1949. (One had been discontinued.) Total feeder airline route mileage was only 2,115 miles in 1945. By 1950, over 30,000 miles of routes had been authorized. A compilation of feeder operations

29. *Ibid.*, p. 34.
30. *Ibid.*, pp. 532–38.

covering data for the second quarter of 1950 listed 547 certificated points (eliminating duplications), of which 377 were to be served exclusively by local service carriers, though many of those were not yet actually being served.[31]

The major check the Board adopted (and the one it used to mollify those who criticized the extent of its feeder route awards) was to grant the feeder carriers "temporary" certificates that would expire automatically after three years. If a city wanted air service, the Board reasoned, then why not grant its request? If traffic didn't develop, the city could be dropped after three years. The majority of the Board seemed unaware of the political difficulties of this course of action, though individual members warned against the consequences.

Restrictions on Service

The typical feeder route granted by the CAB began and terminated in cities already receiving scheduled air service. In many cases there was already nonstop service between the two terminals. The Board recognized that the new carriers would have a strong incentive to ignore their smaller intermediate stations and concentrate on terminal-to-terminal service, thereby entering into direct competition with the established trunkline carriers for this traffic. The feeling that the trunklines, if granted feeder routes, would give them token service at best was one of the major reasons why the Board had created the "specialist" feeder carriers. Fear of feeder competition was one of the major reasons for the opposition of existing carriers to the creation of the new carriers. Therefore, in order both to assure that the local carriers would remain "local" and to protect the trunks from new competition, the Board decided to place severe restrictions on the character of the service it would allow the feeders to offer.

The examiners in the Investigation of Local, Feeder, and Pick-Up Air Service had anticipated this problem. A number of witnesses had suggested that a certificate issued to a feeder should contain a provision requiring the feeder to stop at every intermediate point on every flight. The examiners did not agree with this recommendation, stating that

The evidence regarding the general pattern of traffic flow appears to militate against this simple solution. . . . A limitation which would require that every point be served on every schedule would place a serious handicap on the operator

31. *Southern Flight*, Vol. 34 (September 1950), pp. 22, 34–35.

in cultivating the business of the traveler who wants to get from a small town to a large town with a minimum of delay. To accommodate this type of traffic, the feeder operator should have some leeway in putting on modified skip-stop schedules. Accordingly, limitations relating to skip-stop or nonstop operations should be prescribed to meet circumstances which will vary in different feeder services. Such limitations might, in one case, prohibit nonstop service between two points which may also be designated in a certificate of an existing carrier; in another, they might fix a maximum nonstop distance, or a minimum number of intermediate points which must be served on any one schedule. Situations may arise where no limitations would be necessary.[32]

The Board chose not to agree with the examiners. In the first major case involving feeder routes (Service in the Rocky Mountain States Area, decided March 28, 1946), the Board adopted the policy of requiring feeder flights to originate and terminate at points designated as terminals on the carriers' certificates and to stop at every intermediate point.[33] This policy was also applied in the Florida Case (decided March 28, 1946), the West Coast Case (decided May 22, 1946), and the New England Case (decided June 13, 1946).[34] It was modified by the Pioneer Air Lines, Inc., Amendment (decided November 14, 1946) to allow this carrier to operate shuttle service between any two points consecutively named in its certificate, although a minimum of two round trips a day over each route segment was required.[35] This modification allowed Pioneer to enter into direct competition with Braniff Airways on its Waco–Fort Worth/Dallas and Houston–Austin routes. Although this possibility brought forth a strong dissent from CAB Member Clarence M. Young,[36] such turnaround authority between consecutively named points was adopted in subsequent area cases and was applied retroactively to some carriers.[37]

The effect on the quality of terminal-to-terminal service of an every-stop-on-every-flight requirement can be illustrated by Southwest's Los Angeles–San Francisco feeder route. In 1948, trunklines were providing nonstop service on this route, using DC-3, DC-4, and DC-6 aircraft. The shortest elapsed time was 1 hour and 45 minutes (DC-6); but most flights were scheduled at about 2 hours. By cutting its time at intermediate stops

32. *Civil Aeronautics Board Reports*, Vol. 6 (July 1944–May 1946), p. 55.
33. *Ibid.*, pp. 732–50.
34. *Ibid.*, pp. 791 and 1001–3, and *ibid.*, Vol. 7 (June 1946–March 1947), p. 27, respectively.
35. *Ibid.*, Vol. 7, pp. 469–74.
36. *Ibid.*, pp. 474–77.
37. Southwest Airways Company, Restriction Modification, February 10, 1948. *Civil Aeronautics Board Reports*, Vol. 9 (January–December 1948), p. 67.

to a minimum (a two-minute stop at Monterey was scheduled), Southwest was able to fly its 401-mile Los Angeles–San Francisco route in 3 hours and 45 minutes. The average trunkline speed over the 327-mile straight-line distance was between 150 and 170 miles an hour. In contrast, Southwest's average speed over the same distance was about 87 miles an hour.[38] The restriction on Southwest's operations apparently had the intended effect, however. According to the March 1949 air traffic survey, only 80 of the 21,164 passengers traveling by air between Los Angeles and San Francisco during that month used Southwest for any segment of their trip, and only 68 traveled the entire way on Southwest.[39] On the other hand, where such restrictions were not a factor, the local carriers cut deeply into the markets that formerly had belonged exclusively to the trunklines. Of the 1,153 passengers traveling between Houston and Austin, Texas, during the March 1949 survey, 651 traveled on Pioneer.

To be sure, the requirement that every flight stop at every intermediate point assured a higher level of service to intermediate points than would otherwise have been provided. Yet the fact that such restrictions were aimed primarily at preventing competition between the feeder airlines and the trunklines was revealed clearly in the Great Lakes Area Case.[40] TWA, a trunk carrier, was granted routes in Ohio and Indiana that were admittedly feeder in character. No restrictions were placed on these routes, however. In rationalizing this decision the Board said:

In authorizing services of a purely local or feeder character, it has been our policy in the past to include in the certificates certain restrictions with respect to skip-stop and nonstop operations. This was done to avoid uneconomical duplication of existing trunk-line services. In the instant case, however, no such restrictions are being imposed and this will enable the carriers authorized to conduct these operations to experiment with a wide variety of nonstop and shuttle services without impairing the quality of their long-haul service. Since the operations will be conducted by trunk-line carriers along the course of their established routes, the element of duplication of services and consequent diversion of revenues from other carriers will not exist. At the end of the temporary period of 3 years we shall be able to assess the value of this type of service in meeting the travel needs of the public, and shall be able to compare it with local feeder service systems which we have authorized in various sections of the country.[41]

Route restrictions specified in the certificates of the local service carriers were not the only protection the Board provided the trunk carriers. In some

38. American Aviation Associates, *Air Traffic Guide* (June 1948).
39. Civil Aeronautics Board, *Airline Traffic Survey, March 1949*, p. 904.
40. *Civil Aeronautics Board Reports*, Vol. 8 (April–December 1947), p. 360.
41. *Ibid.*, p. 392.

cases designation of the carrier that would service a particular route was also influenced by a desire to protect the trunk carriers. United and Western Air Lines opposed the creation of a single feeder carrier to serve the entire area from Los Angeles to Seattle. They contended that

> the volume of traffic to be developed at small intermediate points located relatively short distances from certificated cities will not be sufficient to support regularly scheduled air transportation with the result that the new operators will eventually be compelled to seek authority to conduct nonstop operations between major cities.[42]

To mollify these trunklines, the Board, in addition to writing in the normal certificate restrictions, decided to certify two carriers in the area rather than one, as additional protection. Southwest was given routes from Los Angeles northward, terminating at Medford, Oregon. West Coast Airlines was given feeder routes north of Medford.[43]

Subsidy for Feeder Carriers

The Board had anticipated that a subsidy would be necessary if the feeder carriers were to survive. The examiners in the Local, Feeder, and Pick-Up Air Service investigation devoted a considerable portion of their report to an estimate of the costs and revenues to be expected in feeder services. On the basis of model routes proposed for various sections of the country by Braniff (a trunk carrier) and by Southwest, Parks Air College, and E. W. Wiggins Airways (all prospective feeder operators), the examiners arrived at a projected total operating cost of approximately 35 cents per revenue aircraft-mile. The cost projections all assumed the use of twin-engine aircraft seating approximately 10 passengers, with a flight crew consisting of only a pilot and a copilot. Direct operating costs in the sense implied in Chapter 3 constituted 45 to 75 percent of the total. Economies in indirect costs were to be obtained by eliminating stewardesses and meals, the use of the copilot to collect tickets and stow baggage, and the use of part-time ground personnel. Total capital requirements for initiating operations were estimated at between $500,000 and $1,300,000, depending on the extent of the route system granted and the proposed number of flights per day.

42. *Civil Aeronautics Board Reports*, Vol. 6 (July 1944–May 1946), p. 980.
43. *Ibid.*, p. 996.

Revenue projections were sketchy, but the general assumption was that fares would be 4 to 5 cents a mile (approximately three times the motor bus fare). The examiners believed that an average load of two passengers was a reasonable target. This would have produced revenue of about 10 cents per revenue-mile. It was assumed that some cargo revenue would also be earned.

On the basis of these projections the examiners recommended the establishment of a maximum mail pay/subsidy rate of 25 cents a mile. This level of subsidy, it was projected, could provide substantial coverage of the United States with scheduled air service at a cost to the government of approximately $57 million a year.[44]

The Board refused to accept the recommendation of a limit either on total mail pay or on the maximum mail pay per mile. Instead it decided to limit the liability of the government by giving the new carriers temporary certificates, stating that this would "serve as a safeguard against a static or progressively increasing dependence on the Government; and will permit of the subsequent giving of permanent status only to such services as have shown during the life of a temporary certificate that they are capable of operating without undue cost to the Government and of a progressive reduction of such costs."[45]

In the first feeder mail rate case, the Board was faced with the problem of implementing the feeder subsidy.[46] During its first months of operation using 9-passenger Lockheed Electras, Essair (which became Pioneer) had experienced costs of 61 to 88 cents per plane-mile, while its revenue had been running between 5 and 25 cents a mile. This implied that it needed between 83 cents (during the first month of operations) and 38 cents (during the second month) per plane-mile to break even. The Board was reluctant to establish a permanent future mail rate on the basis of such widely fluctuating operating results, but it was equally reluctant to put the airline on a temporary rate subject to future readjustment, which in effect would have placed the carrier on a "cost-plus" subsidy system.[47]

44. *Ibid.*, pp. 54–55.
45. *Ibid.*, p. 5.
46. Essair, Inc., Temporary Mail Rate case, decided March 22, 1946. *Ibid.*, p. 687. Essair became Pioneer Air Lines a few months later.
47. *Ibid.*, pp. 689–90. The Board said, "Heretofore we have refused to establish future mail rates on a tentative basis subject to later readjustment. We have held that the adoption of a method of mail rate determination patterned upon a 'cost plus' system would tend to destroy a carrier's incentive to maintain costs at a reasonable level and to develop its nonmail business." (P. 690.)

In spite of the admitted drawbacks the Board decided to establish a "temporary" subsidy rate of 25 cents a mile, to be paid for mileage not exceeding 2,732 a day (two round trips over Pioneer's 683-mile route). If Pioneer chose to fly more than an average of 2,732 miles a day in any month, the rate was to be reduced proportionately. In March 1947 the Board increased the rate to 35 cents a mile[48] and raised the mileage limit to 8,106 a day (2.87 round trips over an expanded system).[49] The 35-cents-a-mile rate was made retroactive to the date when Pioneer began operations; and for the period from that date until February 1, 1947, the maximum mileage restriction was removed.

As other feeder carriers were established in various route cases, the Board also placed them on temporary rates. The rate generally established was 60–65 cents a mile for the first six months. Thereafter, it was supposed to decline in graduated steps, eventually reaching a minimum of 35 cents a mile.

In July 1947 the Board sought to place Pioneer on a "final" rate.[50] This rate was to have been applied retroactively and was to have applied in the future. In the proceeding, the Board examined Pioneer's costs, disallowed some as unwarranted, and established a final rate (including a 7 percent rate of return on investment) of 53 cents per plane-mile for the period August 1, 1945, to August 31, 1946. For the period September 1, 1946, to May 31, 1947, the Board established a final rate of 60 cents per plane-mile. For the future "permanent rate" the Board established a sliding-scale rate, based on load factor. The basic rate was 45 cents a mile. However, for each percentage point increase in load factor above 35 percent, the rate of mail pay was to be reduced by 0.5 cent per revenue-plane-mile. Thus, if Pioneer achieved a 50 percent load factor, its mail pay would be 37.5 cents a mile. This sliding scale was designed to stimulate Pioneer to increase its load factor. It was not successful, since the incentive involved was slight.[51]

In December 1948 the Board found it necessary to reopen Pioneer's "final" rates.[52] The new rate established was 48 cents a mile, to be paid if the load factor was 31.99 percent or less. For each percentage point increase above 32 percent the rate was to be reduced by 0.65 cent per plane-mile. Under the new "permanent" rate Pioneer would receive only 36.3

48. *Civil Aeronautics Board Reports*, Vol. 7 (June 1946–March 1947), pp. 973–74.
49. *Civil Aeronautics Board Reports*, Vol. 8 (April–December 1947), p. 191.
50. *Ibid.*, p. 175.
51. *Ibid.*, pp. 187–88, 191, 193.
52. *Civil Aeronautics Board Reports*, Vol. 9 (January–December 1948), p. 880.

cents a plane-mile if its load factor were 50 percent (as against 37.5 cents under the old rate), but the subsidy would be increased at all load factors below 41 percent. In 1948 Pioneer's actual load factor was about 30 percent, and thus the new rate increased its subsidy by 3 cents a mile.

The problems the Board faced in setting a "permanent" subsidy rate for Pioneer were typical of the period. At any one point in time only a few carriers were on a "permanent" rate, and a "permanent" rate seldom lasted for more than a year. Most of the time the carriers were on the "open" rate and thus effectively on a "cost-plus" subsidy. Table 4-3 shows total mail payments and mail pay per revenue-mile for the years 1946–51. Throughout the period, mail pay was never less than twice the limit proposed by the examiners in the Local, Feeder, and Pick-Up Air Service investigation. The increase in total payments resulted primarily from increases in miles flown rather than from increases in the rate per mile. The rates generally were greatest during a carrier's first months of operation and stabilized at a lower level thereafter. Toward the end of the period the subsidy per mile began to fall a bit as carriers gained operating experience, and the rate at which new carriers were established declined.

In formulating their recommendation for a maximum 25-cents-a-mile operating subsidy, the examiners had assumed that commercial revenues would average about 10 cents a mile. This in turn was based on an average load of two passengers and an average fare of 5 cents a mile. In practice, commercial revenues proved to be in excess of this, except for the weakest carriers; yet all carriers required subsidy substantially in excess of 25 cents a mile.

Table 4-3. U.S. Mail Revenue Accruing to Local Service Air Carriers, 1946–51[a]

Year	Mail revenue (thousands of dollars)	Revenue-miles flown (thousands)	Mail pay per revenue-mile (cents)
1946	720	1,277	56
1947	5,000	8,353	60
1948	9,941	16,279	61
1949	13,961	24,539	57
1950	17,403	33,022	53
1951	19,144	37,983	50

Sources: Civil Aeronautics Board, *Annual Airline Statistics,* issues for calendar years 1946, 1947, 1948; CAB, *Handbook of Airline Statistics, Calendar Years 1949–56* (1960), pp. 21, 117.

a. Data for 1946–48 exclude All American Aviation, the predecessor of Allegheny Airlines, which operated only a mail pick-up service during those years. Data for 1948 exclude Chicago Helicopter Airlines, which was classified as a feeder carrier for reporting purposes that year.

The problem was on the cost side. While the examiners had presumed that operating costs could be kept at about 35 cents a mile, total operating costs for the feeder lines averaged 62 cents a mile in 1946 and rose to 87 cents by 1948. In part, this discrepancy can be traced to over-optimism on the part of those who had presented estimates in the Local, Feeder, and Pick-Up Air Service investigation. Table 4-4 compares actual operating expenses for Florida Airways in 1948 with the estimates presented by Braniff in its original feeder proposal. Florida used the Beechcraft 18-S. Braniff proposed to use a similar, though slightly larger, aircraft. While Florida's costs were above Braniff's estimate in every category, the widest discrepancy was in the area of indirect costs. Perhaps Braniff's low estimate of these costs had been based on the assumption that many of the "overhead" costs would be borne by the nonfeeder part of its system. In any case, Braniff had assumed that ground equipment and personnel at intermediate stations would be kept to a minimum. Although it proposed to serve eighty-four points, it planned to have a full-time employee at only six intermediate stations. Florida, serving twelve cities in 1948 (three terminal and nine intermediate) employed twenty-six local managers, superintendents, and ground-service employees. (Some of these may have been part-time employees, however.)

Some of the cost difference was largely outside Florida's control and could be attributed rather to the restrictions on feeder operators laid down

Table 4-4. Operating Expenses of Florida Airways, 1948, Compared with Braniff's Estimate in the Local, Feeder, and Pick-up Air Service Investigation, 1943, by Type of Expense

Cents per revenue-mile

Type of expense	Florida Airways, actual	Braniff's estimate
Pilot and copilot salaries	11.8	7.7
Fuel and oil	6.2	4.2
Aircraft and engine maintenance (wages, repairs, and materials)	10.4	10.8[a]
Depreciation (flight and ground equipment)	10.8	3.1
Insurance	2.2	1.9
Ground and indirect expenses (excluding depreciation on ground property)	42.5	7.4

Sources: Braniff, *Civil Aeronautics Board Reports*, Vol. 6 (July 1944–May 1946), p. 33; Florida, derived from CAB, *Annual Airline Statistics, Calendar Year 1948* (1950), pp. 21, 49–50.
a. Includes wages for operations personnel not connected with maintenance.

by the Board, but not anticipated in the 1943 proposals. Braniff had proposed to establish loop-type routes and provide each of the eighty-four points with a minimum of two trips a day. More important traffic generating centers were to receive as many as six flights a day. Braniff felt that in order to maximize the possibility of success, "a type of certificate [should] be granted to the operator which would . . . be sufficiently flexible to permit the operator to change his method of operation as the traffic potential actually developed."[53]

Florida was bound by the requirement that it stop at every point on every flight regardless of traffic; and under the system of subsidy compensation established, flights in excess of the two round trips per station per day would have reduced its subsidy per mile. These restrictions on Florida's costs had three effects: (1) Aircraft utilization was restricted, and under the depreciation rules adopted by the Board requiring a fixed life for equipment regardless of use, this meant that depreciation expenses per mile were increased.[54] (2) Efficient pilot utilization was made more difficult. (Florida's pilot cost per hour was higher than that of any other feeder for the twelve months ending September 30, 1948.) (3) Finally, to the extent that indirect costs were fixed costs, indirect costs per mile were increased.

The costs of other carriers were higher than had been anticipated in 1944 because they were offering a different type of service than the examiners had anticipated when they made their recommendation to proceed with the local service experiment. The presentations made in the Local, Feeder, and Pick-Up Air Service investigation all had envisioned the use of about 10-seat aircraft. The cost estimates of feeder service reflected this assumption. A major consideration favoring the creation of new carriers to provide feeder service had been that the Board thought the existing carriers would offer service to new communities with the aircraft they were using elsewhere on their route systems. However, the Board refused to require as a condition of certification that equipment suitable for feeder routes actually be used. It said, "We believe that more can be accomplished by leaving the details [of economies to be effected] to the ingenuity of the operators, and confining our function at present to fostering over-all economies."[55]

53. *Civil Aeronautics Board Reports*, Vol. 6 (July 1944–May 1946), pp. 31 and 32.

54. Another Board regulation served to increase Florida's depreciation cost even further. Braniff had apparently assumed an equipment life of five years. The Board required the feeder carriers to write off their equipment over the three-year span of their temporary certificates.

55. *Civil Aeronautics Board Reports*, Vol. 6 (July 1944–May 1946), p. 4.

The first feeder carriers certified did begin service with small twin-engine aircraft. Essair (later Pioneer) began operations in August 1945 with three 9-passenger Lockheed 10-As. In August 1946, however, Pioneer replaced its Lockheeds with four 24-passenger DC-3s. Empire began service in September 1946 with 10-passenger Boeing 247s, but had replaced them with DC-3s by 1948. Some carriers never operated smaller aircraft at all but began their operations with DC-3s.

There seems to be little evidence to suggest that the traffic loads of the feeder carriers were so much in excess of the level anticipated that the smaller aircraft were inadequate. During the thirteen months ending August 31, 1946, Pioneer was averaging 5.05 passengers in its 9-seat Lockheed L-10 Electras, for an average load factor of 54.08 percent. Its load factor fell to 30.61 percent during its first months of DC-3 operation, though its average passenger load rose to 7.35. During 1947, Empire Air Lines averaged 2.77 passengers in its 10-passenger Boeing 247Ds, giving it a load factor of 28 percent. During 1948, when it was operating largely a DC-3 fleet, its load factor was 25 percent. The highest load factor experienced by any DC-3 operator during 1948 was West Coast's 36 percent, which implied an average passenger load of slightly less than 7.

The DC-3 could by no stretch of the imagination be called a feeder transport. The CAB itself considered it "inherently uneconomical for local air service."[56] When it was introduced into airline service in 1936, it was the last word in high-capacity, long-range aircraft. Configured as a sleeper with room for 14 passengers, it flew across the continent with only three or four intermediate stops. Why then was it chosen by the local carriers as their standard aircraft?

The primary virtue of the DC-3 from the point of view of the local service carriers was its low initial price. The fact that war surplus C-47s (the military designation of the DC-3) could be purchased from the War Assets Administration for only about $18,000 and made suitable for airline service for an additional $50,000 was a factor that could not be overlooked by carriers that were starved for capital. The existence of a pool of war surplus spare parts and mechanics and pilots familiar with the aircraft meant that inventory and training costs would be low. Furthermore, although the DC-3 was being phased out of the trunkline fleet at the time, it still was present in substantial numbers. (In 1948, trunklines operated 368 DC-3s.) To operate the same aircraft as the trunklines would both improve the

56. *Civil Aeronautics Board Reports*, Vol. 8 (April–December 1947), p. 191.

public image of the feeder carriers and give them equipment parity with the trunks in those cases in which some competition for trunkline traffic was possible. This factor was of particular importance to Pioneer, the first local carrier to acquire DC-3s.

A final reason for adopting such a large aircraft was that a small one, such as the Electra, gave the airlines little cushion with which to meet the peaks in demand to which they were subject. It was noted in Chapter 2 that flights leaving at certain hours of the day have higher load factors than those leaving at other times and that this is true particularly of short-haul business traffic. The local carriers were anxious not to have to refuse service to anyone because of a lack of seats at these peak periods; and the more seats their aircraft had, the more likely it was that peaks could be met.

The route restrictions placed on the local carriers served to accentuate the peaking problem. The requirement that all route segments be served on every flight did not allow carriers to provide extra service to strong route segments and use smaller aircraft on a skip-stop basis on weaker ones. Thus a carrier might find that traffic on one particular segment was extremely heavy and that it could fill even a DC-3, while traffic on other segments of the route would not half fill even an Electra. The case of Robinson Airways (Mohawk) illustrates this problem. Robinson's routes ran from Niagara Falls, New York, to New York City with intermediate stops at Buffalo, Rochester, Ithaca, and Binghamton. Table 4-5 shows the average eastbound and westbound load factors for the various segments on Robinson's route. (Robinson was allowed to operate extra flights between Ithaca, Binghamton, and New York.) If Robinson was to meet traffic demands on its Binghamton–New York segment, a DC-3 was necessary.

Table 4-5. Robinson Airline Load Factors between New York City/Newark and Niagara Falls, by Route Segment, March 1949

Route segment	Revenue passenger load factor on segment	Average[a] passenger load on segment
New York/Newark–Binghamton	50.5	10.6
Binghamton–Ithaca	31.3	6.6
Ithaca–Rochester	25.4	5.3
Rochester–Buffalo	20.4	5.3
Buffalo–Niagara Falls	1.7	0.4

Source: Civil Aeronautics Board, *Airline Traffic Survey, March 1949*, p. 1321.
a. Assuming 21 seats.

Table 4-6. Estimated Direct Operating Costs, Excluding and Including Depreciation, for the B-247D, L-10B, and DC-3, Based on 1936 Trunkline Experience

Cents per aircraft-mile, 1954 dollars

Type of aircraft and depreciation status	Number of seats	Stage length (miles)		
		100	200	300
Boeing B-247D				
Excluding depreciation	10	57.0	47.6	44.4
Including depreciation		74.1	64.7	61.5
Lockheed L-10B				
Excluding depreciation	10	35.4	29.6	27.7
Including depreciation		47.0	41.2	39.3
Douglas DC-3				
Excluding depreciation	21	63.8	53.1	50.0
Including depreciation		82.1	71.4	68.3

Source: Derived from Almarin Phillips, *Technology and Market Structure: A Study of the Aircraft Industry* (D. C. Heath, 1971), Tables 6-2 and 6-6, pp. 95, 99.

Thus the larger DC-3 had several important advantages for the local carriers over its smaller counterparts. It had one important disadvantage—it was relatively expensive to operate. Table 4-6 compares the per-mile operating costs of the DC-3 with those of two other aircraft operated by the locals, the Boeing B-247D and the Lockheed L-10B Electra.[57] Clearly, on an aircraft-mile basis, operating costs for the DC-3 (even excluding depreciation) were substantially above those for the L-10B. The DC-3 did have a cost advantage over the B-247D, if depreciation expenses are *excluded* for the DC-3 (which is appropriate, perhaps, considering the low initial cost of the used DC-3s) and *included* for the B-247D. The average direct flight costs (corresponding roughly to direct operating costs) for Pioneer's L-10s was 34 cents per aircraft-mile, while these costs averaged 47 cents per aircraft-mile during the first three months of DC-3 operations. Other costs were higher with DC-3s also. Pioneer had been operating its L-10s with no stewardesses and no food service. During 1945 its passenger service expenses were 0.8 cent per aircraft-mile. It staffed its DC-3s with stewardesses and served refreshments to its passengers. By 1947, the first complete year of DC-3 operations, passenger service expenses had risen to

57. Lockheed built two aircraft called the Electra, the L-10 (which was a twin-engine aircraft designed for short-haul, low-density routes), and the four turboprop L-188—the aircraft with which most people are familiar. The L-10 first entered airline service in August 1934. Its cruise speed was 185 miles an hour, approximately the same as that of the DC-3.

4.5 cents a mile. Adding these costs to direct flying costs brings the cost difference for the DC-3 over the L-10 to 16.8 cents a mile. Thus for a 50 percent increase in operating costs, Pioneer bought 160 percent higher seating capacity and a much more competitive aircraft.

The Board looked somewhat askance at Pioneer's DC-3 acquisition, observing that the increase of only 2.2 in average passenger load that Pioneer had experienced during its first four months of DC-3 operations failed to cover even the increase in direct flying costs that resulted from operating the larger aircraft. Yet it failed to exercise its authority to refuse to increase Pioneer's subsidy and concluded "since the advantages of the DC-3 over the Electra aircraft cannot be accurately evaluated until after a reasonable period of experience, we conclude that the conversion was a reasonable exercise of managerial discretion. . . ."[58]

The Board's acquiescence to Pioneer's DC-3 purchase signaled to the other feeders that the additional operating costs of this aircraft would not be an obstacle. When the time came for renewal of the original local service certificates, the DC-3 had become the backbone of the local service fleet. By 1948 the local carriers operated forty-four of these aircraft and eleven smaller twin-engine aircraft. While the local service carriers sometimes operated their DC-3s at a somewhat higher seating density than the trunks had done, the standard of service offered by these carriers by the late 1940s was fully competitive with the service offered by the smaller trunklines.

Recertification—the End of the "Experiment"

By the time the Board faced the question of whether to renew the temporary certificates of the local carriers, enough evidence had been amassed to indicate that the Board and the examiners had been correct in 1944 in finding that the traffic potential at small cities was not encouraging. The subsidy necessary to support the extensive services that the Board had established was far higher than anticipated, primarily because the costs of providing such services had been greatly underestimated. To quote one Board member, "Operations of the local service carriers, when viewed as an 'experiment,' have been of value only in proving that at the present state of the art short-haul local service is a field generally ill-adapted to air transportation."[59] The Board could have terminated the local carriers merely

58. *Civil Aeronautics Board Reports*, Vol. 8 (April–December 1947), p. 181.
59. *Civil Aeronautics Board Reports*, Vol. 12 (September 1950–April 1951), p. 631.

by refusing to renew their certificates when they automatically expired, charging the subsidy already spent to experience. It did not do this, however. The certificates of all but three operating carriers were renewed. The renewal proceedings revealed much about the CAB's attitude toward the carriers it had created and about the political pressures to which such a regulatory agency is subject.

As was mentioned above, the fact that local service subsidy payments were going to be substantially above their anticipated 25-cents-a-mile rate was apparent almost as soon as the carriers started operation. In fact, as early as September 1947, only two years after the first feeder carrier had begun operations, Harllee Branch, a member of the Civil Aeronautics Board, dissented from the awarding of any feeder routes to all but two of the petitioners in the Great Lakes Area Case and announced his intention to vote against all future feeder awards because of the high levels of subsidy required by the carriers that were already established. Branch argued that the Board should await the outcome of the experimentation it had already authorized before proceeding further. He pointed out the political problems that were sure to arise if the Board decided to let the experiment lapse, and added that increasing the number of services authorized would only make this problem more difficult.[60]

In the first renewal case, decided on March 7, 1949, the Board refused to renew the certificate of Florida Airways. Florida operated two flights a day using 8-passenger Beech 18s over a two-segment route—one segment between Jacksonville and Orlando with two intermediate stops, the other between Orlando and Tallahassee with five intermediate stops. The two segments were connected between Gainesville and Jacksonville. Six of the stations served by Florida received their only air service from it; it served three others jointly with trunklines. During March 1948, these six cities generated 577 arriving and departing passengers. The three stations that were served jointly generated 346 arriving and departing passengers. Clearly Florida was acting primarily as a feeder carrier.

During March 1948 Florida Airways received $28,881 in mail pay. This means that the government was paying $50.05 in mail pay for each passenger traveling to or from a city that received its only air service from Florida. The Board lay more stress, however, on the fact that in 1948, Florida's first and only full year of operation, the government paid more than $7 in mail pay for every dollar paid by a passenger on Florida. As Table 4-7 shows,

60. *Civil Aeronautics Board Reports*, Vol. 8 (April–December 1947), pp. 360, 419–24.

Table 4-7. Operating Revenue and Expenses per Passenger and per Revenue-mile, Florida Airways, 1948

Item	Per passenger (dollars)	Per revenue-mile (cents)
Passenger revenue	7.45	11.2
Total nonmail revenue	8.45	12.7
Mail revenue	53.48	80.2
Operating expenses	56.39	84.5

Source: Civil Aeronautics Board, *Annual Airline Statistics, Calendar Year 1948* (1950), pp. 21, 38, 50.

this implied a mail pay of 80 cents a mile—over three times the limit recommended by the examiners in 1944. In its opinion, the Board said:

Although applicant has made efforts to reduce operating costs, route No. 75 is short and its pattern, resulting in duplication of mileage and frequent stops, militates against the economical operations that might be expected from a longer route with a more flexible pattern.

The conclusion is inescapable that route No. 75 is an uneconomical route, that no substantial increase in nonmail revenues can be expected in the reasonably foreseeable future and that further expenditures of public funds will not avail to develop it into a route that can be operated at a reasonable cost to the Government commensurate with the service rendered.[61]

Florida Airways, believing that many of its problems could be traced to the inadequacies of its routes, had petitioned the Board to add fifteen new cities to the twelve it already served. This would have expanded Florida's route system from 470 to 1,733 miles. The carrier claimed that a larger route would allow it to spread its overhead and increase its equipment and pilot utilization. It predicted that average plane-mile costs would be reduced by about 25 percent,[62] to 63 cents. The Board refused, noting that more than 83 percent of the population of the state of Florida already lived within ten miles of a point receiving scheduled air service and that ten of the fifteen cities Florida Airways proposed to add already were certified for trunkline service. The Board noted that "this decision places the applicant in an unenviable position," but added, "As we approach the expiration date of our commitment and view the fruits thereof, we are obliged to face the realities."[63] In November 1949 Eastern Airlines was granted the

61. *Civil Aeronautics Board Reports*, Vol. 10 (January–November 1949), pp. 96–97.
62. *Civil Aeronautics Board Reports*, Vol. 9 (January–December 1948), p. 447.
63. *Ibid.*, pp. 451–52.

Table 4-8. Comparison of Operations of Pioneer Air Lines with All Other Feeders and with Selected Small Trunklines, Year Ended March 31, 1949

Item	Pioneer Air Lines	Average for all feeders excluding Pioneer	Small trunklines			
			Colonial Airlines	Northeast Airlines	Conti- nental Airlines	Mid- Continent Airlines
Revenue plane-miles flown (thousands)	3,754	1,617	3,311	3,473	5,810	8,202
Route miles operated[a]	1,625	974	1,025	1,110	2,298	2,875
Daily aircraft utilization (hours and minutes)	7:41	6:14	6:18	6:00	7:14	7:38
Revenue passengers (thousands)	100	43	152	279	169	323
Revenue passengers per station	4,448	2,477	8,757	11,129	6,488	11,123
Revenue passengers per plane departure	2.39	1.71	5.94	7.23	4.40	5.86
Revenue passenger-miles per revenue plane-mile	7.39	4.96	12.55	15.41	10.59	11.73
Average stage length	89	71	129	90	152	149

Source: *Civil Aeronautics Board Reports*, Vol. 12 (September 1950–April 1951), pp. 55–56.
a. Weighted average.

right to serve Ocala and Gainesville, the two strongest of the points previously receiving their service exclusively from Florida Airways.[64]

Florida was generally admitted to be one of the weakest of the local carriers. At the other end of the scale was Pioneer. While Florida operated the type of feeder operation the Board had envisioned in 1944, Pioneer had many of the attributes of a small trunkline. Table 4-8 compares Pioneer with four of the smaller trunks and with the other feeder carriers. While Pioneer's routes were less dense than those of the smaller trunklines, their density was considerably higher than that of most of the other feeder carriers. Furthermore, Pioneer's routes differed from those of the other local carriers in that they allowed Pioneer to enter into significant competition with trunkline carriers. In terms of passenger-miles operated, Pioneer's route system was more than 50 percent competitive with the services of other air carriers.[65] A survey conducted by Pioneer during the summer of 1948 revealed that only 21 percent of Pioneer's passengers traveled on that airline because it was the only service available. Had Pioneer's service not been available, 26 percent of the respondents said that they would have flown on another airline.[66] Because of its access to relatively lucrative

64. Florida Trunk Line Case, Temporary Ocala–Gainesville Service. *Civil Aeronautics Board Reports*, Vol. 10 (January–November 1949), p. 901.
65. *Civil Aeronautics Board Reports*, Vol. 12 (September 1950–April 1951), p. 23.
66. Of Pioneer's passengers, 70 percent were found to be businessmen. *Ibid.*, p. 24.

trunkline markets, Pioneer required substantially lower mail pay per mile than had Florida. During 1949 it received about 45 cents a mile in mail pay—about half of what Florida had received in 1948. Yet its operating expenses were about 79 cents a mile, almost as high as those of Florida. The difference, of course, lay in its denser routes.

One may legitimately ask whether the public benefits received for the $1.7 million in mail pay paid to Pioneer in the year ended March 31, 1949 (to provide air service that largely supplemented that of existing trunk carriers), were substantially greater than those received for the $656,000 in mail pay required to keep Florida Airways operating in 1948. In deciding whether or not to renew Pioneer's certificate, the Board should have considered the relative costs and benefits of air service only to those city pairs that would have been without air service had Pioneer's service been unavailable. Table 4-9 shows such an estimate for all carriers operating during the full year 1949. The next to last column shows the ratio of mail pay to nonmail revenues and shows Pioneer to be among the more self-sufficient

Table 4-9. Mail Revenue per Originating and Departing Passenger at Exclusively Served Stations, March 1949, and Mail Revenue as a Percentage of Nonmail Revenue, 1949

Airline[a]	Exclusively served stations	Mail revenue	Arriving and departing passengers, exclusive stations[b]	Passengers arriving and departing at exclusively served cities as a percentage of total passengers	Mail revenue per passenger, exclusive stations	Rank	Ratio of mail revenue to nonmail revenue	Rank
Challenger Airlines	7	$ 88,809	1,305	64.4	$ 68.05	6	2.08	4
Empire Air Lines	8	56,297	1,636	59.7	34.41	8	1.97	5
Monarch Air Lines	9	104,857	1,330	73.5	78.84	4	2.43	3
Piedmont Aviation	3	100,727	391	7.0	257.61	1	1.04	9
Pioneer Air Lines	8	157,352	1,385	15.9	113.61	2	1.06	8
Robinson Airlines	1	36,738	1,470	49.0	24.99	10	0.98	10
Southwest Airways	15	111,360	4,282	53.8	26.01	9	1.09	7
Trans-Texas Airways	10	128,125	1,764	57.5	72.63	5	3.06	2
West Coast Airlines	10	119,829	3,305	73.8	36.26	7	1.35	6
Wisconsin Central Airlines	10	81,692	932	58.9	87.65	3	3.80	1

Sources: Civil Aeronautics Board, *Air Traffic Survey, March 1949; American Aviation*, Vol. 12 (May 15, 1949), pp. 54–55, Vol. 13 (July 1, 1949), p. 48, and Vol. 13 (April 15, 1950), pp. 26–27; CAB, *Handbook of Airline Statistics, Calendar Years 1949–1956.*

a. Includes only airlines operating throughout 1949. Allegheny Airlines initiated passenger operations in March 1949; Bonanza Air Lines in December; Central Airlines in September; Lake Central Airlines in November; Mid-West Airlines in October; Southern Airways in June; and E. W. Wiggins Airways in September. Florida Airways ceased operations in March 1949.

b. Adjusted to exclude passengers traveling between exclusively served points.

of the carriers when ranked on this basis.[67] Yet the eight stations served exclusively by Pioneer generated a total of only 1,385 passengers in March 1949—only 16 percent of Pioneer's total passengers. Attributing Pioneer's mail pay to these passengers, the ones who would have been without scheduled air service had Pioneer not existed, gives a mail pay per passenger figure of $113.61, the second highest among the local carriers, and significantly more than the cost per passenger to the government of supporting Florida's service in 1948. (In March 1948 the cities served exclusively by Pioneer generated 1,012 arriving and departing passengers. Pioneer's mail pay was $100,255 during the month, so mail pay per passenger was $99.07, twice the level for Florida Airways.) At a cost of more than $100 a passenger, it would have been cheaper for the government to charter a plane every time someone from one of these towns wanted to fly somewhere. The Board did not bother to consider this alternative and instead voted to renew Pioneer's certificate for another five years because of its "encouraging progress toward commercial self-sufficiency."[68]

The Pioneer and Florida cases were the polar certificate renewal cases. In deciding to recertify Pioneer, which in many respects resembled one of the smaller trunks, and not to recertify Florida, the Board established a precedent for future cases. The only question was where to draw the line. The Board seemed to want to draw it so as to exclude Trans-Texas Airways (another feeder carrier operating in Texas), since on April 4, 1949, it issued an order directing Trans-Texas to "show cause" why its certificate should not be allowed to expire.[69] During fiscal 1950 the taxpayer had contributed 72 cents of every dollar it cost to operate Trans-Texas, and in addition had paid a return on investment. Trans-Texas had the lowest load factor of any DC-3 operator during fiscal 1950 (20.11 percent) and the lowest daily number of passengers per route-mile.[70] Board Member Harold A. Jones made an analysis for Trans-Texas similar to the one from which the data presented in Table 4-9 were derived and concluded that:

During [the third quarter of 1949] Trans-Texas served a total of 174 pairs of points. Approximately 60 percent of these pairs, 102 out of 174, produced *less than one passenger every three days*, and accounted for only 5 percent of the total traffic. Of this group, 23 pairs of cities and towns were dependent entirely upon

67. The Board stressed the fact that Pioneer's ratio of mail pay to commercial revenues was the lowest of all the local carriers. This statement apparently referred to an earlier period, since data for 1949 show that Robinson (which later became Mohawk) had the lowest ratio of mail pay to commercial revenues: 0.98 to 1.

68. *Civil Aeronautics Board Reports*, Vol. 12 (September 1950–April 1951), p. 5.

69. Trans-Texas Certificate Renewal Case, in *ibid.*, p. 608.

70. *Ibid.*, p. 620.

Trans-Texas for air service. These pairs produced 37 percent of the traffic, and represented *1.65 passengers per city per day*. Only three of the pairs of points served exclusively by Trans-Texas produced more than four passengers per day.

In sum, Trans-Texas carried 89 passengers per day who did not have competitive air service available, which is the measure of the public benefit represented by its passenger service. During the same period the carrier received $4,212 per day in mail pay.[71]

The Board's "show cause" order announcing its intention not to renew Trans-Texas's certificate provoked considerable controversy and confirmed the fears earlier expressed by Board Member Branch. Letters were received from forty-four U.S. senators and congressmen expressing interest in the case, and six congressmen appeared before the Board during the oral argument to urge the recertification of Trans-Texas.[72] In early 1951 the Board decided that Trans-Texas's certificate should be renewed after all, citing "continuing improvement for the system in recent reports."[73] In his dissent, quoted in part above, Jones observed:

If Trans-Texas warrants further extension, there will be few, if any, of the other local service carriers who will not deserve similar treatment. . . .

On paper, these renewals will of course be limited to a further period of fixed duration. But there should be no blinking the fact that an extension for a term of years, regardless of how it is hedged about with language calling it an "experiment," amounts to a *permanent* authorization. To insist otherwise is to ignore realities. Thus the nationwide short-haul air-route network will become a fixture of our transportation system.[74]

Jones was correct.[75] The certificates of all but Florida and two other carriers were renewed. Like Florida Airways, those two carriers operated equipment smaller than a DC-3. All DC-3 operators were recertified, but no carrier that did not operate DC-3s was. In 1955 Congress fulfilled Jones's prophecy by directing the Board to grant permanent certificates to the local carriers. This legislation has been cited as ending the experimental phase of the local carriers' operations. In fact, the "local service experiment" had ended years earlier.

Table 4-10 ranks the local service carriers operating during the second quarter of 1950 by number of stations to which they provided exclusive service. It reveals that seven of the sixteen local carriers could have been

71. *Ibid.*, p. 637.
72. *Ibid.*, p. 628, note 18. The six congressmen appearing before the Board represented the 3rd, 9th, 12th, 14th, 15th, and 16th districts of Texas (*ibid.*, p. 607).
73. *Ibid.*, p. 609.
74. *Ibid.*, pp. 609, 620.
75. The only possible exception to this was the alleged attempt by the Board in 1954 to carve up the local carriers and hand over their routes to trunklines. For details, see below, p. 154–55.

Table 4-10. Points Served and U.S. Mail Revenue of Local Service Air Carriers in Order of Points Served Exclusively, Second Quarter 1950

Dollar amounts in thousands

Carrier	Number of points served	Number of points served exclusively	Mail revenue	Mail revenue per exclusive point
Piedmont Aviation	23	1	$368	$368
Robinson Airlines[a]	9	2	297	149
Bonanza Air Lines	8	4	137	34
Turner Airlines	11	5	115	23
Southern Airways	20	7	262	37
E. W. Wiggins Airways	16	7	50	7
Pioneer Air Lines	24	8	272	34
Empire Air Lines	16	9	150	17
West Coast Airlines	15	10	174	17
Central Airlines	23	13	159	12
Wisconsin Central Airlines	22	15	305	20
Mid-West Airlines	29	16	140	9
Southwest Airways	25	16	272	17
Trans-Texas Airways	26	17	442	26
All American Aviation[b]	34	18	379	21
Frontier Airlines	43	25	508	20

Sources: *Southern Flight*, Vol. 34 (September 1950), pp. 34–35; CAB, *Handbook of Airline Statistics, 1969 Edition* (1970), pp. 503–06.
a. Became Mohawk Airlines in 1952.
b. Became Allegheny Airlines in 1953.

eliminated with the loss of airline service to only thirty-four cities. These seven carriers, serving 20 percent of the exclusively served cities, received 37 percent of the total mail pay—$1.5 million during the second quarter of 1950.

Under the criterion adopted by the Board as an indication of the degree to which a carrier was meeting the Board's goals—the ratio of mail pay to total commercial revenue—Piedmont Aviation ranked as a carrier much more deserving of continued federal support than did Frontier Airlines. During the second quarter of 1950 Piedmont's ratio of mail pay to nonmail revenues was 0.86 while Frontier's was 2.19. But in the second quarter of 1950, in return for the same amount it cost for air service at the one point Piedmont served exclusively, the government received air service at twenty-five such points from Frontier. Many of these were in isolated areas without other satisfactory means of transportation. Yet it was carriers such as Piedmont and Robinson (later Mohawk) that had no trouble in securing renewal of their certificates.

CHAPTER FIVE

Route Strengthening—Within Limits

THE CIVIL AERONAUTICS BOARD, having decided to renew the certificates of most of the local service carriers in spite of the disappointing results of the "local service experiment," then faced the difficult task of deciding just where these carriers were to fit into the nation's air transportation network. The Board had created a separate group of carriers to specialize in providing short-haul, low-density air service primarily because it felt that a group of "specialist" carriers would provide the smaller cities with service of a better quality at a lower cost than would trunkline carriers. The dilemma facing the Board was that, as far as the level and quality of service provided was concerned, the local service carriers by the early 1950s differed little from the smaller trunklines. This could be blamed in large part on the regulatory policies the Board had followed. Furthermore, the local carriers appearing to come closest to the Board's goal of financial self-sufficiency were those with routes most like those of the trunklines. The Board decided, therefore, that the routes of the local carriers needed to be "strengthened." Route restrictions were gradually loosened, though the general policy of discouraging direct trunk–local service competition was maintained, except in a very few cases, by preventing local carriers from offering nonstop service in markets where they competed with trunkline carriers.

Another phase of CAB route policy during this period was the transferral of a large number of the weaker trunkline points to the local carriers and the suspension of trunklines at many points where joint trunk–local service was offered. The ostensible purpose of this policy also was to strengthen the local carriers. While the cities added did indeed generate a considerable amount of traffic for the locals, in retrospect it is difficult to determine which carrier group benefited more—the locals, which acquired some stronger cities in the process, or the trunklines, which were relieved of the burden of serving many points that undoubtedly had been losing money for them.

Third, a "use-it-or-lose-it" policy was adopted that gave the local carriers a means for ridding themselves of their least profitable stations—those generating fewer than five passengers a day. By June 1967, eleven years after the use-it-or-lose-it policy first took shape,[1] 101 cities had been dropped.[2] Nevertheless, the policy was not applied rigorously, and as late as 1966, fifty-four cities that did not meet even these minimal standards of traffic were still being served. Many of these cities had been below the 5-passenger-a-day level for many years without any action being taken.[3]

Finally, a certain amount of "route weakening" took place, particularly during the late 1950s, when many stations that had never before received air service were added to the local service route system.

In the late 1950s and early 1960s the Board and Congress took a number of steps aimed at strengthening the financial position of the carriers. The purpose of these actions was to enable the carriers to replace their DC-3s with aircraft better suited to their operations. A bill offering government-guaranteed loans to the carriers for the purchase of flight equipment was passed in 1957. In 1958, legislation was enacted exempting from tax the capital gains of local airlines if they were used to purchase new flight equipment. In 1960 the Board increased the rate of return allowed local service carriers and modified the method by which it was calculated to encourage the use of equity financing. Finally, in 1961 the Board adopted a new method of subsidy compensation that both increased the level of subsidy paid and altered some of the more perverse incentives that existed under the system. In response to the new routes acquired and the new financial incentives the carriers set about replacing their DC-3s. However, in all but one case the aircraft acquired to replace the DC-3 was substantially larger than the one it replaced, which itself had been too large for many of the routes over which it had operated.

If "route strengthening" was designed to reduce the carriers' dependence on federal subsidy, it clearly failed. Subsidy levels increased dramatically throughout the 1950s and early 1960s. There were four reasons for this:

1. The policy of removing route restrictions allowed the local carriers

---

1. It was not formalized until the Seven States Area Investigation in 1958. *Civil Aeronautics Board Reports*, Vol. 28 (December 1958–February 1959), pp. 680–819.

2. *Flight Magazine*, Vol. 56 (June 1967), p. 67.

3. See "Use-it-or-Lose-it Analysis," *Flight Magazine*, Vol. 55 (June 1966), pp. 76–78, 87.

to compete more effectively against the trunks and led them to concentrate attention on their stronger and more competitive markets. This caused a rise in costs, and traffic at the marginal stations did not grow enough to offset it.

2. The majority of the stations that were transferred from the trunks to the locals to strengthen the latter had been operated by the former carriers at a loss. With the ending of the trunkline subsidies in the early 1950s, the burden of supporting these stations shifted from the federal government to the trunks' customers who flew on the denser, long-haul routes. When these stations were transferred to the local carriers, the burden of subsidizing these points was shifted back to the federal government.

3. The aircraft that the local carriers obtained to replace and augment their DC-3s were for the most part ill suited to short-haul service, yet under the cost-plus system of subsidy compensation in effect until 1961 the government stood ready to pay the additional costs of operating these aircraft. Even when a method of subsidy compensation was adopted, it initially contained a strong incentive to use inefficient aircraft—an incentive that was not changed until 1963.

4. A large number of the communities that were granted air service for the first time failed to develop the traffic that would even come close to paying the cost of providing the service. Yet the Board, in the face of strong pressures, moved slowly to implement the policies it had established when granting those services that would have assured their termination if their operation proved too expensive.

In the wake of this subsidy increase, the Board came under pressure from President Kennedy "to develop . . . a step-by-step program, with specific annual targets, to assure sharp reduction of operating subsidies. . . ."[4] The Board's plan, announced in 1963, failed to achieve its goals, and by early 1966 the Board found itself again in the process of reassessing its policy concerning the role of the local service carriers.

Liberalization of Route Restrictions

It was noted in Chapter 4 that the Board, overriding the objections voiced by its examiners, decided that the only way in which a proper separation between the local service carriers and the trunklines could be

4. *The Transportation System of Our Nation*, Message from the President of the United States, H. Doc. 384, 87 Cong. 2 sess. (1962), p. 7.

achieved was to require the local carriers to fly between designated terminals and to land at every intermediate point on every flight, even if no
passengers or freight were to be loaded or unloaded.

As early as November 1946, little more than a year after the first feeder
carrier began operating, and in spite of a strong dissent from one of its
members, the Board began to recognize that such a policy "prevented full
exploitation of the traffic potentialities of [a] route" and restricted the carrier from obtaining the maximum utilization of its equipment.[5] It decided
to modify Pioneer's certificate to allow it to operate shuttle service between
any two points named consecutively in its certificate. This allowed Pioneer
Air Lines to operate nonstop service between Houston and Austin and
between Fort Worth, Dallas, and Waco. Both of these segments already
were receiving service from trunklines. The Board was careful to emphasize, however, that this modification in no way was to be taken as a signal
of its intention not to maintain restrictions in the certificates of the short-
haul carriers "which will insure maintenance of the short-haul characteristics of such carriers."[6] Partially to assure this, the Board required Pioneer
to offer a minimum of two round trips a day over its entire route.

A related modification was granted Southwest Airways in February
1948, when this carrier was given the right to begin or terminate trips short
of designated terminal points provided every flight stopped at each point
named in Southwest's certificate between the point of origin and the point
of termination.[7] This modification not only allowed Southwest to offer
shuttle service between any two points named consecutively in its certificate, but also allowed the carriers to limit service to weak "stub-end"
terminals.[8] Again the Board said that its only reason for allowing the
modification was that the every-stop, every-flight, terminal-to-terminal
restriction "deterred full exploitation of the traffic potentialities of the
route through inability of the carrier to operate additional schedules over
more heavily traveled segments of the route without continuing such
schedules over the entire segment. The record shows that traffic has been
'unabled' [refused service] on some of the more heavily traveled portions,
that the public has suffered from a lack of adequate passenger facilities,

5. *Civil Aeronautics Board Reports*, Vol. 7 (June 1946–March 1947), p. 472.
6. *Ibid.*, p. 473.
7. *Civil Aeronautics Board Reports*, Vol. 9 (January–December 1948), p. 72.
8. The primary "stub-end" terminal on Southwest's route was Medford, Orgeon.
Medford, it was noted above, was created as a "stub-end" in order to allay fears on the
part of the trunklines of excessive competition from local service carriers. (See p. 88.)

and that the carrier has been prevented from improving its record of equipment utilization."[9] The Board again stated its intention to keep the local carriers "local" and required Southwest to operate a minimum of two schedules a day over the entire route.

Southwest did not delay in implementing its new authority—particularly on its stub-end Medford–San Francisco route. While it continued to operate three flights a day over its Sacramento Valley Division (Medford to San Francisco via Sacramento), it originated its other three daily flights at the intermediate points of Redding and Chico and at Sacramento. Southwest's aircraft utilization rose from 4.39 hours a day in 1947 to 5.33 hours a day in 1948, and expenses per revenue-mile fell from $1.16 in 1947 to $0.97 in 1948.

The next major liberalization occurred in January 1949 in the Middle Atlantic Area Case.[10] All American Aviation (which later became Allegheny Airlines) was granted a route between Pittsburgh and New York, with six intermediate stops. The Board concluded that competition between trunk and local service carriers would be adequately discouraged if All American were required to make a maximum of three intermediate stops and were prevented from operating nonstop between Scranton/Wilkes-Barre and either New York/Newark or Pittsburgh—cities between which trunk service already was offered.

A similar right was granted to Southwest in June of the same year. The Board noted:

Obviously all [intermediate] points do not need the same frequency of schedules daily, and to serve each point on all flights would unnecessarily delay a substantial number of passengers and tend to minimize the advantages of air over surface transportation. Requiring four stops between Los Angeles and San Francisco would give the trunk-line carrier a substantial time advantage and should be sufficient to prevent effective competition. If Southwest, with stops at four intermediate points, can divert sufficient terminal-to-terminal traffic from the through carriers to have any substantial effect thereon, it would indicate a deficiency in those carriers' services which might be improved by such competition.[11]

The Board also decided that a minimum of three stops on the San Francisco–Medford route was sufficient.

In the same decision the Board deleted the requirement that Southwest actually land at an intermediate point even if no traffic were enplaning or

9. *Civil Aeronautics Board Reports*, Vol. 9 (January–December 1948), p. 70.
10. *Civil Aeronautics Board Reports*, Vol. 10 (January–November 1949), pp. 46–47.
11. *Ibid.*, p. 428.

deplaning; that is, Southwest was given the right to serve intermediate points on a "flag stop" basis. "Since Southwest will still be required to follow a flight path that will make possible a landing at each scheduled stop in the event traffic is available, it appears that no serious competitive implications are presented." The minimum daily frequency that Southwest was required to offer to intermediate points was reduced from two round trips to one.

The Board was not entirely deaf to the protests of United and Western that the progressive liberalization of Southwest's operating rights was a competitive danger to them. In August 1951 the Board rejected a proposed merger of Southwest and West Coast, a merger that would have created a single local carrier operating from Seattle to Los Angeles. The Board rejected the claim of United Air Lines and Western Airlines that the merged carrier "would lose the attributes of a local-service system and eventually become in effect a long-haul carrier basically indistinguishable in size and scope from Western's and United's operations on the west coast." It pointed to its intention to continue restrictions on the operations of the local carriers but stated that "[we] will remove the fear expressed by the trunklines in this case" by disallowing the merger.[12]

The Board's examiner had estimated that the merger would have involved an annual saving in operating expenses of $211,600 and an annual increase in commercial (nonmail) revenue of $35,000. In 1950 the operating expenses of the two carriers were $2.6 million, while their commercial revenues were $1.8 million.

Similar liberalizations of operating authority were incorporated in other local service carriers' certificates at the time of their renewal. In the Wisconsin Central Renewal Case the Board deemed only two intermediate stops necessary on some of that carrier's routes ". . . in view of the fact that there are involved longer distances between terminals and greater route circuity, so that the relative superiority of Northwest's [a trunkline] faster equipment is accentuated."[13]

In the Ozark Certificate Renewal Case[14] the Board adopted a general policy of requiring local carriers to make only two intermediate stops be-

12. Southwest–West Coast Merger Case, decided August 7, 1951. *Civil Aeronautics Board Reports*, Vol. 14 (May–December 1951), pp. 357–58.
13. *Civil Aeronautics Board Reports*, Vol. 19 (August 1954–January 1955), p. 105.
14. Decided August 20, 1954. *Civil Aeronautics Board Reports*, Vol. 19 (August 1954–January 1955), p. 105.

tween designated terminal points. However, the Board placed specific restrictions against the offering of nonstop service by Ozark Air Lines in competition with trunks where adherence to the above restriction still might allow such service to be offered.

The precedent established in the Ozark case was maintained until the start of the second round of area cases. In the Seven States Area Investigation,[15] the Board overruled its examiner, who had recommended awarding the new routes in the case under the two-stop "Ozark restriction" and stated that henceforth it would be its general policy to allow locals to offer nonstop flights between noncompetitive terminals and to make only one intermediate stop between competitive terminals. Where this would allow direct trunk-local competition, additional restrictions would be imposed. The Board said that its concern in restricting local service operations was no longer primarily the financial health of the trunk carriers but rather "to exclude the local-service carriers from participation in markets where the need for direct competitive service has not been shown and where the likelihood is that the effort by the local carrier to compete would jeopardize the soundness of the local carrier's operations." The Board argued that granting such authority should result in lower costs "since it is manifest that longer hops and the elimination of unnecessary stops minimize operating costs."[16] To assure adequate service to intermediate points, the Board did require that the local carriers provide each with a minimum of two round trips a day.

The general policy on route restrictions adopted in 1958 stood essentially unchanged until 1966. In those relatively few cases where local-service carriers were allowed to offer nonstop service in markets where they competed directly with a trunkline, the Board took pains to emphasize any extenuating circumstances and cautioned against the decision being taken as a sign of weakening on its part.

Note that this pattern of liberalization of route restrictions had as its primary goal to allow the local carriers to offer improved service on their more heavily traveled routes. This trend in policy both reflected and encouraged the increasing interest shown by the local carriers in these more important routes and tended to lower the quality of service offered to the smaller communities.

15. Decided December 8, 1958. *Civil Aeronautics Board Reports*, Vol. 28 (December 1958–February 1959), pp. 680–819.
16. *Ibid.*, pp. 760–61.

Suspension of Trunk Carriers and Replacement with Local Service Carriers

Another step taken by the CAB during this period was to suspend the trunk carriers at many points where they were certificated to offer service. During the years 1949–64 a trunk was suspended and replaced by a local carrier at at least seventy-eight stations. During the same period trunks were suspended entirely from fifty-one stations where joint local-trunk service had been provided, and at sixteen stations that were served by two or more trunks and one local, one of the trunks was suspended. Finally, at eight stations that had been served by at least two trunks, one of the trunks was suspended and replaced by a local carrier.[17]

In some cases these suspensions were contested bitterly by the trunk carriers involved. Both United and Western filed suits against the Board charging that it had no legal power to suspend a carrier at a point at which it was permanently certified and that such a suspension included the taking of property without due process of law.[18] The Board was upheld in both cases although the court specifically refused to try to determine the boundaries of the Board's suspension powers, restricting itself merely to finding that in the instances before the court the Board had not exceeded its statutory authority.

In the majority of cases, however, the suspensions were either supported by, or only lightly contested by, the trunks, though the cities involved often complained bitterly about being downgraded.[19] At one point it was even alleged that the Board had solicited from the trunks a list of stations that they wanted to drop, which it was using as a guide to its suspension policy.[20]

Why were the trunks willing and even anxious to drop these stations— stations that they earlier had tried so hard to get permission to serve? In

17. James G. Ray, "More Traffic Where Locals Replace Trunks," *Flight Magazine*, Vol. 54 (June 1965), pp. 90–91.

18. *Western Air Lines, Inc.* v. *Civil Aeronautics Board*, 196 F. 2d 933; *United Air Lines, Inc.* v. *Civil Aeronautics Board*, 198 F. 2d 100.

19. For example, see statement by Wilmer J. Garrett, Superintendent of Airports, Fresno, California, in *Review of the Local Air Carrier Industry*, Hearings before the Aviation Subcommittee of the Senate Committee on Commerce, 89 Cong. 2 sess. (1966), pp. 346–51.

20. Reference to the alleged letter is made in *Aviation Daily*, Vol. 131 (Dec. 14, 1960), p. 262.

some cases stations had been needed regardless of traffic as fueling stops for the trunk carriers' DC-3s. This was the reason why Douglas, Arizona, was on American Airlines' route. Once aircraft range had been improved, such stops were no longer required. The primary reason, however, was that advanced by Richard E. Caves,[21] who observed that as long as the government stood willing to subsidize the trunks it was in their interest to expand service to as many cities as possible. If a city proved to be a good traffic producer, then the airline benefited. If it did not, it cost the airline little.

Once the trunks began to go off subsidy in the late 1940s and early 1950s, however, the situation changed. The marginal stations proved a heavy burden on the trunklines, and without the government subsidy the costs of operating them had to be covered by revenues generated in the more lucrative markets. If the trunklines could get rid of their low-traffic points, they would be free either to reduce fares in denser markets if they felt demand would respond sufficiently, or to make use of the revenues that had been used to cover the costs of the marginal stations either for advertising or to upgrade the quality of their services in the denser, longer-haul markets. United and Western fought suspension, for they believed that local service was not a viable proposition and that the Board gradually was creating a group of potential competitors. Yet even these opponents of suspension eased their opposition as they began to realize the advantages to them of discontinuing service to the smaller cities.

Although the stated purpose of the trunk suspensions was route strengthening for the local carriers, it is an open question which group of carriers benefited more—the trunks or the locals. The seventy-eight points at which a trunk was suspended and replaced with a local each generated an average

21. As Caves noted, if subsidy was paid on a rate-of-return basis, a regulated firm could increase its total allowable profits by such entry if in doing so it increased the investment base on which the rate of return was computed. This incentive would continue until interest payments (paid out of the rate-of-return element of the subsidy) used up the entire rate-of-return element. *Air Transport and Its Regulators: An Industry Study* (Harvard University Press, 1962), pp. 327–29.

Caves's analysis is similar to, but less formally presented than, the standard case of the regulated firm acting under a rate-of-return constraint presented in Harvey Averch and Leland L. Johnson, "Behavior of the Firm under Regulatory Constraint," *American Economic Review*, Vol. 52 (December 1962), pp. 1052–69.

The same factors that influenced the trunks to seek to continue to serve money-losing points apply to the local carriers. As long as they felt that Congress was willing to subsidize them with little argument, they fought any suggestion that some of their stations might better be served by air taxis. Once pressure for subsidy reduction began to be felt and their interest began to turn more toward competition with the trunklines, they began to welcome such transfers.

of only about 9.5 passengers a day during the trunks' final year of operation. To be sure, in some cases this was due to the fact that the trunks had been providing many of these communities with only token service, and at inconvenient times of day. While these stations were marginal to the trunks, in several cases they represented major new sources of traffic to the locals, which sought to cultivate traffic by increasing frequency and improving the general quality of service offered.

An analysis of about 200 cities involved in a trunkline suspension or deletion between 1949 and 1965 indicated that in the first year following the suspension of the trunk the number of flights scheduled increased at 142 (71 percent) of the cities served. At 117 of these cities frequency of flights increased by 50 percent or more. The median increase was 168 percent. Frequency declined at only 15 cities. As would be expected in view of the evidence presented in Chapter 2, this increase in service led to increased numbers of passengers. At 102 of the cities, passenger volume grew by 50 percent or more. The median increase in traffic was 140 percent at the 131 cities with increases.[22] Some of the more spectacular results were obtained at Aberdeen, South Dakota, where traffic increased from 3,356 to 8,108 passengers between Braniff Airways' last year and North Central Airlines' first year of operation, and Bridgeport, Connecticut, which jumped from 1,129 passengers a year under American to 13,140 passengers under Allegheny Airlines—an increase of more than 1,000 percent! On the other hand, not all cities reacted favorably to the switch from trunk to local service. By the end of 1964 the locals themselves had been suspended from eight of the seventy-eight cities mentioned above, and at eight additional stations traffic was below the 1,800-passenger-per-year use-it-or-lose-it level.

The suspension of trunk carriers in cities formerly receiving joint service by a trunk and a local service carrier was of more help to the local carriers. In general, these were more important traffic centers to begin with. During the last year of joint local-trunk operations the fifty-one cities averaged 31.2 passengers a day, or more than three times the traffic of the above

---

22. Civil Aeronautics Board, "Historical Review of Trunkline Suspensions and Deletions at Points Served by Local Service Carriers, January 1, 1949 through December 31, 1963" (CAB, 1964; processed), and Supplement for 1966, especially p. 1.

Ironically these data were cited by an air taxi seeking to justify transferral of routes from a trunkline and a local service carrier to itself. Systems Analysis and Research Corporation, "Proposal by Executive Airlines for Improving Scheduled Airline Service in Maine, New Hampshire, Vermont and Massachusetts" (Cambridge, Mass.: SARC, 1969; processed), p. 2.

seventy-eight cities. After the trunk suspension, average daily passenger originations rose to 36.6, but, more important, this traffic now all went to the local carrier. For example, Atlantic City, New Jersey, originated 19,511 passengers during the twelve months ending December 31, 1962, of which 10,620 flew on Allegheny and 8,891 flew on Eastern Airlines. Eastern was suspended from Atlantic City during the second quarter of 1963. In the twelve months ending December 31, 1964, there were 20,248 passenger originations from Atlantic City, all of them on Allegheny.

In some cases total airline traffic from a station fell when a trunk was suspended, but the remaining traffic represented an increase for the local carrier. During the fourth quarter of 1961, Eastern and United were both suspended at Winston-Salem, North Carolina, leaving Piedmont Aviation as the sole carrier. Total passenger originations dropped by almost 30 percent, but Piedmont's originations rose from 9,633 passengers during the calendar year 1961 to 20,150 in calendar 1962.

Certification of New Points

A third facet of the CAB's route policy during this period was the extension of air service to communities that had not previously received it. If it can be assumed that route expansion had been proceeding with some rationality, then the cities added could come only from among those with even poorer traffic potential than the cities that the local carriers had been certified to serve. This in fact proved to be the case. Fifty-six cities that had not received scheduled air service in 1951 were receiving it in 1959. None of these cities ranked among the top two hundred in passenger-mile volume in 1959. Only twenty-two ranked in the top four hundred. One of the most extreme instances of expansion by the CAB of service to new cities occurred in the Seven States Area Investigation.[23] Sixteen cities that had not previously received air service were added to Frontier Airlines' routes. By 1965, ten of these sixteen had been dropped by Frontier, having failed to generate the minimum levels of traffic required under the use-it-or-lose-it policy. In that same year the remaining six generated a total of 28,241 passengers for Frontier, of which 13,991, or almost half, came from one station—Rapid City, South Dakota. The other five stations each generated

23. United Research Incorporated, "Federal Regulation of the Domestic Air Transport Industry," Prepared for the U.S. Department of Commerce (Cambridge, Mass.: United Research, 1959; processed), Table B-17.

an average of 7.8 passengers a day—not substantially above the use-it-or-lose-it level.

In their 1963 report on subsidy reduction the local carriers themselves pointed out the low quality of the many stations added. In 1958 the average local station generated 27 passengers a day. The seventy-nine stations added in 1959 (largely as a result of the Seven States Area Investigation) averaged only 4 passengers a day. The forty-two stations added in 1960 generated an average of 6 passengers a day, while the forty-seven stations added during 1961 generated 11 passengers a day on an average. These added stations include trunkline transfers as well as points that had not previously received service, and in general the former group of stations generated considerably more traffic than did the latter.[24]

Suspension of Marginal Stations

Although the Board's use-it-or-lose-it policy was not formalized until the Seven States Area Investigation in late 1958, long before that date the Board allowed local service carriers to drop cities that failed to generate even a minimal level of traffic. For example, in the Trans-Texas Certificate Renewal Case[25] seven of Trans-Texas Airways' stations were dropped, and two were consolidated.

The standard of 5 passengers a day, which was adopted by the Board, did not result from an analysis of any such factor as the minimum avoidable costs of serving marginal stations. The Board merely offered its opinion that such a standard seemed "reasonable." In September 1955, in the Southwest Airways Company Permanent-Certificate Case, it said:

The experience of the Board with local-service carriers in the past has indicated that, in general, on-line intermediate points generating in the neighborhood of 300 passengers on and off monthly have borne a reasonable share of the expense incurred by the carrier in providing service to the intermediate point on existing flights. The results of past operations have also led the Board in ordinary circumstances to conclude that local-service carrier points generating in the neighborhood of 5 or more enplaned passengers per day have warranted recertification.[26]

The fact that a station enplaned fewer than 5 passengers a day did not mean that it would automatically be dropped, and as late as 1967, 41 of 473

24. Association of Local Transport Airlines, "Report of the Local Service Committee on the President's Transportation Message" (ALTA, 1963; processed), p. 2.

25. *Civil Aeronautics Board Reports*, Vol. 12 (September 1950–April 1951), p. 606.

26. *Civil Aeronautics Board Reports*, Vol. 21 (June–October 1955), p. 835.

local service points fell below the use-it-or-lose-it standard. Cities fought tenaciously to keep from losing their air service. Most argued that the fault lay with the carriers for providing service of such poor quality. Some contended that they generated a great deal of cargo and that this should make up for a lack of passengers. Some held that their remote location justified air service. Others pointed to the importance of their community for national defense. When all else failed, cities sometimes resorted to the law. At one time, both Bonanza Air Lines and Frontier faced injunctions ordering them to continue air service to communities in Nevada and Nebraska even though the Board had authorized them to drop the cities in question.[27]

Effects of Route Strengthening on Local Service Carriers

Were the routes of the local service carriers "stronger" after the end of the Board's route strengthening than before it? The bulk of the evidence suggests that they were, though the evidence clearly is not entirely on one side. This section attempts to summarize and weigh this evidence.

The policy of removing route restrictions clearly had the effect of allowing the local carriers to compete more effectively for passengers in markets that were served also by trunklines. Table 5-1 shows the increase by carrier over the 1955–65 period in the percentage of local service passenger-miles generated in competitive markets. (A market is defined as competitive if no one carrier carries more than 90 percent of the passengers traveling in it.) In only one case did the importance of competitive traffic decline substantially. In one case it remained constant, and in one it rose only slightly. In the other ten cases it rose substantially, and for the local carriers as a whole it increased by 74 percent over the ten-year period. By 1962 several carriers were approaching the point where nearly half of their traffic was generated in such markets.[28] Note particularly the increase in the proportion of Pacific's traffic originating in competitive markets. It is little wonder that United and Western continued to feel uneasy about Pacific and continued to fight strenuously any relaxation of that carrier's route restrictions.

27. "Frontier Caught Between CAB, State Rulings," *Aviation Daily*, Vol. 130 (Sept. 15, 1960), p. 85; and "Bonanza Fights State Service Order," *Aviation Daily*, Vol. 130 (Sept. 22, 1960), p. 130.

28. The 19 percent of local service passenger-miles generated in competitive markets made up only 0.5 percent of total trunkline passenger-miles in 1955, and the 33 percent in 1965 constituted 1.8 percent of trunkline revenue passenger-miles. The failure of the local carriers to increase the proportion of their traffic generated on competitive routes between 1962 and 1965 may reflect an increased interest on the part of the trunks in upgrading the quality of their short-haul services during this period. (See pp. 157–58, below.)

Table 5-1. Percent of Passenger-miles Generated in Competitive Markets by Local Service Air Carriers, 1955, 1962, and 1965

Carrier	Percent of passenger-miles generated in competitive markets[a]		
	1955	1962	1965
Allegheny Airlines	26	50	46
Bonanza Air Lines	7	33	30
Central Airlines	22	20	32
Frontier Airlines	13	27	34
Lake Central Airlines	15	42	43
Mohawk Airlines	16	39	33
North Central Airlines	24	23	24
Ozark Air Lines	30	23	11
Pacific Air Lines	8	45	44
Piedmont Aviation	21	30	23
Southern Airways	27	40	35
Trans-Texas Airways	19	37	31
West Coast Airlines	18	31	45
Average, all carriers	19	34	33

Sources: United Research Incorporated, "Federal Regulation of the Domestic Air Transport Industry," Prepared for the U.S. Department of Commerce (Cambridge, Mass.: United Research, 1959; processed), Table B-19; *Flight Magazine*, Vol. 52 (June 1963), pp. 48–49; Civil Aeronautics Board, *Competition Among Domestic Air Carriers*, Vol. VI-5 (1965), Table 6.

a. A market is defined as competitive if no one carrier carries more than 90 percent of the passengers traveling in that market.

The removal of route restrictions aided the locals' penetration of trunkline markets. The transfer of trunkline cities to the locals improved traffic significantly at the cities to which they provided exclusive service. Table 5-2 breaks down local service originations by class of originating station for the years 1949, 1954, and 1964 and shows strikingly the importance of the trunk transfers. In 1949 each station served exclusively by local service carriers generated 1,390 passengers—approximately 3.8 passengers per station per day. By 1964 this had risen almost five times to 7,909 passengers a year, 22 passengers per station per day. However, much of this growth came through the transfer of 113 stations from joint trunkline–local service or from exclusively trunkline service to exclusively local service. In 1964 these 113 stations generated more passengers than did the 204 stations which were served exclusively by the locals but which had never received trunkline service. At these latter points, the number of passengers per station grew at a rate of only 10 percent a year, compared with 15 percent a year at the stations receiving joint trunkline–local service.

Finally, the number of dense city pair markets grew as a result of route

Table 5-2. Airline Passenger Originations, by Class of Station, 1949, 1954, and 1964

Item	1949[a]	1954	1964
All stations			
Number	161	361	479
Originating passengers (thousands)	599	2,381	10,457
Passengers per station (thousands)	3.7	6.6	21.8
Joint stations[b]			
Number	79	146	162
Originating passengers (thousands)	485	1,746	7,950
Passengers per station (thousands)	6.1	12.0	49.1
Exclusive stations[b]			
Number	82	315	317
Originating passengers (thousands)	114	635	2,507
Passengers per station (thousands)	1.4	3.0	7.9
Exclusive stations transferred from trunks			
Number	0	25	113
Originating passengers (thousands)	0	142	1,275
Passengers per station (thousands)	0	5.7	11.3
Exclusive stations never served by trunks			
Number	82	188	204
Originating passengers (thousands)	114	492	1,232
Passengers per station (thousands)	1.4	2.6	6.0

Sources: Civil Aeronautics Board, *Airline Traffic Survey, March 1949; Flight Magazine*, Vol. 44 (June 1955), pp. 35–38, and Vol. 54 (June 1965), pp. 94–97, 100, 102.

a. Includes only airlines operating throughout 1949. See Table 4-9, above, note a. Data for March 1949 were expanded to a full year by multiplying by 12.

b. A "joint station" is an airport served by both a trunkline and a local service carrier. An "exclusive station" indicates a city served exclusively by a local service airline.

strengthening. In 1960 (the earliest year for which the data have been assembled), 319 of the 5,114 city pairs served by the local carriers had a density of over 10 passengers daily. Thirty-nine of these city pairs generated over 50 passengers daily. By 1964, 561 city pairs were generating more than 10 passengers daily, and 93 were generating over 50 passengers a day. By 1966 these 561 city pairs accounted for 78 percent of the local carriers' traffic.

These measures indicate a strengthening of routes. The following measures indicate the reverse. During the same period mentioned above, 1960–64, the number of city pairs generating *fewer* than 10 passengers a day rose from 4,795 to 6,142. In 1960 they made up 94 percent of total local service city pairs. By 1964 they still constituted 92 percent of all local service city pairs.

Another indication that the Board's success in route strengthening was somewhat limited is provided by the fact that while in 1955, 90 local service stations receiving a full year's service generated less than the 5-passengers-a-day use-it-or-lose-it minimum and 225 generated fewer than 20 passengers a day, in 1966 there were still 41 stations below the use-it-or-lose-it level, and 186 stations below the 20-passengers-a-day level. In fact, as late as 1960, there were 122 cities that did not meet the use-it-or-lose-it standards, a reflection of the "route weakening" aspects of the area cases.

Thus, by 1966 the route system of the local carriers was both stronger and weaker. It was stronger in that the locals had access to an increasing number of dense markets. These markets were supplying a growing proportion of their total traffic. However, the route system was weaker in that it contained a large and only slowly declining number of very low-density routes—routes too thin to be served even with a DC-3. Furthermore, the routes that were growing the most slowly were in general the ones that the locals had been established to serve. In part this stagnation was the result of the route strengthening policies, since the locals, having been freed from their obligations to serve every city and every stop, concentrated their attention on areas where traffic was growing. Flight frequencies at smaller cities were cut back, and traffic suffered as a result.[29]

Financial Policies

The actions taken by Congress during the 1954–60 period to increase the financial strength of the local carriers and improve their access to the capital markets were mentioned in Chapter 3. These included directing the Board (over strong CAB objections) to grant permanent certificates to the locals, the passage of guaranteed loan legislation, and the granting of favorable capital gains treatment to the local airlines. The most important Board actions in this area were the setting of a higher "fair and reasonable" rate of return on investment for the local carriers and the establishment of a new system of subsidy payment. These two steps combined to both raise and stabilize the rate of return earned by the locals. In Chapter 3 the details

29. Concern over the results of these cutbacks was expressed in *Flight Magazine*, Vol. 50 (June 1961), pp. 54–55, and again in *Flight Magazine* in 1967. The latter article pointed out that at the 475 points the locals served in 1966 they provided 176,000 (14 percent) more aircraft departures than they did in 1964. But 142,000 of these additional departures were provided to the top one-third of the local service points ranked by number of passengers per departure. The bottom one-third received 888 fewer departures than did equivalent-ranked cities in 1964. E. H. Pickering, "Seeds of Trouble in Apple-Rosy Outlook?" *Flight Magazine*, Vol. 56 (June 1967), p. 66.

were presented on the rate-of-return decision, and thus no further discussion of that topic is needed here. The change in the method of subsidy compensation was treated only briefly, so the earlier discussion of this important policy change is expanded below.

In Chapter 4 it was pointed out that the Board, because of its admitted inability to forecast with any degree of accuracy the costs and revenues of local service airlines during their initial period of operation, had agreed reluctantly to put these carriers on temporary "open" rates until final subsidy rates could be established. The Board previously had refused to allow carriers to be subsidized in this way, arguing that "the adoption of a method of mail rate determination patterned upon a 'cost plus' system would tend to destroy a carrier's incentive to maintain costs at a reasonable level and to develop its nonmail business."[30] It was also pointed out, however, that the Board was unsuccessful in establishing "final" rates and that the final rate for Pioneer Air Lines (formerly Essair) had to be reopened almost as soon as it became effective.

The Board's success in placing local carriers on final rates and keeping them there did not improve as the local carriers gained experience in airline operations. Changes in equipment, route patterns, and economic conditions all conspired to cause rates to be reopened almost as fast as they were made final.[31]

Between 1958 and 1960 the local carriers were on an open rate status 80 percent of the time, in spite of strenuous efforts by the Board to put them on final rates.[32] A rate could be opened at the request either of the carrier or of the Board. Once a carrier went onto an open rate, its allowable rate of return was lowered to 7 percent. The 7 percent rate applied during the period when the rate remained open. During the time when it was on the open rate, however, the carrier could draw subsidy sufficient only to cover its deficiency in operating expenses plus interest payments on long-term debt. The 7 percent return on investment and any additional breakeven need was carried on the carrier's books as an account receivable. Only when the Board and the carrier got around to closing the rate again was the return on investment and additional breakeven need actually paid. At this time also, the Board scrutinized the carriers' costs incurred during the open rate period in order to determine whether any should be disallowed as being not consistent with "honest, economical, and efficient manage-

30. *Civil Aeronautics Board Reports*, Vol. 6 (July 1944–May 1946), p. 690.

31. See figures in Frederick P. Kimball, "For Locals, Inefficiency Can Pay Off," *American Aviation*, Vol. 22 (Aug. 11, 1958), p. 56.

32. *Civil Aeronautics Board Reports*, Vol. 34 (June–December 1961), p. 430.

ment." (F.C.A. 49, sec. 485b.) In theory this power allowed the Board to have substantial control over a carrier's operations. In practice such power was severely limited. While minor inefficiencies could be held against a carrier and the associated expenses disallowed, to disallow a major portion of its expenses would mean bankruptcy for the carrier—which the Board wanted to avoid. Thus, while the Board could, and often did, disallow as excessive such items as a portion of executive salaries or mileage flown by the carrier, and such disallowals did have a substantial effect on carrier profits, the Board was extremely reluctant to disallow such important items as the expenses incurred through the use of equipment that was too large on low-density routes. As a result, a situation developed where, to quote the title of the article by Kimball that was cited above, "For Locals, Inefficiency Can Pay Off."

In addition to lowering a carrier's cost consciousness, the system of subsidy compensation described above had a major impact on a carrier's ability to raise capital funds. Once a final reckoning took place between the Board and the carrier, the latter might end up owing the former money or vice versa—no one ever knew in advance. The impact on the financial position of a local service carrier while on an open rate is illustrated by the following example cited by Richard H. Vaughan:[33] As of December 1960, North Central showed a net worth of $1.9 million. The carrier had been on an open rate since 1956 and believed itself due over $600,000 in unpaid breakeven need and return on investment for the open rate period. It carried this amount on its accounts as an account receivable. North Central at this time was negotiating a $2.5 million loan for the purchase of five additional Convairs. The lenders could not be assured that expense disallowances might not substantially reduce the $600,000, seriously impairing North Central's working capital and net worth. As a result the carrier was able to buy the aircraft only on extremely unfavorable terms.[34]

Table 5-3 shows for the years 1954 to 1961 the subsidy paid to North Central during each calendar year, the subsidy the carrier actually earned (including the rate-of-return element) as finally determined by the Board, and the rate of return on total investment computed from the subsidy figures. It is apparent that the rate of return based on the subsidy actually

33. "A Financial Assessment of the Class Mail Rate Subsidy Formula for the Local Service Airlines" (thesis, Stonier Graduate School of Banking, Rutgers University, 1963), pp. 51–52.
34. When the 1956–59 claims finally were disposed of during 1961, over $300,000 was disallowed.

Table 5-3. Subsidy and Rate of Return, North Central Airlines, 1954–61
Dollar amounts in thousands

Year	Subsidy received during year	Rate of return on total investment when subsidy received is included (percent)	Subsidy earned[a]	Rate of return on total investment based on subsidy earned (percent)
1954	$2,141	13.88	$2,075	8.05
1955	1,502	12.60	1,498	12.29
1956	1,297	3.71	1,384	10.16
1957	2,482	−8.15	2,623	1.93
1958	3,312	−5.33	3,403	2.02
1959	5,847	2.83	5,603	−4.93
1960	6,708	−22.70	7,672	6.32
1961	8,032	45.85	7,613	36.69

Source: Civil Aeronautics Board, *Handbook of Airline Statistics, 1965 Edition* (1966), p. 262. The last column was computed by the author.
a. Final subsidy as determined by Civil Aeronautics Board.

earned is both higher and more stable than the rate of return based on subsidy actually paid to the airlines during each calendar year. This was of little help to North Central, however, for while it was on an open rate, it could show only the latter figure to potential investors. The carrier always had to treat its financial results while operating under an open rate as preliminary and subject to uncertain future adjustments.

Given the uncertainty involved in being on an open rate, it is easy to see why it was in the interest of both the government and the carrier to settle on a final rate. The higher rate of return allowed the carrier while operating under a final rate also served to increase its attractiveness. More than outweighing this, however, was the advantage to the carrier under the open rate of being able to recoup the costs of new equipment or additional schedules, and to the Board of being able to recapture for the government any excess profits. Therefore, in spite of efforts by the Board to keep the carriers on final rates, open rates prevailed.

The Class Rate

The Board realized the need to change the method of subsidy compensation and in January 1958 instructed its staff to develop a subsidy program to cure the deficiencies of the one then existing. At approximately the same time, the airlines themselves engaged United Research Incorporated to do the same. From the efforts of both, the class rate was developed.

The class rate established a single subsidy rate schedule for all the local service carriers. It was determined that a relatively stable relationship existed between subsidy requirement per available seat-mile and revenue plane-miles per station per day, a measure of traffic density.[35] To establish the total monthly subsidy to be paid a carrier, revenue plane-miles flown per month (excluding trips flown as extra sections, trips flown on routes not eligible for subsidy, or trips flown over routes on which the Board had authorized the carrier to suspend service) were computed and converted to available seat-miles per month by multiplying miles flown by the number of seats on the aircraft used to fly the route. (The Board established a standard seating capacity for each aircraft for this purpose.) The number of available seat-miles multiplied by the appropriate rate, given the particular carrier's density factor (miles per station per day), represented the gross subsidy due the carrier.[36] This gross subsidy, however, was subject to reduction based on the carrier's experienced rate of return. Each carrier's fair rate of return was to be the weighted average rate of return arrived at by applying the ratios of 21.35 percent to the common stock equity, 7.5 percent to the preferred stock equity, and 5.5 percent to the debt components of "recognized" investment. This fair rate of return was not to exceed 12.75 percent after taxes nor to be below 9.0 percent. In no event was it to be less than the equivalent of 3.0 cents per revenue plane-mile flown. In cases where a carrier's after-tax actual earnings exceeded its calculated fair rate of return, the carrier was to refund a portion of the excess profits to the government. If the actual rate of return fell somewhere between the fair rate of return and 15 percent, 50 percent of the additional profits were to be refunded. If it was greater than 15 percent, the refunded share rose to 75 percent.[37]

The Board claimed several advantages for the class rate:

1. Although it was recognized that in future periods some adjustment of the class rate formula might be necessary, the Board and the carriers would be spared the protracted periods of open rates. The current class rate would prevail until a new one was established. Thus both the carriers and the Board would know in advance how much subsidy would be paid.

2. It was recognized that carrier incentives under the new system would

35. *Civil Aeronautics Board Reports*, Vol. 34 (June–December 1961), p. 438.
36. *Ibid.*, p. 444.
37. *Ibid.*, pp. 444–45.

be improved. A carrier could reap the benefits of cost reduction (within the limits of the profit-sharing provisions) without being afraid that the Board would attempt to recapture its gains if it were on an open rate or lower its subsidy rate if it were on a closed one.

3. The adoption of the class rate would end the distasteful task of having the Board scrutinize carrier costs during open rate periods. The carriers had always resented intrusions by the Board into areas they considered to be legitimate concerns only of their managements, yet because of the "cost-plus" feature of the open rate system, such scrutiny was necessary if any pretext of subsidy control was to be maintained.

The class rate has required several revisions and has been altered so much by adjustments pertaining only to particular carriers that it may be stretching the definition to refer to it as a class rate today;[38] yet it has achieved its purpose of providing a method of subsidy disbursement that allows all sides to know with much greater certainty the amount of subsidy the carriers will be receiving.

Aircraft Choice

By the early 1950s, the local service airlines, in spite of their low passenger loads, had standardized their fleets on the 21-passenger DC-3. The few smaller single- and twin-engine aircraft remaining in the local service fleets after 1950 either were rapidly phased out or belonged to the carriers that the Board refused to recertify. The year 1952 marked the first use by the locals of equipment that was larger than the DC-3. During that year Pioneer replaced its entire fleet of eleven DC-3s with nine 36-passenger Martin 202 aircraft. By the early 1960s the importance of the DC-3 was fast fading, and even the 36- to 52-seat piston and turboprop aircraft that had succeeded it were being replaced by the first of the local service jets. The aircraft problems of the local service carriers can be divided into two categories: (1) how to replace the DC-3 with a more efficient aircraft on short-haul, low-density routes and (2) what aircraft to buy for use both on their denser routes and on the new routes being acquired from the trunklines. The first problem never was solved. The second was not solved satisfactorily until late in the period.

38. On December 2, 1969, Frontier Airlines petitioned to be taken off the class rate, claiming that the subsidy it provided was unrealistically low. "Industry, CAB to Review Subsidy Program," *Aviation Week and Space Technology*, Vol. 90 (Dec. 8, 1969), p. 38.

The DC-3 Replacement

At first glance it would appear to have been easy to find an aircraft better suited than the DC-3 to the short-haul, low-density routes of the local carriers. The DC-3 had been derived from the DC-1, which first flew in 1933. The DC-3 itself had first entered airline service in 1936 and was at that time the ultimate in a long-range, high-capacity aircraft.

Indeed there were several U.S.-designed aircraft—Lockheed's L-10, L-14, and L-18 and Beech's Model 18, for example, which entered service at about the same time as or even later than the DC-3—that were designed specifically to provide short-haul, low-density service and to do it efficiently. By the time the DC-3 was adopted by the local carriers (for reasons suggested in Chapter 4) it was considered obsolete, and the Civil Aeronautics Administration had set December 30, 1950, as the date for its retirement from scheduled domestic airline service.

If the statements of the local carriers are to be believed, they looked upon the DC-3 strictly as an interim aircraft. They realized that in flying their routes the DC-3 was being called upon to perform a task for which it had not been designed. The locals believed that considerable operating cost savings could be achieved by an aircraft designed specifically for feeder operations.

Yet with one exception, no true DC-3 replacement ever was purchased by the local carriers.[39] The most likely explanation for this would be that local service traffic grew so much that aircraft smaller than the DC-3 were no longer needed. But this was not the case. To be sure, traffic on many routes reached levels where aircraft larger than the DC-3 clearly were required. However, throughout the period under study a need remained for small, short-haul aircraft. The number of low-density routes increased substantially as a result of route strengthening, presumably increasing the need for a DC-3 replacement. (See page 119, above.)

The scope of this role was perhaps best brought out in a study performed in 1964 for the Federal Aviation Agency, Aircraft Development Service, by the Systems Analysis and Research Corporation (SARC). SARC forecast local service airline traffic through 1975 and found that it could be divided into two parts—a group of longer, higher-density routes on which traffic

39. The exception was the twelve Nord 262s purchased by Lake Central Airlines in 1965 and 1966. The Nord was a 28-passenger, turboprop-powered, French-built "DC-3 replacement." The Nord was phased out in 1969 by Allegheny, the company that in 1968 acquired Lake Central.

was growing relatively rapidly and a large group of low-density, short-haul routes on which traffic was growing very slowly.[40] It was assumed that the local carriers would be required to provide service to these lower-density stations at least through 1975. SARC then attempted, by means of a simulation of local service operations, to find the optimum aircraft size to use on such routes. To quote from SARC's findings:

The determination of the operating profit or loss of each routing's daily financial results indicate that in 1975 there should be more widespread use of smaller aircraft than is presently [March 1964] made of the DC-3. Current DC-3 operations of the local carriers account for some 46.5% of total routings operated by the local carriers [in 1963 DC-3 aircraft miles constituted 36% of the total], whereas in 1975, even with the greater traffic volumes which are forecast, 61% of the local industry routings will be most economically operated with aircraft of less than 40-seat capacity.[41]

Depending on the load factor and utilization rate assumed, SARC foresaw a market for from three hundred to five hundred 20-seat aircraft (the optimal size) among the local service carriers.[42]

It is apparent, then, that unless SARC's estimate of traffic growth on the low-density segments was substantially too low or the local carriers were to be allowed to drop their short-haul, low-density segments, the local carriers would need a 20-seat DC-3 replacement even into the mid-1970s.

The need existed. Aircraft technology was not a major bar to development. Although there was relatively little interest in light turboprop engines in this country until the Army's Light Observation Helicopter competition in the late 1950s, engines of a sort that could have powered or been modified to power a DC-3 replacement were available from the early 1950s on. In 1951, Continental Motors Corporation obtained a license to manufacture a 400 h.p. turboprop engine from the one manufacturer in the world who showed a continuing interest in such powerplants, Turbomeca of France. At the time of the agreement, Continental stated that the engines were "not experimental but ready for production."[43] The 825 h.p. Lycoming XT53 was an engine produced in 1955 partially for the purpose of powering a DC-3 replacement that was never built.[44]

40. Systems Analysis and Research Corporation, "Economic Analysis of the Short-Haul Transport" (Cambridge, Mass.: SARC, 1964; processed), pp. 21–27. The SARC forecast is consistent with the results reported above in connection with the analysis of the effects of route strengthening.

41. "Economic Analysis of the Short-Haul Transport," p. 29.

42. *Ibid.*, p. 70.

43. *Aviation Week*, Vol. 55 (Oct. 15, 1951), p. 32.

44. *Aviation Week*, Vol. 63 (Sept. 19, 1955), pp. 7, 17.

A brief description of how two of today's foremost builders of light turboprop engines, the Garrett Corporation and United Aircraft of Canada, got into the business demonstrates that technological constraints were not controlling. The Garrett Corporation has long been a producer of turbine-powered auxiliary power units, air turbine starters, and air-conditioning systems for aircraft. In 1959 it was working on a power source for a 300-kilowatt generator when company planners decided that the power source could be configured as an aircraft or helicopter propulsion powerplant, for which they thought there might be a market. The engine was successful and is today being produced in four power configurations from 575 to 840 h.p. United Aircraft's Canadian Division had served essentially as a sales, overhaul, and spare parts manufacturing organization for Canadian customers until a small design group was formed in 1956. By late 1958 this group had produced the design for the 500 h.p. PT6 turboprop, later used to power a wide range of helicopters and business and commuter aircraft.

If a lack of engine availability was not a problem, airframe technology was even less of a constraint. All of the 15- to 20-passenger commuter aircraft produced in the 1960s were of highly conventional design. De Havilland Aircraft of Canada produced its 20-passenger Twin Otter by adapting an airframe it had been producing for years. The Beech Model 99, which was developed in response to a 1963 local carrier appeal for a DC-3 replacement but was not purchased in quantity by the local carriers, was derived from a Beech business aircraft. Swearingen's 20-passenger Metro was a modification of the Swearingen Merlin corporate light twin.

It is true that the local carriers had difficulties in raising funds to purchase equipment. This was a problem particularly during the early and middle 1950s. Yet both Congress and the Board showed themselves willing to take actions to aid the carriers in acquiring DC-3 replacements. In 1950 the Congress passed a bill appropriating funds for a period of five years "to promote . . . the development of improved transport aircraft . . . suitable for feeder-line operation, by providing for temporary Government assistance in the testing and minor experimental modification of such aircraft."[45] Congress granted the local carriers permanent certificates in 1955, at least partially in the hope that this would make it easier for the carriers to raise capital and would thus encourage the aircraft industry to produce a DC-3 replacement. The passage of legislation in 1957 to guarantee loans for the purchase of aircraft was aimed directly at this problem.

45. Public Law 867, 81 Cong. 2 sess. (Sept. 30, 1950), 64 Stat. 1091.

The ability of the local carriers to increase their assets in the form of operating property and equipment from less than $10 million in 1954 to over $250 million in 1966 attests to the success of these financial strengthening activities. Yet, with the one exception mentioned above, no DC-3 replacements were acquired. The 1950 prototype aid legislation expired in 1955 and was not renewed. The local carriers in 1952 had said that no federal aid was needed and had withdrawn their request for funds.[46] As of the end of 1966, the federal government had guaranteed loans for forty-seven aircraft worth almost $38 million, yet in no case were the proceeds of the loan used to purchase an aircraft of less than 36-passenger capacity.

The conclusion one is inescapably drawn to is that no DC-3 replacement was purchased because none was really desired by the local carriers, and that none was desired because the regulatory environment offered little or no incentive for the carriers to acquire such an aircraft. Beginning in 1947 the Board had shown itself willing to support the use of DC-3s by local carriers, even though they were far larger than the traffic warranted. As will be seen below, after 1955 the Board adopted the same policy with respect to larger aircraft. Under the cost-plus subsidy system that was in effect prior to 1961, there was no incentive for a carrier to draw on its meager financial resources to purchase an aircraft that would at most benefit the government through a reduction in subsidy. Furthermore, even when the class rate was introduced in 1961, it contained a strong incentive to use larger, not smaller, aircraft (see below, page 134), an incentive that was removed in 1963. After that, the Board tried to make the subsidy "neutral" as between aircraft, and it resisted an attempt by Lake Central to establish a rate for the Nord that would have made the use of this aircraft more attractive.[47] Under the Federal Aviation Act the Board is prevented from prescribing the type of aircraft that a carrier may use on a route, but it can establish a subsidy system that creates a strong economic incentive to use a particular type of aircraft.[48]

Larger Aircraft—Piston vs. Turboprop

The aircraft that the local carriers did buy, both to replace the DC-3 and to serve their denser markets, ranged in capacity from 36 to 52 seats. The

46. Robert E. Peach, "The Search for a Better Local Transport Design," *Flight Magazine*, Vol. 37 (June 1952), pp. 31, 45.
47. *Civil Aeronautics Board Reports*, Vol. 41 (August 1964–January 1965), p. 145.
48. *Civil Aeronautics Board Reports*, Vol. 39 (September 1963–February 1964), p. 73.

majority of these aircraft were Convair 240s, 340s, and 440s and Martin 202s and 404s, purchased second-hand from the trunklines. When they were acquired, these aircraft were powered by piston engines, but by the mid-1960s most had been retrofitted with turboprops. A number of turboprop-powered F-27s also were purchased by the local carriers.

The shift to larger aircraft was led by Pioneer, the same carrier that had led the switch to DC-3s from smaller twin-engine aircraft in 1946. In June 1952 Pioneer replaced its entire fleet of eleven DC-3s with nine 36-seat Martin 202s, purchased second-hand for $300,000 each from Northwest Airlines.[49] Later the same year Southwest Airways acquired four Martin 202s for approximately $285,000 each and on April 26, 1953, placed them in service on its Los Angeles–San Francisco route. Both carriers predicted that the introduction of these larger aircraft would temporarily raise subsidy requirements but claimed that the transition was necessary if they were eventually to achieve self-sufficiency. However, when each carrier applied to the Board for an upward adjustment in its mail pay to cover the higher costs, the Board refused to approve it.

Caves has attributed the Board's action in these cases to an "economy drive."[50] This may be a partial explanation, but there were other important reasons involved. Both United and Western had long fought the easing of Southwest's route restrictions, particularly on the Los Angeles–San Francisco route. They believed that the actions of the Board would enable Southwest to offer them substantial competition on this important route. The Board, in easing Southwest's restrictions, had assured the trunk carriers that its aim was merely to allow Southwest additional flexibility in its local services, not to create a rival to them. The adoption by Southwest of the Martin 202, an aircraft designed for trunkline operations which would place Southwest on a par with the trunks in equipment, may have struck the Board as a severe blow at its "specialist doctrine"—a blow too strong to tolerate. In any event, the Board did not want to place itself in the position of increasing Southwest's subsidy so it could better compete with United and Western.

The case of Pioneer seemed to the Board to be an even stronger blow at the specialist doctrine.[51] The Southwest re-equipment involved only a few

49. Pioneer sold its DC-3s for $100,000 each. This was about 50 percent more than it had cost the company to buy each DC-3 and prepare it for airline service five years earlier. *Flight Magazine*, Vol. 37 (June 1952), pp. 23–24.

50. *Air Transport and Its Regulators*, p. 261.

51. *Civil Aeronautics Board Reports*, Vol. 17 (March–September 1953), pp. 499–534.

aircraft and would have applied to only the most heavily traveled routes. Southwest's load factor in 1951 was the highest of all the locals, and it did not decline after the introduction of the Martin 202s. Thus, traffic increases more than matched capacity increases. Finally, the additional subsidy required was small, and the transition was expected to be almost self-supporting. Pioneer, on the other hand, completely replaced its DC-3s even though on many routes passenger loads were far from the level at which the capacity even of a DC-3 would be strained. Pioneer's overall revenue-passenger load factor in 1951 was 45 percent—lower than three other local carriers (Piedmont Aviation, Mohawk Airlines, and Southwest Airways) and not substantially above that of five other locals (Allegheny Airlines, Bonanza Air Lines, Mid-Continent Airlines, North Central Airlines, and West Coast Airlines). During 1953, the first full year of the Martin 202's operation, Pioneer's load factor fell to 42.7 percent. However, Pioneer's load factor was becoming strained on some of its most important competitive routes. For example, it was running at 73 percent of capacity on its Dallas–Waco segment. The Board admitted that on certain routes at certain times of the day the limited capacity of the DC-3 caused Pioneer to have to refuse service to customers, but remarked that "it is well recognized that the economics of a transportation enterprise may well inhibit a carrier from providing sufficient capacity to meet all peak traffic movements where such traffic demand will not by itself support additional capacity."[52]

Of more consequence to the Board was the fact that Pioneer's management had admitted that one of the considerations that had led it to adopt Martin aircraft rather than to increase flight frequencies with its DC-3s was its desire to maintain, for competitive reasons, equipment parity with trunkline carriers that served some of the points authorized to Pioneer.[53] The Board commented: "Pioneer's authority to provide service over route No. 64 was not granted for the primary purpose of competing with trunk carriers, and we do not recognize competitive considerations as a significant justification for new equipment."[54] Finally, the amount of additional subsidy needed to support Martin aircraft operations over five years was substantial—$1.8 million if Pioneer's figures were to be believed and $3.4 million if the Board's figures were correct.

Southwest continued to operate its Martins without any increase in mail

52. *Ibid.*, p. 514. Contrast this statement with the Board's concern over "unables," reflected in its easing of Southwest's route restrictions in 1948. See above, p. 108.

53. *Ibid.*, p. 513.

54. *Ibid.*, pp. 513–14.

pay. Pioneer, however, sold its Martins and reacquired DC-3s. In 1955 it merged with Continental Air Lines, a trunkline and one of its chief trunkline competitors.[55]

The next move to larger equipment took place in 1955, when Mohawk Airlines acquired three 40-passenger Convair 240s and Allegheny acquired four 40-passenger Martins. Both carriers stressed the fact that the equipment was being acquired not as a replacement for their DC-3s but in order to handle traffic loads that had become too large for a DC-3 on certain segments.[56] Furthermore, Mohawk contended that in spite of the fact that the Convair cost three times as much per hour to operate as the DC-3, its operating results actually would be better because of the Convair's greater revenue potential. Mohawk forecast a reduction in its break-even need of $44,000 a year if it had a mixed, as opposed to an all-DC-3, fleet, but admitted that "return and tax liability on the additional capital invested in Convair equipment may raise the over-all subsidy requirements during our first year of Convair operation."[57]

Allegheny and Mohawk were not unaware that the acquisition of such equipment would place them more on a parity with the trunklines operating in their area. Allegheny played this aspect down, stating: "While Allegheny is aware of the public relations and sales appeal of faster and more modern equipment, the company's decision in this instance was primarily a matter

55. Several of the local carriers opposed this as a first step in the dismemberment of the feeder system (see Chap. 6, below). A trunkline representative also noted this possibility. The Board's Bureau of Air Operations supported the operation. V. Rock Grundman, appearing for the Bureau at hearings, said that "because of the many similarities of routes and services rendered by Continental and Pioneer, Continental would be able to serve Pioneer's routes adequately and without any loss in the character and quality of this service." "CAL-Pioneer Merger Stirs Feeder Protest," *Aviation Week*, Vol. 61 (Sept. 20, 1954), p. 96.

In 1963 several of Pioneer's old routes were given back to two local carriers, Frontier and Trans-Texas, as part of the Board's "route strengthening" policy.

56. The president of Mohawk stated: "While we feel the Convair 240 is our best available transport, we realize it does not solve the problem of the need for a short-haul aircraft which will carry maximum loads over short distances (the Convair has a 40,500-lb. gross take-off limit but its landing weight limit is only 38,600 lbs. and a [rate of fuel consumption] of 200 gals. hourly means a Convair at full gross [weight] must fly an hour and 30 mins. before it can land). This problem cannot be solved until aircraft engineers are convinced of the economic requirement of and market for a short-haul transport designed to carry more passengers economically over a shorter distance, rather than designed for expansion to carry the same number of people a greater distance." (Robert S. Peach, "Convairs for Mohawk," *Flight Magazine*, Vol. 43 [June 1955], pp. 34, 54.) Mohawk never did acquire a "DC-3 replacement."

57. *Ibid.*, pp. 54–55.

of keeping pace with its own growth and development."[58] Significantly, Mohawk listed as one advantage of the Convair that "in our area the public has already accepted the 240 as standard short-haul equipment on American's schedules."[59]

The Board was apprehensive about the results of these equipment acquisitions, but it did not deny the additional subsidy that they entailed. The position of the Board appears to have been influenced by the strong congressional show of support for the local carriers that resulted from passage in the summer of 1954 by the House and Senate Commerce Committees (over CAB objections) of legislation directing that permanent certificates be issued for these carriers. The bill did not finally pass both houses until 1955, but even before then the CAB began to sense the way the political wind was blowing. In an order adopted November 10, 1954, it reversed itself and allowed Southwest a higher subsidy rate for its Martin 202s, overruling an objection by Bonanza that it could operate Southwest's routes more economically with DC-3s than Southwest could with a mixed DC-3/ Martin 202 fleet. The Board was careful to hedge its position, stating that "we must emphasize, however, that the findings contained herein as regards the operation of several M-202s by Southwest relate solely to this carrier and are based upon the particular circumstances in this case at this time."[60] William V. Henzey noted the apparent shifting of the Board's position, attributed the shift in part to pressures from Senator A. S. Monroney and Representative Carl Hinshaw, and predicted that the Board would approve use of larger aircraft in the future, even if this meant that "the locals' subsidy bill must go up before it can come down."[61] Henzey predicted, however, that such permission probably would be forthcoming only for the use of new aircraft, such as the F-27, and not if the carriers proposed to acquire used Convairs and Martins.[62]

However, on July 22, 1958, the Board adopted an order authorizing the substantially higher subsidy rates required by Mohawk's Convairs over the

58. Leslie O. Barnes, "Martins for Allegheny," *Flight Magazine*, Vol. 43 (June 1955), p. 33.

59. Peach, "Convairs for Mohawk," p. 34.

60. *Civil Aeronautics Board Reports*, Vol. 19 (August 1954–January 1955), p. 333.

61. "Locals to Get Aid in Buying New Fleets," *American Aviation*, Vol. 64 (Feb. 13, 1956), pp. 92–93.

62. In presenting its case for the acquisition of Convairs, Mohawk took pains to stress the immediacy of its need for larger aircraft, observing that, although the F-27 looked like a better aircraft, it was at that time at least three years away from being ready to enter service. Mohawk also stressed the low initial cost of the used Convairs. Peach, "Convairs for Mohawk," pp. 33–34. (But see p. 39, above.)

strong protests of Members G. Joseph Minetti and Harmar D. Denny. The majority of the Board had argued that its granting of a higher rate was only temporary and was subject to readjustment after the rate was made final. Denny scoffed at this, asking, "If the carrier is not capable of survival as alleged, then how can the Federal Treasury seriously anticipate the recoupment of overpayments?" He accused the carrier of expanding its operations regardless of the costs involved and asking the government to pick up the tab.[63]

By the end of 1959 there were fifty-two Convairs and Martins in the local service fleet, and they supplied 24 percent of the fleet's total revenue passenger-miles. Between 1955 and 1959 the only carriers using such aircraft were Southwest, Allegheny, and Mohawk. In 1959, armed with the knowledge that the CAB would pay any "reasonable" increase in subsidy that resulted, two more carriers (North Central and Frontier) acquired Convairs. As Table 5-4 shows, this year marked the beginning of an upsurge in the importance of these aircraft that was to last until about 1963.

The local carriers were particularly active in acquiring large piston aircraft between 1960 and 1963. One possible reason for this was the incentive to use large aircraft built into the class rate system of subsidy payment in effect during that period. Under Class Rate I, carriers were paid a rate per seat-mile based on the number of miles flown per station per day. For example, if a carrier averaged 500 aircraft-miles per station per day, its subsidy rate would have been 2.07 cents per seat-mile. A DC-3 was assumed by the Board to have 24 seats, a large piston aircraft, 40 or 44 seats. The direct operating cost per aircraft-mile for the DC-3 in 1962 was 60.1 cents, and it was 93.6 cents for the larger piston aircraft as a group. (This ignores the 23-mile difference in average stage lengths between the DC-3 and large piston aircraft for 1962, but taking it into account would strengthen the argument.) If the Systems Analysis and Research Corporation report cited above is followed and it is assumed that total operating costs are approximately 175 percent of direct operating costs, a total cost per mile of $1.05 for the DC-3 and $1.64 for the large piston aircraft is obtained.[64] Assume the passenger fare to be 7.8 cents a mile, the 1962 local service average. If a carrier received the same subsidy for flying the Convair as it did for the

63. *Civil Aeronautics Board Reports*, Vol. 27 (July–November 1958), p. 31. CAB Member Louis J. Hector, while voting to allow the higher subsidy, agreed with Denny concerning the futility of the cost adjustment procedures and called for a new method of subsidization.

64. "Economic Analysis of the Short-Haul Transport," p. 48.

Table 5-4. Relative Importance of DC-3s, Large Piston, and Turboprop Aircraft in Local Service Air Carrier Fleet, 1953 and 1957–68

Year	DC-3		Large piston		Turboprop[b]	
	Number[a]	Percent of revenue passenger-miles	Number[a]	Percent of revenue passenger-miles	Number[a]	Percent of revenue passenger-miles
1953	150	n.a.	2	n.a.	0	0.0
1957	202	n.a.	24	n.a.	0	0.0
1958	203	76.7	25	19.3	n.a.	4.0
1959	220	56.5	52	24.0	31	19.5
1960	215	47.5	59	28.9	35	23.4
1961	216	35.2	98	41.2	38	23.5
1962	179	25.0	153	55.9	35	19.0
1963	172	21.2	180	59.8	40	19.0
1964	149	25.0	193	59.5	51	25.0
1965	118	11.7	201	54.4	68	30.0
1966	97	6.6	160	38.8	116	38.2
1967	58	2.4	92	16.9	186	48.7
1968	10	0.1	55	6.9	228	42.7

Sources: *Flight Magazine*, Vol. 41 (June 1954), p. 53, and various later June issues; Civil Aeronautics Board, *Handbook of Airline Statistics, 1967 Edition* (1968), p. 419, and *Handbook of Airline Statistics, 1969 Edition* (1970), p. 413.
n.a. Not available.
a. During fourth quarter.
b. Excludes Nord 262. Data on pure jets (1965–66) are not included.

DC-3, it would cover total costs with an average DC-3 load of 7.1 passengers, while the large piston aircraft would require 14.6 passengers to cover total costs. However, under the subsidy formula contained in Class Rate I, the DC-3, given the assumptions above, would receive a subsidy of 50 cents a mile, while a 40-seat large piston aircraft would receive a subsidy of 83 cents a mile. Thus a large piston aircraft would be profitable on a larger number of routes—any route on which the average expected passenger load was at least 10.4. This incentive was removed when Class Rate II was adopted in March 1963, making the subsidy neutral as among aircraft.

Another explanation for the number of larger piston aircraft purchased during this period is the number of trunkline suspensions that took place during these years.[65] These suspensions left the trunklines with a surplus of large piston aircraft. The local carriers did not want to alienate the communities they had just received from the trunklines (in many cases because

65. Between 1959 and 1963 there were 97. *Flight Magazine*, Vol. 54 (June 1965), pp. 90–91.

they had promised better service) by "downgrading" them to DC-3 service, so they purchased large piston aircraft from the trunklines. The most interesting case occurred in 1961, when the Board transferred many of Eastern's short-haul routes in the northeast to Mohawk. Mohawk bought from Eastern the aircraft that Eastern had been using on the routes; it hired Eastern's personnel and took over Eastern's leases.[66]

Turboprop Aircraft

With the exception of Lake Central's Nord 262s, the turboprop aircraft operated by the local service carriers during this period fell into two classes: the Fairchild F-27 and the turboprop conversions of the Convair aircraft mentioned above. The local carriers realized early the great advantages turboprop power has for the type of services they offer, in addition to any inherent passenger appeal it possesses.[67] The retention of the propeller means that the turboprop can still land at many of their airfields that would be closed to jets, yet the turboprop has many of the features that make the jet so attractive. It is mechanically much more simple than the piston engine, which means that it has substantially lower maintenance costs. It is virtually vibrationless, which both improves passenger comfort and prolongs airframe life. A turboprop engine weighs about half as much as a piston engine of equal horsepower. And, as was seen in Chapter 2, although it burns somewhat more fuel than does a piston engine, its fuel is substantially cheaper. The net result is that fuel expenses are lower.

The one major drawback to a turboprop engine is its higher initial cost, as was indicated in Table 3-3. While a new set of engines and propellers for a Convair 240 cost about $45,000 in 1969, a set of engines and propellers for the turboprop Convair 600 cost $290,000, or more than six times as much. A set of engines and propellers for the DC-3 cost $14,000; a set for a Nord 262, a turboprop aircraft of roughly equivalent capacity, cost $132,000— nine times as much. In a world of relatively perfect capital markets this would be no problem. If the lower operating costs of the turboprop engines (suitably discounted) more than compensated for the higher capital costs, they would be used. However, in an industry where credit rationing exists, or where operating costs are low and capital costs high, due to the method of subsidy payment, one might observe different behavior. Both of these factors would tend to lower the present value of cost savings through the use of turboprops and bias the decision in favor of piston aircraft. Actions

66. *Review of the Local Air Carrier Industry*, Hearings, p. 425.
67. *Flight Magazine*, Vol. 36 (October 1951), p. 26.

to reduce the degree of credit rationing to an industry or to increase the benefit from cutting operating costs would work to ameliorate this bias. Finally, if the rate of return allowed by the regulatory agency were greater than the cost of capital to the industry, and the industry were one that sought to maximize dollar profits, an Averch-Johnson effect would introduce bias in the direction of the more capital-intensive turboprops.[68]

THE FAIRCHILD F-27. The first turboprop aircraft operated by the local carriers was the Fairchild F-27, which was designed by Fokker Aircraft of Amsterdam and built in the United States under license. The history of the evolution of the F-27 design illustrates the shift in aircraft interests of the local service carriers during the 1950s and adds further evidence that these carriers did not want a true replacement for the DC-3. The F-27 was designed as a 28- to 36-passenger aircraft.[69] By the time the aircraft was ordered into quantity production, its capacity was 36 to 40 passengers. The announced price of the 28-passenger version was approximately $400,000. In 1956 the price for the 36- to 40-passenger version was $540,000.

During 1958 and 1959 twenty-nine of these aircraft were placed in service by five local carriers. Twenty-three of the twenty-nine were financed by government-guaranteed loans. While most of the F-27s were used merely to supplement the DC-3 (as was the case with the Convairs and Martins), one carrier, Bonanza, replaced its entire fleet of DC-3s with F-27s by November 1960, thereby becoming "the nation's first all-jet airline."

The F-27 cost more to operate than did the DC-3. In 1957, Bonanza's last year of all-DC-3 operations, direct costs were 54 cents per revenue-mile for an average stage length of 113 miles. During 1961, Bonanza's first year of all-F-27 operations, direct expenses were 82 cents a mile over an average stage length of 127 miles. Yet the F-27 looks considerably better when compared with the large piston aircraft. During 1961 the average operating cost for all large piston aircraft was 97 cents a mile (over a stage length of 106 miles).

In spite of its operating-cost superiority over the larger piston aircraft, the F-27 sold poorly. Sales slumped in 1959, the year in which large piston sales began to boom. In April 1960 the Fairchild factory went on a five-days-a-week, one-aircraft-a-month schedule. In November, production

68. Averch and Johnson, "Behavior of the Firm under Regulatory Constraint." The authors demonstrate that when the rate of return allowed by the regulatory agency exceeds the cost of capital to the firm, the firm will be able to increase its total dollar profits by adopting excessively capital-intensive production processes.

69. *Flight Magazine*, Vol. 41 (June 1954), p. 33.

was shut down, and the company announced that it had ten aircraft on hand for immediate delivery. Production did not begin again until 1964, coinciding with the increase in local service carrier interest in turboprop conversions.

TURBOPROP CONVERSIONS. The other large turboprop aircraft operated by the local carriers were the turboprop conversions of their large piston aircraft. Both the Convair 340 and the Martin 404 were designed originally to be turboprop-powered. The 340 was designed around the Allison 501 engine, but the engine was unavailable for civilian use at the time because of the Korean war. The 340 thus was built as a piston-engine aircraft with provision for later conversion. The same was true of the Martin 404. The first Allison-powered Convair flew in 1951. In 1954 the Air Force conducted extensive tests on the aircraft. Between 1955 and 1957 the Military Air Transport Service operated turboprop Convairs over a pattern of routes that was designed to simulate an airline's operations. The purpose of the tests was to obtain data on the reliability and costs of operation of turboprops. By 1958 Allison was offering conversion kits to the airlines.

Yet the first Allison-powered Convair did not enter local airline service until June 1, 1964. Frontier introduced the Convair 580—the converted Convair 340—and enjoyed such success with it that by the end of 1966 Frontier had converted all eighteen of its piston-powered Convairs. Other airlines joined the rush to convert, and Pacific Airmotive Corporation, the firm performing the conversions, was forced to double production. By the end of 1969, 107 of the conversions had been completed.

The interest of the airlines in turboprop conversions led Convair itself to develop a kit based on the Rolls-Royce Dart turboprop engine. The kits were designed for all Convair models, but the locals converted only Convair 240s to Dart power. By 1968 all thirty-five Convair 240s in the local service fleet had been converted to Convair 600s, as the Dart-converted 240 was called.

The converted Convairs offered substantial savings in operating costs over their piston-powered counterparts. In 1966 the local carriers operated sixty Convair 340s and 440s and twenty-six Convair 580s. Direct operating costs per aircraft-mile for the 340/440s was $1.22 over a 100-mile average stage length. Over that same stage length the Convair 580s cost 98 cents a mile to operate (*including* depreciation)—a saving of almost 20 percent.[70] During 1966 the average Convair 580 flew about 760,000 revenue-miles.

70. The actual operating cost figure for the Convair 580 in 1966 was 90 cents over a 150-mile stage length. This was adjusted to the figure shown, using information from *Review of the Local Air Carrier Industry*, Hearings, Chart 3, p. 136.

If the same number of revenue-miles were flown using piston-powered Convairs, operating costs would have been higher by $175,000 per aircraft per year. The cost of conversion was between $500,000 and $650,000 per aircraft, indicating a payout period (excluding interest costs on capital) of between 2.9 and 3.7 years.

The favorable experience of the carriers with both the F-27 and the Convair conversion raises the question why larger piston-powered aircraft remained in the local service fleet for such a long time. The F-27 was available for immediate delivery in 1960. The Allison-Convair was available as early as 1958. Yet between 1958 and 1966, local carriers bought approximately 150 larger piston aircraft and flew them 400 million aircraft-miles.

It was suggested above in connection with the "DC-3 replacement" problem that the regulatory environment did not make it in the carriers' interest to undertake cost-reducing innovations. Yet this is what turboprop conversion or the acquisition of turboprop equipment represented. Under the cost-plus subsidy system that prevailed until 1961, savings in operating costs were of little value to the carriers, but savings in capital funds, given the severe capital rationing to which these firms were subject, were of great value. Thus it is not difficult to understand the general reluctance of the carriers to acquire turboprop aircraft, at least until 1961.

The establishment of the class rate in 1961, which for the first time put a positive value on cost reduction, should have stimulated the acquisition of turboprops. In particular, the incentive to use the larger aircraft that were in Class Rate I should have been particularly strong, since the Convair 580 seats 52, compared with 44 for the 340.

Unfortunately, another facet of Board policy tended to discourage turboprop acquisitions during the early 1960s. As was seen above, during the 1958–63 period the Board was engaged in "strengthening" the local carriers through a series of major route awards. Merely to buy the equipment to serve the additions to their systems the local carriers were having to raise larger sums of money than they had ever raised before. A large piston aircraft could be purchased at between one-half and one-third the price of a turboprop. Thus, for a given amount of money, greater capacity could be purchased if larger piston aircraft were acquired. For example, in its proposal made in 1960 in the Southwestern Case, Central Airlines estimated that its capital requirements for equipment needed to provide the services it was requesting were $5.1 million for a DC-3/Convair 340 package and $9.3 million for a DC-3/F-27 package. At this time Central's total assets were only $2.4 million, and its stockholder equity was $751,000. Furthermore, in 1960 Central was on an open subsidy rate, and $850,000 of its assets were in the form of accounts receivable, primarily subsidy payments which Central considered the government owed it but which it had not yet collected.

An illustration of how the subsidy system and excessive route awards combined to thwart one carrier's attempt to acquire efficient turboprop equipment is provided by the case of Lake Central. In January 1960 the airline ordered five Allison Convairs, becoming the first domestic carrier to do so. At the same time it took an option on ten more. The first was to be delivered by "late summer," the remainder "prior to the end of the year."[71] On May 13, 1960, Lake Central contracted for the purchase of five Convair 340s from United, presumably to provide the airframes for the conversion. During May and June the Board settled Lake Central's temporary mail pay for the period since January 1, 1957. Lake Central had claimed substantially more subsidy than the government finally allowed and had argued that any adverse adjustment in its claims would complicate its financing of the turboprop Convairs.[72]

On July 27 in the decision in the Piedmont Local-Service Area Investigation,[73] Lake Central was awarded new routes in Indiana, Ohio, and Illinois. In August it was awarded even more new routes throughout the Midwest in the Great Lakes Local Service Investigation.[74] These awards increased Lake Central's route mileage and cities served—each by more than 60 percent.[75] In order to provide service on these routes, Lake Central had to acquire immediately ten additional DC-3s. Then on October 11, 1960, the Board put Lake Central on a final mail rate. Lake Central had requested a rate of 2.07 cents per passenger-mile; the CAB set the rate at 1.65 cents. On November 28, *Aviation Daily* announced: "Lake Central won't convert five Convairs to Allison turbine power immediately. Company will move conservatively, make certain that traffic forecasts for its expanded system work out." (*Aviation Daily*, November 28, 1960, p. 152.) In fact, Lake Central's Convairs were not converted to Allison power until 1967.[76]

71. "Lake Central Orders Five Allison Convairs," *Aviation Daily* (Jan. 22, 1960), p. 127.
72. *Civil Aeronautics Board Reports*, Vol. 31 (May–September 1960), p. 101. As it turned out, for the years 1957–60, Lake Central had to refund $154,000 in overpaid subsidy.
73. *Ibid.*, p. 306.
74. *Ibid.*, p. 442.
75. *Flight Magazine*, Vol. 49 (June 1960), p. 78; Vol. 50 (June 1961), p. 30.
76. In 1967 Lake Central's Convair 580s, operating with an average stage length of 135 miles, had operating costs (including depreciation) of $1.06 per aircraft-mile, while its Convair 340s, with a 109-mile stage length, had operating costs of $1.49 per aircraft-mile.

It might be argued that Lake Central's Allison-Convair order was merely a ploy to help it obtain new routes. In presentations before the Board, a carrier sometimes tends to make somewhat extravagant claims concerning the type of service it will offer if only it, and not another carrier, is awarded the route in question. In fact, Lake Central had based its presentation on a mixed fleet of F-27s and DC-3s. However, the evidence in the case would indicate that Lake Central was serious in placing its order. It was unable to follow through when the Board reduced its subsidy to the point where it could not obtain the loans needed to finance the conversion and at the same time granted it a massive increase in routes, which required the carrier to deplete its meager financial resources to obtain the equipment needed to serve them. Vice Chairman Chan Gurney of the Board recognized this possibility in his dissent from the Lake Central awards in the Great Lakes Local-Service Investigation.[77] Gurney argued that the route awards would make Lake Central into a regional, as opposed to a local, carrier. He said:

A 400-mile extension of Lake Central's route into Washington, D.C., is completely unjustified. It is contended that the extension will strengthen the carrier and in the long run materially assist it in the goal of subsidy reduction. The strengthening argument is basically unsound at the time when Lake Central has just been awarded the Cincinnati-Detroit Route (order E-15365, 31 CAB 63) and is being awarded other substantial new route mileage by this decision. Lake Central should be given time to digest these new routes without being saddled with more than it can develop with its limited resources. Extensive route awards can be detrimental to a carrier such as Lake Central at this critical time in its development. Its debt-equity structure is unfavorable now, and the additional financing to inaugurate service on the West Virginia routes will put a further strain on its financial condition. This factor certainly is not in the best interest of either the carrier or the public.[78]

Thus, in spite of the strong incentive to conversion created by the class rate subsidy system, and in particular by the formula embodied in Class Rate I, the locals were unable to finance conversion of their aircraft until about 1964. By this time they had begun to digest the massive route awards made in the area cases and the improved source of subsidy support resulting from the class rate. Furthermore, the higher rate of return allowed had begun to convince lenders that larger sums could be loaned to these carriers. In its eagerness to strengthen the local carriers (and the trunklines) during the 1958–63 period, the Board probably prevented the carriers from obtaining the aircraft that would have allowed them to achieve substantially greater benefits from this strengthening. To be sure, the local carriers,

77. *Civil Aeronautics Board Reports*, Vol. 31 (May–September 1960), pp. 487–89.
78. *Ibid.*, p. 489.

with CAB acquiescence, acquired too many larger aircraft too rapidly, but this mistake was compounded by the type of larger aircraft they acquired.

Subsidy Levels

The stated goal of the Board's program of route strengthening was to lessen the local carriers' dependence on federal subsidy. Table 5-5 shows that, on the contrary, subsidy increased substantially between 1954 (when it was first officially separated from mail pay) and 1963. Table 5-5 also shows that after the latter date the composition of subsidy began to change. Break-even need, defined as the difference between operating revenues (excluding subsidy paid) and operating costs (including depreciation) began to decline in importance relative to the return on investment and income tax element of the subsidy. This latter element rose because of the increase in local service investment during the early 1960s and because of the higher rate of return allowed after 1960. This substantial rise in total local service

Table 5-5. Local Service Air Carrier Subsidy, Break-even Need, and Return on Investment and Equity, 1954–66

Dollar amounts in thousands

Year	Adjusted subsidy	Break-even need[a]	Break-even need less aircraft depre- ciation	Interest, taxes, and return element[b]	Rate of return on stockholder equity[c] (percent)	Rate of return on total in- vestment[c,d] (percent)
1954	$23,807	$22,409	$20,497	$ 1,398	14.16	13.47
1955	22,051	20,540	18,785	1,511	7.54	7.48
1956	24,960	23,793	21,702	1,167	−4.44	−0.32
1957	31,071	30,411	27,574	1,660	−11.43	−2.62
1958	32,938	31,089	27,709	1,849	10.73	9.24
1959	43,252	41,544	36,244	1,708	0.52	4.95
1960	54,837	51,954	46,230	2,883	14.82	9.12
1961	61,920	53,578	46,452	8,342	21.23	11.05
1962	66,776	54,574	46,857	12,202	19.25	11.04
1963	67,043	55,923	47,079	11,120	13.05	8.88
1964	63,559	48,813	39,306	14,746	16.29	10.08
1965	62,618	41,921	30,214	20,697	19.30	12.08
1966	56,439	31,457	15,080	24,982	16.74	7.87

Sources: Civil Aeronautics Board, *Handbook of Airline Statistics, 1965 Edition*, p. 233; *1967 Edition*, pp. 225, 383, 385; *1969 Edition*, pp. 205, 371, 373.
a. Operating revenues (less subsidy paid) minus operating costs.
b. Adjusted subsidy minus break-even need.
c. Including investment tax credits.
d. Before interest payments.

investment was also reflected in the composition of break-even need itself; more of this began to be accounted for by aircraft depreciation expenses. The last two columns in Table 5-5 show the rate of return on stockholder equity (after taxes and interest expense) and the rate of return on total investment (after taxes but before interest) and show the effect both of the class rate and the higher rate of return allowed on each of these items.

The increase in subsidy was greatest during the 1958–62 period, the years of greatest route strengthening activity.[79] As was suggested above, it is questionable whether a substantial portion of the Board's route strengthening activity actually strengthened the local carriers. It has also been argued that the route awards led the carriers to purchase aircraft that were unsuited to their routes. The features of the class rate subsidy have been outlined and the Board's action in raising the allowable rate of return has been mentioned. It is clear that each of these elements had a hand in the subsidy increase. Ideally their effects could be separated out statistically. Unfortunately this is not possible. A carrier has usually acquired its larger aircraft in order to provide service on newly awarded routes. An improved rate of return makes the purchase of aircraft easier. In short, collinearity proves an insurmountable problem. Consequently, the relative impacts will have to be inferred as accurately as possible directly from the available data.

The Systems Analysis and Research Corporation report, referred to above, provides the only available information concerning the effect on costs that results merely from the use of excessively large equipment. SARC's estimates of 1975 operating results for the industry's lower-density routes as a function of the size of aircraft used on these routes are:[80]

Number of aircraft seats	Operating profit or loss (thousands of dollars)
14	−2,688
16	−742
18	+247
20	+802
22	−361
24	−1,644
26	−2,852
28	−5,174
30	−8,086

79. Nine of the twelve Area Cases were decided in the 1958–60 period.

80. Systems Analysis and Research Corporation, "Economic Analysis of the Short-Haul Transport" (Cambridge, Mass.: SARC, 1964; processed), p. 64.

It is apparent that relatively small variations in the size of aircraft used on such routes do have an important impact on costs and that this impact increases more than in proportion to the increase in size of aircraft used.

The data for the industry as a whole conceal a great deal of information, and it is useful to look closer at particular carriers. This study will concentrate on Frontier—a carrier which has one of the weakest of the route systems but which provides essential services to many isolated communities. Data on Frontier for the 1954–66 period are presented in Table 5-6. The carrier received important route awards in the Seven States Area Investigation.[81] A number of trunkline points were turned over to Frontier, and several cities that had not previously received scheduled air service were added to its routes. In 1956, before this route strengthening, only fourteen (35 percent) of Frontier's stations generated fewer than the standard of 1,800 passengers a year.

Not all stations generating more than 1,800 passengers a year produced profits for Frontier. The 1959 United Research study included an estimate that the minimum avoidable costs of serving an on-line intermediate station with one round trip a day were approximately $40,000 a year.[82] Raising the frequency of service to two round trips a day—the frequency generally required by the Board—would increase this figure to $65,000 a year. Both of these amounts are based on the assumption that the service is provided by a DC-3. If the two round trips a day were in fact provided by a Convair 340 or 440, the minimum avoidable cost would rise to $115,000 a year. A station that just barely met the 1,800-passenger-a-year standard would have generated $25,560 a year in revenue (1,800 passengers times Frontier's average fare of $14.20 per enplaned passenger in 1958). Thus the annual increase in subsidy due to the addition of a single marginal intermediate point that generated just 1,800 passengers a year would have ranged between $40,000 and $90,000, depending on the aircraft used to provide the service. The addition during the years 1957 through 1960 of fifteen stations that generated *fewer* than 1,800 passengers a year added a minimum of $600,000 to $1,350,000 to Frontier's subsidy. Of course, to the extent that a frequency of service exceeding two round trips a day was provided or the stations generated fewer than 1,800 passengers a year, subsidy was increased by an even larger amount. In 1960 Frontier's twenty-

81. Decided December 8, 1958. *Civil Aeronautics Board Reports*, Vol. 28 (December 1958–February 1959), p. 680.

82. "Federal Regulation of the Domestic Air Transport Industry," pp. 56–59.

Table 5-6. Financial and Traffic Statistics for Frontier Airlines, 1954–66

Dollar amounts in thousands

Year	Total subsidy (1)	Break-even need (2)	Break-even need less depreciation expenses[a] (3)	Percentage of aircraft-miles with DC-3 aircraft (4)	Percentage of aircraft-miles with large piston aircraft (5)
1954	$2,652	$2,560	$2,519	100	0
1955	2,564	2,527	2,482	100	0
1956	2,471	2,262	2,190	100	0
1957	2,513	2,561	2,476	100	0
1958	2,841	2,894	2,737	100	0
1959	5,712	5,660	5,136	90	10
1960	6,251	6,081	5,454	81	19
1961	6,835	6,146	5,495	69	31
1962	7,135	6,496	6,023	60	40
1963	7,639	6,414	5,854	39	61
1964	7,118	5,775	5,058	33	55
1965	6,840	4,091	3,091	26	17
1966	5,095	1,800	410	11	0

	Percentage of aircraft-miles with turbine aircraft (6)	Average passenger load (7)	Number of stations			
			Originating fewer than 1,800 passengers (8)	Originating 1,800– 8,000 passengers (9)	Originating more than 8,000 passengers (10)	Total (11)
1954	0	8.5	n.a.	n.a.	n.a.	n.a.
1955	0	9.4	14	20	7	41
1956	0	10.0	14	19	7	40
1957	0	10.5	14	19	7	40
1958	0	10.1	19	19	9	47
1959	0	8.7	33[b]	28	11	72
1960	0	9.5	27	29	12	68
1961	0	10.4	26	26	14	66
1962	0	9.9	25	24	12	61
1963	0	12.5	17	31	18	66
1964	12	14.6	12	27	22	61
1965	57	16.5	12	23	25	60
1966	89[c]	20.9	11	21	29	61

Sources: Mileage data are from Civil Aeronautics Board records; other data are from CAB, *Handbook of Airline Statistics, 1965* and *1967 Editions*, and *Flight Magazine*, various issues.

n.a. Not available.

a. Depreciation expenses of flight equipment only.

b. Includes twenty-two stations added during year and not receiving full year's service.

c. Includes 4 percent of aircraft-miles flown by pure jet equipment.

nine stations that generated fewer than 1,800 passengers averaged 862 passengers a year.

With the cost data reported above, it is possible to determine that an ntermediate, on-line station would have to have generated approximately 4,500 passengers a year, each paying Frontier's average fare of $14.20, in order to have produced enough revenue to cover the avoidable costs of serving it with two-round-trips-a-day DC-3 service. Alternatively, a station would have had to generate approximately 8,000 passengers a year in order to have covered the costs of providing it with Convair service. In 1957 Frontier had seven stations that generated more than 8,000 passengers a year. Five generated between 4,500 and 8,000, and fourteen generated between 1,800 and 4,500. By 1960, two years after the Board's attempt to strengthen Frontier's routes, the number of stations generating more than 8,000 passengers a year had risen to twelve, the number generating between 4,500 and 8,000, to ten, and the number generating between 1,800 and 4,500, to nineteen. Thus between 1957 and 1960, as a direct result of route strengthening, the number of stations that were unable to support even a minimal DC-3 service had risen from twenty-eight to forty-six, while the number of stations that were unable to support a minimal Convair service had risen from thirty-three to fifty-six. In view of this, it is not surprising that the examiner in the Seven States Area Investigation estimated that the additional subsidy necessary to support routes granted to Frontier, Ozark, and North Central in that case was $3.2 million a year.

Once the CAB began to enforce its use-it-or-lose-it policy, things began to look up for Frontier. The number of submarginal stations was reduced by half between 1962 and 1964, due primarily to the dropping of seven of these stations in 1962 and 1963. This both strengthened Frontier's route system and allowed it to be more competitive on its longer-haul flights. Yet even in 1969 Frontier reported that 40 percent of its points produced fewer than fifteen passengers daily (approximately 5,500 passengers a year).[83]

If "route strengthening" substantially weakened Frontier's routes and resulted in subsidy increases, the carrier itself compounded the problem by the aircraft it used to serve these routes. At the time of the Seven States Area Investigation route awards, Frontier acquired its first large aircraft— Convair 340s. By 1962, when its average passenger load was no higher than it had been in 1955 with an all-DC-3 fleet, Frontier was flying 40 percent

83. *Aviation Week and Space Technology*, Vol. 91 (Dec. 8, 1969), p. 38.

of its total aircraft-miles with Convairs. During 1962 its DC-3s, operating over an average stage length of 92 miles, had direct operating costs of 59 cents a mile. Its Convairs, operating over an average hop of 148 miles, at a higher rate of utilization, were costing 84 cents a mile to operate. Yet the Convairs, presumably operating over Frontier's most lucrative routes, were averaging only a 36.3 percent load factor (14.9 passengers).

Frontier could have alleviated some of this cost disadvantage by converting its Convairs to turboprop power. Total direct expense (including depreciation) for Frontier's turboprop Convairs in 1964 was 68 cents a mile (with an average hop of 158 miles), 16 cents a mile less than for the piston-powered Convairs. As Table 5-6 showed, once the turboprop Convairs were acquired, break-even need began to fall dramatically, though this was hampered by the use of excessively large aircraft on Frontier's low-density routes. By 1966 DC-3s flew only 11 percent of Frontier's aircraft-miles—2.3 million miles, down from 7.5 million in 1960. The SARC study mentioned above predicted that even in 1975 Frontier would need to fly 9.1 million miles with aircraft of less than 40-seat capacity.[84] The optimum-sized small aircraft for Frontier was found to be one of 16-passenger capacity, the smallest of all the locals except for Central, whose optimum-size small aircraft was also a 16-passenger one. Furthermore, SARC forecast a $1.8 million increase in Frontier's operating loss in 1975 if aircraft of 30-passenger capacity were used to serve its low-density routes rather than 16-passenger aircraft.[85]

The above picture of Frontier during the late 1950s and early and mid-1960s serves to illustrate the point that a combination of mistaken "route strengthening" policies and improperly timed acquisition of excessively large flight equipment to serve these routes was chiefly responsible for the substantial increase in the carrier's subsidy after 1958. Once the route policy began to be rectified and more efficient large equipment was acquired (although still in too large amounts), subsidy turned down sharply. By 1966 federal subsidy was being paid to Frontier primarily to cover depreciation expenses and rate of return on the larger investment involved in the turboprop Convairs. In that year Frontier acquired its first jets, and a new round of route strengthening began. In 1967 Frontier merged with Central, one of the weakest of the local carriers. In 1967 the favorable trend in Frontier's financial position reversed sharply.

84. "Economic Analysis of the Short-Haul Transport," p. 61.
85. *Ibid.*, p. 64.

Subsidy Reduction

The substantial post-1956 increase in the local service subsidy led President John F. Kennedy to include in his 1962 transportation message a request for the CAB to develop a subsidy-reduction program.[86] The local carriers responded with a proposal that would have resulted in the abandonment of the Board's longstanding general policy against direct trunk–local service competition.[87] The Board expressed a reluctance to embark upon such a course at that time and instead put forward a plan more in line with its traditional thinking.[88]

The largest cause of subsidy reduction—$43.5 million over five years—was the continuing growth in local service revenues, which expanded twice as fast as operating costs. A saving of $26.8 million over five years was to be achieved by a gradual reduction in the number of flights per day that the government was prepared to subsidize. In the first year, subsidy was not to be paid for more than seven round trips a day. For the third and subsequent years, the limit was to be reduced to four daily round trips. Offsetting this to some degree was the proposal that virtually all intermediate points receive a minimum of two daily round trips. A program to consolidate airports which were relatively close together, but which produced little traffic, was to result in a $6.9 million saving over five years. Finally, continued application of the use-it-or-lose-it policy was to save $4.3 million.

But the program did not work out as planned. A modest reduction of $3 million was achieved in 1964, and the reduction in 1965 amounted to less than $1 million. The use-it-or-lose-it program made progress, with eleven points dropped in 1964 and six in 1965; but as of June 1, 1966, sixty points were still being served that did not meet the use-it-or-lose-it standards. The airport consolidation plan, which was to have eliminated forty-four airports, failed to achieve its goal when it ran into strong congressional and community opposition.[89]

On the other hand, revenues and operating costs had moved as predicted. Between 1963 and 1965, revenue rose by 43 percent while operating

86. *The Transportation System of Our Nation*, p. 7.

87. There was also a flurry of interest in developing a "true DC-3 replacement." This led to the SARC study referred to above. The interest on the part of the locals was short-lived, however.

88. Civil Aeronautics Board, "Report to the President on Airline Subsidy Reduction Program pursuant to Transportation Message of 1962" (CAB, June 1963; processed).

89. See Ronald D. Dockser, "Airline Service Abandonment and Consolidation—A Chapter in the Battle Against Subsidization," *Journal of Air Law and Commerce*, Vol. 32 (Autumn 1966), pp. 496–525.

costs rose by only 25 percent. However, interest charges rose by 33 percent, and total investment, on which a rate of return had to be paid, rose by 62 percent. As Table 5-5 showed, break-even need dropped substantially between 1963 and 1965, but the rate-of-return element increased almost as fast, as the local carriers acquired their Convairs, Martins, and F-27s and began acquiring the first of their jets. By 1965 some were beginning to convert their Convairs to turboprop power—an action that reduced break-even need but raised total investment. Offsetting the reduction in break-even need was the phasing out of the DC-3 without an adequate replacement, in spite of the continuing need for the services of aircraft of this size. Aircraft-miles flown by DC-3s dropped from 44 million in 1963 to 26 million in 1966.

By early 1966, it was clear that the Board's policy was not going to achieve its goals, and the Board, under its newly appointed chairman, Charles S. Murphy, was beginning to rethink its position on subsidy reduction. In a series of hearings held in February and March 1966 before Senator A. S. Mike Monroney's Subcommittee on Aviation, both Murphy and former Board Chairman Alan Boyd, who had since been appointed under secretary of commerce for transportation, expressed sympathy for the program that had been espoused by the local carriers in 1963. Murphy said:

The local carriers have requested that the Board strengthen their systems by relaxing present route and operating restrictions, by allowing them to compete with trunklines in denser markets, and by awarding them new operating authority over potentially profitable routes. This avenue for strengthening the local carriers, and hopefully reducing their dependence upon subsidy support, is one which the Board views with favor and which it plans to pursue on a case-by-case basis. [90]

The policy of strengthening the local carrier's routes while keeping them local carriers had only made the local service subsidy payments higher. In 1966 break-even need, even excluding depreciation, was at only about the same level as it had been twelve years earlier. [91] The total subsidy bill was more than twice that of 1954. In spite of the experience of the previous decade and a half, the Board was now prepared to embark on another program of "route strengthening"—but this time with no restrictions.

90. *Review of the Local Air Carrier Industry*, Hearings, pp. 35–36. Alan S. Boyd's statement appears on pp. 13–27.
91. The substantial improvement in local service results in 1966 may have been in part because of traffic they received during the 43-day strike that shut down several of the trunklines during July and August of that year. See "Strike Cost $93 Million Revenue in July," *Aviation Week and Space Technology*, Vol. 85 (Oct. 3, 1966), p. 45.

CHAPTER SIX

Transition to Trunkline Status

BY EARLY 1966, the Civil Aeronautics Board (CAB) was rapidly changing its mind about the policies it should follow to reduce the local service subsidy. Since the early 1960s the carriers had contended that what was required was an end to the Board's policy of generally not allowing trunk-local competition. The Board had resisted this proposal,[1] trying instead to reduce the subsidy by consolidating or eliminating marginal airports, reducing the frequency of service for which subsidy would be paid, and working to hold down local service operating costs. While break-even need (the difference between operating revenues and operating costs, including depreciation) did decline after 1963, the increase in the local carriers' total investment on which a rate of return had to be paid prevented any significant reduction in overall subsidy levels through 1965. In the hearings held in early 1966 before the Senate Aviation Subcommittee, Chairman Murphy was forced to admit ". . . if we continue to follow past policies, I would think we might reasonably expect the total subsidy for the local carriers to remain near current levels."[2] These Senate hearings foreshadowed the shift in Board policy that was formalized in December 1966, when the Board issued a policy statement on the matter of direct trunk–local service competition.[3]

Since December 1966 the Board has undertaken an expansion of local service operating authority unparalleled since the series of area cases that established the local carriers in the late 1940s. Nonstop rights in competition with trunklines (and even in competition with other locals) have been granted in many markets. Local carriers have been chosen over trunklines

1. See examiner's initial decision (*Civil Aeronautics Board Reports*, Vol. 35 [January–March 1962], p. 196), decided January 23, 1962.

2. *Review of the Local Air Carrier Industry*, Hearings before the Aviation Subcommittee of the Senate Committee on Commerce, 89 Cong. 2 sess. (1966), p. 33.

3. Civil Aeronautics Board, Docket 18022, "Nonstop Authority for Local Service Carriers in Markets on their Respective Lineal Route Segments: Notice of Proposed Rule Making," PSDR-16 (Dec. 8, 1966).

to provide new nonstop service in relatively dense short- and medium-haul markets. Finally, the locals have been given permission to overfly traditional traffic hubs where they formerly transferred passengers to the trunklines. Instead they will fly directly to major traffic centers, such as New York, Washington, Chicago, and Los Angeles—cities sometimes more than a thousand miles outside their traditional areas of operation.

The change in CAB route policy was reflected also in the three local service mergers, involving seven of the thirteen carriers, that occurred in 1967 and 1968. Two of the smaller and financially weaker carriers were acquired by larger local carriers, and there was one consolidation of three relatively strong carriers. While some cost savings were claimed for these purposes, their undeniable effect was to widen substantially the scope for route strengthening under the post-1966 CAB route policies.

The local carriers have responded to their new operating authority by acquiring new flight equipment on an unprecedented scale. Between 1966 and 1968, local service industry assets in the form of property and equipment more than doubled, from $254 million to $552 million. (In 1960 it was $59 million.) As of the end of 1969 the local carriers were operating 138 pure jet aircraft, with seating capacities ranging from 69 to 144 passengers. Fifty-one of these aircraft were delivered in 1968 and 41 in 1969. By the end of 1970, the local service carriers had 157 pure jets in service. (See Table 6-1.) During the same period the local carriers virtually completed the upgrading of their 36-seat to 52-seat capacity aircraft to turboprop power, either through conversion or through new purchase. The last local service DC-3 was retired in 1969; the Nord was phased out in 1970.

The movement of the local carriers into direct competition with the trunks and the concurrent shifting of their attention to these potentially lucrative markets was paralleled by the rise of a new group of air carriers whose interest lay primarily in the relatively lower-density, short-haul end of the air transportation market. These so-called "third-level" air carriers began to move into many of the local service markets. They used small (up to 20-seat), efficient, turboprop aircraft that the local carriers, for all their supposed interest in a "DC-3 replacement," generally disdained to purchase. The attitude of the local carriers toward these "upstarts" was ambivalent. At first they reacted to the third-level carriers as the trunks originally had reacted to the proposed creation of the local carriers. They argued that the service these new carriers proposed wasn't needed, but if it was needed, the local carriers should provide it. However, it was not long before the locals began to look on the third-level carriers as a potential

Table 6-1. Fleet of the Local Service Air Carrier Industry, by Type and Model of Aircraft, 1966–70

Type and model of aircraft	Number in service on December 31				
	1966	1967	1968	1969	1970
Piston					
Douglas DC-3	97	58	10	—	—
Convair CV-240	27	8	—	—	—
Convair CV-340/440	56	27	11	4	—
Martin 202/404	77	57	44	38	27
Piper PA-31	—	4	4	4	0
Beech 99	—	—	—	—	3
	257	154	69	46	30
Turboprop					
Nord N-262	0	12	12	1	0
Fairchild F-27/27J	57	44	41	33	28
Fairchild Hiller FH-227	8	48	48	48	47
Convair CV-600	17	28	35	25	25
Convair CV-580	34	66	96	107	107
Nihon YS-11	—	—	8	14	21
	116	198	240	228	228
Turbojet					
British Aircraft Corporation BAC-111	9	10	14	20	23
Douglas DC-9-10	9	21	31	30	34
Douglas DC-9-30	—	7	35	65	73
Boeing B-727	4	8	11	6	5
Boeing B-737	—	—	6	17	22
	22	46	97	138	157
Total	395	398	406	412	415

Source: *Flight Magazine*, Vol. 60 (June 1971), pp. 30–31, and preceding June issues for 1967–70.

dumping ground for their unwanted routes and began to promote route transfers to these carriers, just as many of the trunks had promoted similar trunkline–local transfers in the 1950s.

In order to assure that its "route strengthening" policies in the late 1960s did not result in the same level of subsidy increase that its route strengthening policies of the 1950s had led to, the Board adopted three safeguards. It awarded the majority of new local carrier routes on a "non-subsidy eligible" basis (although the problem of allocating indirect and overhead costs to particular routes apparently has not yet been solved). It reduced to two the number of flights per day that it would subsidize on those routes that were eligible for subsidy. Finally, it changed its subsidy recapture plan from one based on profit-sharing to one based on revenue-sharing. The result was, from the Board's point of view, the desired one. In 1968, total subsidy amounted to only $43 million, down from the 1963 peak of over $67 million. However, the 1968 subsidy payments were $8 million short of covering merely break-even need, and a subsidy of $124 million would have been necessary in 1968 to cover total break-even need and provide the 9 percent rate of return on the local carrier's $809 million in total assets that the Board considered to be a minimum fair and reasonable level. Federal subsidy payment "bottomed out" at $36 million in 1969 and thereafter began to rise again, reaching $41 million in 1970.

Changes in CAB Route Policies

The changes that have occurred in CAB route policies during recent years have taken several forms. Liberalization of route restrictions has continued until local service carriers have found themselves with authority to compete with trunklines on an unrestricted basis. Local service carriers have been granted "by-pass" authority, which has permitted them to pick up traffic over their low-density routes and fly these passengers directly to their ultimate destination, by-passing the points at which this traffic formerly had been handed over to the trunks. Finally, the Board in some cases has granted local service carriers the right to compete directly with each other.

Route Restrictions

The CAB's policy of using profits generated on one route to cover losses incurred on another is not a newly adopted one. As the local carriers were quick to point out, it was just such a policy that the Board had followed to eliminate the trunkline subsidy in the late 1940s and 1950s. At that time the Board deliberately favored weaker trunklines in route awards, with a view to giving them access to profits, which could be substituted for federal subsidy. In general, such awards meant favoring a smaller over a larger trunk, either as the carrier to provide a new service or as the carrier to provide additional service on a route already served by another trunkline. The Board was particularly active in this sort of route strengthening between

1955 and 1958. According to Cherington, before 1955 nearly 60 percent of the four hundred most important air travel markets were noncompetitive. By mid-1958, competitive service had been authorized in 87 percent of these markets. Additional competition was authorized in markets already having more than two carriers operating, and the average number of carriers authorized in each of the four hundred markets rose from 1.5 to 2.2.[4] Partially as a result of this policy, by 1959 all the trunklines were off subsidy (although Northeast Airlines was to return to subsidized status in 1963).

That the Board should follow a similar course of action with respect to the local service subsidy had been argued by some since the Investigation of Local, Feeder, and Pick-Up Air Service in 1944. Implicit in the argument in favor of using the existing trunk carriers rather than new carriers to provide the proposed extension of service was the feeling that this would allow the overhead costs of the operation to be carried by the more lucrative routes.[5]

In his dissent in the Trans-Texas Certificate Renewal Case,[6] Board Member Harold A. Jones argued against the Board's creating a permanent class of subsidized air carriers, pointing out that it would be "consistent" with the established principles of public utility regulation to use profits from "high-value, low-cost service" to cover losses incurred in providing "lower-value, higher-cost service."[7] In 1953 Senator Edwin C. Johnston of Colorado wrote to the chairman of the CAB urging that rather than reacting to the high profits the trunks were then making by compelling them to reduce fares, the Board instead should compel the profit-making carriers to assume the burden of providing some of the services then being provided by the subsidized carriers. Finally in its 1954 report on civil air policy, the President's Air Coordinating Committee recommended that "where the public interest requires the continued maintenance of uneconomical services, increased emphasis should be placed upon the inclusion of such operations within route systems that are capable of absorbing their cost without subsidy."[8]

4. "The Status and Economic Significance of the Airline Equipment Investment Program," A Report by Paul W. Cherington prepared for President Eisenhower's Special Assistant for Aviation (June 30, 1958).

5. *Civil Aeronautics Board Reports*, Vol. 6 (July 1944–May 1946), pp. 29, 30. "The existing carriers, at least in some instances, would be able to operate a local route which might be unprofitable in itself by absorbing such losses with profit from long-haul services."

6. *Civil Aeronautics Board Reports*, Vol. 12 (September 1950–April 1951), pp. 606–63.

7. *Ibid.*, p. 634.

8. *Civil Air Policy*, A Report by the Air Coordinating Committee by Direction of the President (1954), p. 8.

In its recommendation on routes, the committee said:

The route structures and certificates of the various local service carriers should be adjusted to provide the maximum opportunity to improve their economic position, within the general scope of their intended type of operation. Where continued and significant progress towards self-sufficiency is not demonstrated by a local service carrier, its operating authority should be terminated in an orderly fashion. To the extent that the services formerly provided by it are clearly required to meet a public need, such services should be furnished by another carrier capable of providing the service without cost or at substantially reduced cost to the government.[9]

The local carriers, which were then still operating under "temporary" certificates, looked on such proposals with alarm.[10] They unsuccessfully opposed a proposed merger between Pioneer Air Lines and Continental Air Lines, feeling that it represented "the first step in the destruction of the two-level trunk and local service air transportation system which the Board has so carefully developed over the past 10 years in this country."[11] They viewed as an even stronger threat the Board's 1954 decision in the "Route No. 106 Renewal Case and Ozark Certificate Renewal Case."[12] Route 106 had been granted to Parks Air Lines in one of the original area cases. Parks failed to provide service, so in 1950 the route was given to Mid-Continent Airlines, one of the smaller trunklines. Braniff Airways acquired Mid-Continent in 1952 and later applied to have Route 106 renewed, but without local service restrictions. The Board voted 3 to 2 to reconstitute Route 106 as a trunkline route and give it to Braniff. It decided further to grant the local service stops on Route 106 to United Air Lines. It refused the applications of Ozark Air Lines and North Central Airlines to be given these routes, on the grounds that to do so would increase their subsidy.[13]

9. *Ibid.*, p. 14.

10. The policy of turning trunkline stations over to locals and removing route restrictions to a limited extent was in fact a policy of internalizing the subsidy. It differed from the policies the locals were proposing in the late 1950s and early 1960s in that it involved a transfer of revenues only within a local carrier's own system (unless removal of route restrictions allowed the local carrier to capture some trunkline traffic).

11. "CAL-Pioneer Merger Stirs Feeder Protest," *Aviation Week*, Vol. 61 (Sept. 20, 1954), p. 96.

12. *Civil Aeronautics Board Reports*, Vol. 20 (February–May 1955), p. 165.

13. Solar feels that it was this talk of dismemberment of the local carriers during 1953 and 1954 that led congressional supporters of the locals to introduce the bill to provide these carriers with permanent certificates. (Donald Solar, "The Federal Interest in Local Air Service: A Study in the Evolution of Economic Policy" [Ph.D. thesis, Columbia University, 1963], Chap. 7.) Whether this is true or not, after the bill passed, the Board agreed to reopen the Route No. 106 Renewal Case and gave Ozark the routes it had previously awarded to United.

Before they received permanent certificates, the locals had been careful to disclaim any interest in direct local-trunk competition. For example, in 1954, while Congress was considering permanent certification for the locals, the President of Allegheny Airlines, Leslie O. Barnes, wrote:

The trunk lines—even those supporting the local service concept—either keep a most watchful eye on their younger brethren, or are downright distrustful of them and their motives, and well they might, too, because unless some pretty careful lines are drawn and a plan of development defined, it is conceivable the local carriers might very well become a serious competitive threat to the trunks. The threat does not lie in our activities at the intermediate cities; this activity is in strict accordance with the initial reason for our creation. Rather, the threat to the trunks is found in the possibility of our ultimately penetrating the non-stop operation between major trading areas.

This is forbidden territory and local carriers have no business invading it. The trunk lines should be insured, so to speak, against this threat for two reasons: First, this is not our role, nor was it ever intended that it would be. Secondly, the ultimate success of the local service concept is dependent upon our concentrating on our particular mission—service to intermediate cities.

It should not be difficult to give this needed assurance to the trunks, because no other course of action makes any real or lasting sense. It must seem obvious that if the survival and growth of the local carriers are dependent upon long-haul business between major trading areas, then the original basis for our creation no longer exists.[14]

Once they were sure of congressional support for their continued existence as operating entities, however, the locals began to apply for nonstop routes in competition with the trunklines. The first instance of such an award occurred in 1957, when Mohawk Airlines was chosen over Eastern Airlines to provide nonstop service in competition with American Airlines in the New York City–Syracuse market.[15] The Board was careful to stress that its decision should not be viewed as a "landmark" case that in any way modified its long-held views concerning the general undesirability of local-trunkline competition. It pointed to particular aspects of the market in question that justified its choice of Mohawk. Nevertheless, it did admit that one reason for choosing Mohawk over Eastern was the adverse effect that nonstop service by the latter carrier would have on Mohawk's share of the New York–Syracuse market, which it then served on a one-stop or two-stop basis. Furthermore, it was anticipated that Mohawk would reap

14. Leslie O. Barnes, "Local Service—Destiny & Definition," *Flight Magazine*, Vol. 41 (June 1954), pp. 26–27, 44–53.

15. Syracuse–New York City Case, decided March 27, 1957. *Civil Aeronautics Board Reports*, Vol. 24 (September 1956–March 1957), p. 770.

a profit on the route, which would "contribute to a decrease in [Mohawk's] subsidy requirements." The route was granted to Mohawk on a "subsidy ineligible" basis.[16]

Although direct local service–trunkline competition was proposed by the local carriers in several of the area cases, the Mohawk case cited above was the only instance, prior to 1962, in which the Board authorized such direct competition. In the Pacific-Southwest Local Service Case,[17] Bonanza Air Lines was granted the right to offer nonstop competitive service in the Los Angeles–Las Vegas market in competition with Western Air Lines, Trans World Airlines, and United Air Lines.[18] In the same case, however, the Board refused to allow Pacific Air Lines to offer nonstop service between Los Angeles and San Francisco, and denied the right either to Bonanza or Pacific to operate nonstop Las Vegas–San Francisco service. The examiner's opinion in this case contained a detailed review of the Board's policy concerning local-trunkline competition and argued that unless exceptional circumstances could be demonstrated, such competition should not be allowed. He said:

The Board pointed out in the *Seven States Area Investigation, supra*, the policy it has adopted is not so much for the protection of the trunklines from diversion. It is more in the nature of requiring local-service carriers to devote their strength to the job at hand without dissipating their energies in a shortsighted engagement with the trunklines for traffic in terminal-to-terminal markets that are mined in advance with economic pitfalls.[19]

In spite of such warnings of possible adverse results, the locals increased their pressure on the Board to allow them to offer unrestricted competitive service with trunklines. One possible explanation for the local carriers' increased interest in removing remaining route restrictions was their realization that the trunklines, having concentrated on their long-haul markets during the late 1950s and early 1960s, were beginning by the mid-1960s to show renewed interest in their short-haul markets. In spite of the prevailing route restrictions, by the early 1960s the locals had established strong competitive positions in several major short-haul markets. Although this penetration involved a relatively small proportion of total trunkline passenger-

16. *Ibid.*, pp. 777, 778. As was noted in Chapter 5, at this time Mohawk was receiving a substantial increase in subsidy due at least in part to its acquisition of larger piston aircraft.

17. *Civil Aeronautics Board Reports*, Vol. 35 (January–March 1962), pp. 50–316.

18. Western was the only unrestricted trunkline in the Los Angeles–Las Vegas market. TWA and United were not authorized to offer turnaround service there.

19. *Civil Aeronautics Board Reports*, Vol. 35 (January–March 1962), p. 202.

miles, competitive markets by 1961 contributed about 34 percent of all local service passenger-miles and 25 percent of total local service revenues.[20] However, by 1964 increased interest in these markets on the part of the trunklines was beginning to make itself felt. In 1962 three competitive markets, Philadelphia-Pittsburgh, Philadelphia-Washington, and Philadelphia-Boston, provided 206,000 of Allegheny's passengers, or about 20 percent of the total. By 1964 Allegheny's share in each of these markets had dropped dramatically because of increased competition from the trunklines. In 1964 Allegheny carried only 164,000 passengers in these markets, 13 percent of its total passengers. North Central's market share in its important Chicago-Milwaukee market (about 13 percent of North Central's total passengers in 1961) dropped from 79 percent in 1961 to 70 percent in 1964.[21] As *Flight Magazine* commented in 1965, "If the local out-carries the trunk airline, then we assume that it does this because the trunk allows it to, for with its superior equipment and service capabilities the trunk can dominate any market it desires. So, where the local is dominant, the trunk is obviously conceding because of more important commitments elsewhere on its system."[22]

By the mid-1960s, however, the trunks had ordered a substantial number of short-haul jets and gave every sign of being no longer willing to concede traffic to the locals.[23] For example, in the 1966 hearings, Mohawk complained that American was intending to drive it out of a number of markets through a combination of jet service with BAC-111 aircraft (which Mohawk intended to match), coach fares (which Mohawk felt it would be unable to match), and nonstop flights (which Mohawk could match in only a few cases).[24] In 1964 only two of the markets, New York-Albany and New York-Syracuse, generated almost 20 percent of Mohawk's passengers.

Complicating the locals' problems was the fact that even if they acquired jets to match trunkline equipment, the requirement that intermediate stops be made would have conspicuously reduced the quality of their service and substantially raised their operating costs. The data presented in Chapter 3 show that jets are extremely expensive to operate over very short stage

20. George E. Haddaway, "At Long Last Local Service Airlines Find Profit Breakthrough," *Flight Magazine*, Vol. 51 (June 1962), pp. 44–49.

21. *Flight Magazine*, Vol. 54 (June 1965), pp. 120–23.

22. *Ibid.*, p. 120.

23. In 1965 the first DC-9s and BAC-111s entered trunkline fleets. By the year 1970 the trunks had about 350 of these twin-engine, short-haul jets in service, completely replacing their Convairs and DC-6s.

24. *Review of the Local Air Carrier Industry*, Hearings, pp. 401–26.

lengths. For example, the total direct operating cost of a 200-mile nonstop flight using a DC-9-30 would be $306, while the comparable cost of a 200-mile flight made up of two 100-mile segments would be $362, an increase of about 20 percent. In short, if they were faced with continued operating restrictions, the locals might be unable to afford to operate the jet aircraft they were then ordering in large numbers. The Board recognized this possibility in its decision to allow direct competition. (See below.)

On the other hand, when restrictions were removed, local penetration of trunkline markets seemed to increase substantially. In the highly competitive Los Angeles–Las Vegas market, Bonanza's market share had risen from 10 percent (26,000 passengers) to 28 percent (107,000 passengers) following the removal of route restrictions in 1962. If the trunks chose to compete with jets in such markets, the locals could match them.

For these reasons it is possible that the increased demand by the locals in the mid-1960s for the removal of nonstop restrictions in competitive markets stemmed not only from their desire to be able to compete on an equal basis for traffic in these relatively lucrative markets but also from a desire to protect an important market position that was threatened with serious erosion if such restrictions were not lifted.

As was noted above, the local carriers sought access to trunkline markets in order to increase their revenues and thus make up for a reduction in their subsidy. While the Board did not accept their proposal in 1963, by 1966 it was convinced that only in this way could the subsidy be reduced, and so it relented. Although this reversal was foreshadowed in the February hearings before the Senate Aviation Subcommittee, not until December did the Board reveal its plan. In a policy statement dated December 8 the Board announced its intention to remove, not on a case-by-case basis, but under expedited procedures, restrictions that prevented locals from offering nonstop flights between terminals already receiving trunkline service.

After detailing the history of its previous liberalization of operating authority, the Board stated that a further liberalization was now warranted, "because such a policy offers promise of a substantial reduction in the total amount of subsidy paid to the local service carriers while rendering improved service to the public." The Board admitted that "a principal consideration in our policy with respect to nonstop authority of local carriers is the fact that all carriers in this class have embarked on a re-equipment program," and that "at 100-mile stage lengths, the small jets [ordered by the locals], even on a seat-mile basis, do not offer an appreciable advantage in direct operating costs over the aircraft which they will replace. But at 200-mile or more stage lengths, the small jets offer a seat-mile direct cost advantage of about 50 percent."[25]

The main thrust of the new policy was to allow local carriers to compete directly with trunklines on routes that they were already allowed to serve. Markets with stage lengths of less than 300 miles were to be the principal target, but the Board said that "the rule will apply to all on-segment pairs of points without regard to their stage lengths."[26]

Concerning the impact of such a policy revision on the trunklines the Board commented, "The current prosperity of the trunkline carriers indicates that they can easily absorb some diversion of traffic in these markets without seriously impairing their earnings. The trunklines' aggregate net profit of $221 million for the year ended December 31, 1965 (which provided a 12.4 percent rate of return), was several times greater than the total local service subsidy."[27] Furthermore, the Board stated that "except where the trunkline carrier can show this [traffic] diversion [by a local service carrier] would be of such magnitude as to impair its entire system operations, we believe the benefits will outweigh adverse consequences of diversion."[28] However, the Board assured the trunklines that their interests would not be ignored, for it stated: "The grant of nonstop authority to local service carriers in these medium-haul hub markets would be experimental in nature. Should the operations [under such authority] not produce the anticipated results, the Board would remain free to rescind the authority."[29]

In order to protect itself, the Board stated that any routes involved in such authorizations would be made ineligible for subsidy.

As further protection, the Board in April 1967 issued a new subsidy formula, Class Rate IV.[30] The previous class rates had contained a profit-sharing provision whereby profits in excess of those necessary to provide a "fair rate of return" were to be shared with the government on a sliding scale basis. The innovation contained in Class Rate IV was the replacement of the profit-sharing plan with a *revenue* growth adjustment scheme. The base period was the twelve months that ended June 30, 1966. If reve-

25. Civil Aeronautics Board, Docket 18022.
26. *Ibid.*, p. 6, note 6.
27. *Ibid.*, p. 8.
28. *Ibid.*, p. 10.
29. *Ibid.*, p. 8.
30. "Board Shifts Policy on Subsidies," *Aviation Week and Space Technology*, Vol. 86 (April 10, 1967), pp. 36–37.

nues increased at a faster rate than during the base period, the government would capture some of the revenue growth in the form of a subsidy reduction. It was estimated that the reduction would amount to 8.6 cents of every "growth dollar."

The locals lost little time in taking the Board up on its offer to liberalize route restrictions. In March 1967 it was announced that North Central had filed for nonstop authority in the Milwaukee-Detroit and Minneapolis-Omaha markets.[31] In June, Frontier was granted nonstop rights between Denver and Kansas City. In the succeeding months Frontier received several more such awards. There followed similar grants of authority to every local service carrier.[32]

The impact of these grants of authority on the routes of the local carriers was revealed by Harold D. Watkins, who noted that between January 1967 and June 1970 the CAB had granted local carriers new authority in 107 route cases and that the bulk of these cases allowed locals to compete directly with trunks on routes of less than 1,000 miles. According to Watkins, as of June 1970, 70 percent of Allegheny's revenues were coming from its competitive routes. The twenty-eight city pairs over which Mohawk and American competed directly, while they comprised only 25 percent of Mohawk's route structure, nevertheless produced 65 percent of Mohawk's revenues. It was estimated that Frontier derived 65 percent of its revenues from competitive routes.[33]

By-pass Authority

The local carriers had long complained that they seemed to be stuck perpetually with the unprofitable part of the air travel market. They performed the job of assembling passengers in larger cities, at which point a trunkline took over and made money flying these passengers to their ultimate destinations. The problem that this might cause for short-haul air carriers had been foreseen as early as the local, feeder, and pick-up service investigation, when one reason advanced for the use of a single carrier to provide both long-haul and feeder service was that "revenue from a passenger pick-up at a 'local' point and continuing beyond a terminal of a

31. Reuben H. Donnelley Corporation, *Official Airline Guide* (March 1967), p. 69.

32. For a listing of these awards see *Flight Magazine*, Vol. 57 (June 1968), pp. 60–61; Vol. 58 (June 1969), p. 43; Vol. 59 (June 1970), p. 39; and Vol. 60 (June 1970), p. 25.

33. Harold D. Watkins, "Locals Expand with Mixed Results," *Aviation Week and Space Technology*, Vol. 93 (July 6, 1970), pp. 25–27.

Table 6-2. Interline Local Service Air Traffic, by Carrier, 1952, 1961, and 1964

Carrier	Interline connecting passengers, as percent of total local passengers		
	1952	1961	1964
Allegheny Airlines	56	28	27
Bonanza Air Lines	50	28	17
Central Airlines	51	51	59
Frontier Airlines	36	37	43
Lake Central Airlines	51	43	51
Mohawk Airlines	21	28	27
North Central Airlines	65	65	54
Ozark Air Lines	62	51	49
Pacific Air Lines[a]	41	24	31
Piedmont Aviation	50	50	50
Southern Airways	61	61	59
Trans-Texas Airways	50	45	46
West Coast Airlines	n.a.	26	26
All local service carriers	49	42	41

Sources: *Flight Magazine*, Vol. 39 (June 1953), p. 24, and Vol. 54 (June 1965), p. 68.
n.a. Not available.
a. Name changed from Southwest Airways, effective March 6, 1953.

local route would be available for the entire journey to the [single] carrier, whereas only that part for the local transportation would be available to a local operator. . . ."[34] The extent of such interline traffic as a percentage of total local service traffic is shown in Table 6-2 for the years 1952, 1961, and 1964. Even in the last of these years, interline traffic was important for many of the local carriers, and in the earlier period it constituted almost half of all local service traffic. The problem faced by the locals could have been solved by an equitable joint fare arrangement that would have compensated the local carriers for the traffic generated for the trunklines. CAB Member Oswald Ryan pointed out this fact as early as 1954.[35] Yet not until 1970 were even the beginnings of a general joint fare arrangement worked out, and then it was put into effect only over the strong protests of the trunklines that they were being forced to "subsidize" the local carriers,[36] and even thereafter in most city-pair markets, the total fare a passenger paid was the sum of the two separate fares.[37]

34. *Civil Aeronautics Board Reports*, Vol. 6 (July 1944–May 1946), p. 30.
35. American Aviation Publications, *Official Airline Guide*, Vol. 10 (1954), p. 10.
36. Harold D. Watkins, "Three Part Fare Review Planned," *Aviation Week and Space Technology*, Vol. 92 (Feb. 9, 1970), pp. 29–31.
37. The joint fare agreement worked out in 1970 was to be effective only in those markets which were not served by a single carrier and which generated at least 200

As is apparent from Table 6-2, it is no coincidence that Central Airlines, Southern Airways, Piedmont Aviation, and Ozark have strongly favored granting local service carriers the right to by-pass traditional traffic hubs and fly passengers directly to their ultimate destination. In his testimony before the Senate Aviation Subcommittee in 1966, M. Lamar Muse, the president of Central, stated the case for the "feeder" group when he contended:

Local service carriers should be authorized to provide long-haul bypass service. . . .

Today 39 percent of our traffic travels less than 100 miles on Central. The bulk of this traffic is being carried a short distance to a major hub to connect to trunkline flights beyond Central's present system.

This proposal will allow Central to carry traffic it is already carrying on a short-haul basis all the way to the major cities where the traffic desires to go anyway. It permits Central to carry passengers from the exclusive cities to their destination—not just to connecting points a short distance away.

Central's bypass proposals sharply improve service at Central's cities. It strengthens Central's routes. It will dramatically reduce its subsidy requirements. Moreover, since Central will bypass competitive markets, these major benefits are attainable without significant new competitive service or diversion from other carriers, and last but not least, it establishes without question the need for jet aircraft on Central's system. [38]

The Board reacted favorably to Central's proposal. Southern was given authority to fly nonstop from Columbus, Georgia, to Washington, D.C., and New York City. Piedmont was allowed to by-pass Washington and fly nonstop from Charlottesville, Virginia, to New York City. North Central was allowed to fly from Milwaukee to New York City. However, perhaps the most conspicuous beneficiary of this policy was Ozark, which was given authority to fly nonstop from Peoria and Champaign, Illinois, to New York City and Washington, D.C. This new route prompted Ozark to place ads boasting "We're two-thirds transcontinental now" and asking the interesting question, "What's Ozark Airlines doing in New York and Washington?"

New Routes

In the 1940s and 1950s the Board had favored the smaller over the larger trunklines in awarding new routes, on the grounds that the former were more in need of route strengthening. In the late 1960s the Board began to apply the same standard in cases involving local service carriers. Local

---

passengers in the second quarter of 1968. This was estimated to include only 2,700 city-pair markets. In 1964 the local carriers alone operated in 6,703 city-pair markets.

38. *Review of the Local Air Carrier Industry*, Hearings, pp. 230–31.

carriers were chosen in preference to trunk carriers and were awarded routes lying far outside their traditional areas of operation on the grounds that such awards would "strengthen" them. In 1969 Texas International was granted a nonstop route from Albuquerque to Los Angeles. Frontier was granted a nonstop Las Vegas–Albuquerque route, and both carriers were granted nonstop Dallas–Albuquerque routes. This final award struck deeply at another long-held CAB view—that subsidized carriers should not to be allowed to compete with each other.[39]

Mergers

Another significant change in Board route policy during this period was the approval and even encouragement of local service mergers. During 1967 and 1968, three mergers involving seven carriers were consummated. In the fourth quarter of 1967, Central was merged with Frontier Airlines. In April 1968, Bonanza, Pacific, and West Coast Airlines merged to form Air West. In July 1968, Lake Central Airlines merged with Allegheny. The approval of these mergers marked a reversal in Board policy. It will be recalled that Pacific and West Coast had tried to merge several times previously but had been turned down. Ozark and Central, as well as Lake Central and North Central, advanced formal merger proposals, but both were withdrawn before the Board was called upon to make a formal reply. In the case of the Pacific Coast carriers, fears on the part of the trunklines that a local service carrier merger could mean serious competition for them were important in preventing the merger. The decision of the Board to allow the mergers was therefore consistent with the Board's new policy that trunklines no longer were to be given protection from local service competition.

In line with the findings of Chapter 3, only limited cost savings were forecast for the mergers. Because the carriers had been operating adjoining but not overlapping systems, there was little duplication of facilities to be eliminated, although a few stations could be consolidated at points where the routes came together. Some limited improvement in aircraft utilization, as a result of being able to schedule through flights, was also anticipated.

The primary potential benefits of these mergers were to be found on the revenue side. Merged carriers had much longer lineal route segments, and

39. The particular route in question was awarded on a nonsubsidized basis.

under the new CAB policy, this meant that they could apply for longer nonstop flights. For example, the Air West merger created a single local service carrier west of Salt Lake City and Phoenix, which was in a position to offer substantial competition to United and Western. In fact, in late 1969 Air West, in being recommended for nonstop authority between Los Angeles, San Francisco, and Seattle, fulfilled the 1946 prophecy of United and Western.

As of the date of this writing, none of the mergers can really be called successful. Difficulties connected with the Frontier-Central merger have been blamed in part for that carrier's recent poor performance.[40] The Allegheny–Lake Central merger, potentially the most profitable of the three, only began to show first signs of success by mid-1970.

The most difficult problems, however, were encountered by Air West. The merged airline found itself operating seven different types of aircraft; an attempt to save money by consolidating maintenance facilities was a disastrous failure; and schedules could not be integrated properly. Finally, the carrier found itself committed to acquiring a very large number of jet aircraft within a very short time. The result was that losses soared, and the airline looked to a takeover by Howard Hughes as its salvation. However, the agreement worked out with Hughes included a stipulation that Air West's net worth be at least $16.2 million at the time of the actual takeover. That was not a problem when the agreement was negotiated, but by late 1969 it was disclosed that the airline actually had a "negative" net worth of $5 million. By March 1970 the airline was trying desperately to raise enough capital to fulfill the terms of the takeover agreement and was stating that if Hughes withdrew, it might have to suspend operations.[41]

Elimination of Smaller Stations

In its 1966 presentation before the Senate Aviation Subcommittee, Frontier, one of the strongest advocates of the kinds of route strengthening outlined above, cited the experience of six smaller trunklines—Braniff, Delta Air Lines, Continental, National Airlines, Northwest Airlines, and Western—as an example of what route strengthening could accomplish in the

40. Richard G. O'Lone, "Difficulties Beset Local Service Mergers," *Aviation Week and Space Technology*, Vol. 90 (March 17, 1969), pp. 27–29.

41. *Wall Street Journal*, Vol. 177 (March 16, 1970), p. 30. Subsequently, Howard Hughes did take over the carrier and changed its name to Hughes Air West.

way of subsidy reduction. In 1938 the routes of these carriers had been little different from those of the local carriers in the 1960s. The Board favored these carriers in route awards, and by the early 1960s all of them were off subsidy and financially healthy. Frontier estimated that it could be off subsidy "within 18 months" if its routes were strengthened to a similar degree.[42]

Frontier did not mention, however, that in addition to having their routes expanded, the six carriers it referred to were replaced by local carriers at eighty-two marginal stations and were suspended and not replaced at others. The financial health of the smaller trunklines cited by Frontier could be attributed both to their entry into stronger routes and to their exit from weaker ones, and it is impossible to say which of the two policies was more important.

The Board was well aware of this. Consequently, it is not surprising that in its effort to reduce the local service subsidy it would look to the elimination of weaker stations. On the other hand, this had to be done very carefully, or congressional ire might be raised. While some of the relief continued to come from applying the increasingly outmoded standards of the "use-it-or-lose-it" policy, more and more during the late 1960s the Board began to look with favor on transferring some of the weaker local service routes to a new and rapidly growing group of air carriers—the scheduled air taxis or "third-level" carriers.

The Third-level Carriers

The category of "air taxi" was created in 1952, when the Board amended its economic regulations to permit carriers operating aircraft of less than 12,500 pounds gross take-off weight to offer unrestricted connecting service between points not served by scheduled commercial carriers, as well as service to such points.[43] Furthermore, if the aircraft operated had a capacity of fewer than 5 passengers, the carrier was relieved of CAB reporting requirements. These special provisions applied initially for a period of only five years, but they were renewed. In 1965, regulations were further lib-

---

42. *Review of the Local Air Carrier Industry*, Hearings, p. 211.
43. The weight limit (one-half the maximum gross take-off weight of a DC-3) was chosen to prevent these carriers from acquiring equipment that would make them competitive with the local carriers. Civil Aeronautics Board, Docket 2176 1, "Part 298 Weight Limitation Investigation: Initial Decision of Examiner Merritt Ruhlen" (Sept. 27, 1971), pp. 1, 19, 25.

eralized to allow air taxis to carry mail and to operate regularly scheduled services over certificated carrier segments; that is, they could compete with trunks or local service carriers provided they used aircraft weighing not over 12,500 pounds.

Several thousand air taxi operators existed at one time or another during the 1950s and 1960s, but most offered only the charter type service typical of ground taxis. A few, however, operated on a set schedule. The attitude of both local service carriers and the Board toward these scheduled air taxis was relatively hostile until the mid-1960s. Two examples are given below:

One of the earliest of the scheduled air taxi operators was TAG Airlines, which began operations in about mid-1956. TAG operated 9-passenger De Havilland Doves between Detroit City Airport and Cleveland Lakefront Airport. Although it had a substantially higher fare than the certificated carriers flying between Cleveland and Detroit, its relatively high frequency of service and its use of close-in airports, which made it convenient for businessmen, allowed it to capture a significant share of the Cleveland-Detroit traffic, although it lost money consistently. In the 1960 Great Lakes Local Service Investigation, the Board amended the certificates of Lake Central and North Central to allow them to operate into the close-in airports if they would obtain aircraft that could be used in such service. However, it would not permit these local service carriers to offer shuttle service between the two airports. TAG had requested that the Board delay consideration of these awards until it had acted on TAG's request for a certificate of public convenience and necessity for the route that would have allowed it to use larger than 12,500-pound aircraft. The Board refused (the certificate was not granted until late 1969), saying:

The effect of these awards upon TAG's operations will be substantial, since the carrier will face stiff competition by subsidized carriers, using larger equipment, charging lower fares, and being well-identified in the market. However, such a consequence is inevitable where, as here, air taxi operations demonstrate that a sizable volume of traffic is seeking more convenient service. The awards to Lake Central and North Central permit this additional convenience to the traveling public to accrue in conjunction with substantial benefits to beyond passengers.[44]

In the early 1960s an air taxi operator, Hi-Plains Airways, proposed that it be allowed to operate routes in Kansas, Colorado, Nebraska, and Missouri that coincided in many cases with those operated by Frontier.

44. *Civil Aeronautics Board Reports*, Vol. 31 (May–September 1960), p. 454.

Frontier was involved in a use-it-or-lose-it investigation covering some of the routes, and the communities affected had countered with a claim of inadequate air service. Hi-Plains proposed to offer service using 7-place Aero Commander aircraft and requested a certificate and subsidy support to do so. Central Airlines intervened in the case and argued that if such a service was to be offered, a local service carrier should provide it. Frontier argued that there was no need for the service. The hearing examiners agreed with Frontier and denied the application.

By about 1967, however, the attitude of the Board and the local carriers toward the scheduled air taxis had begun to change. The aircraft sponsored by the local service airlines as the "true" DC-3 replacement was appearing along with several other new aircraft, all weighing under the 12,500-pound limit, but having a seating capacity of up to 20 passengers.[45] Yet the local service airlines themselves showed little interest in purchasing such aircraft. They were preoccupied with their new jets and large turboprops and their newly won rights to compete with the trunklines.

About this time Allegheny Airlines proposed to the Board that it be allowed to turn over its operating rights at Hagerstown, Maryland, to an air taxi operator that would operate the route under contract with Allegheny. Reservations would be handled through Allegheny's reservation system, the aircraft to be used—the Beech 99—would be equipped according to full airline standards, and high performance levels would be guaranteed. In return for the Board's permission to undertake the experiment, Allegheny would forgo subsidy for Hagerstown. Finally, if the experiment did not succeed, Allegheny would reestablish its services. The Board agreed, and Allegheny Commuter began operating in November 1967.

The experiment was successful. By offering a higher frequency of service than Allegheny to Baltimore and thus indirectly to Washington (Hagerstown's principal communities of interest), the commuter carrier was able to increase traffic from 6,128 to 12,317 passengers in the first year. The Board was impressed with the results of the experiment and agreed to suspend Allegheny at five additional points: Salisbury, Maryland, Hazleton, Pennsylvania, Danville, Illinois, Du Bois, Pennsylvania, and Mansfield, Ohio—in order that it might be replaced by air taxis. In late 1969 Allegheny published a report on these suspensions, citing substantial increases in traffic in all cases and estimating subsidy savings of $324,000 a year as a

45. The Beech 99 was reportedly developed in accordance with the local airline standards for a DC-3 replacement. Allegheny Airlines, *Allegheny Commuter* (Allegheny Airlines, 1969; processed), Chaps. 1, 5.

result.[46] In mid-1970, Frontier was granted permission by the CAB to discontinue service to eight communities in Montana and North Dakota after having worked out an agreement with Apache Airlines, an Arizona air taxi operator, to take over its scheduled service. (This arrangement proved to be unsatisfactory, however. See p. 196, below.)

Finally, in 1970, the CAB approved a plan whereby Northeast's (a trunk carrier) and Mohawk's low-density routes in upper New York State and New England were turned over to an air taxi. In late 1969, Northeast's medium-density New England routes were turned over to Mohawk. Similar requests are expected from other carriers. A foreshadowing of this was a proposal by Eastern's President, Floyd D. Hall, that airlines "be permitted by the Civil Aeronautics Board to swap routes to achieve greater efficiency." Hall said that one-third of Eastern's 116 communities produced all the company's profits, on one-third it broke even, and one-third did not produce enough revenues to cover their costs.[47] In line with this proposal, Eastern earlier had turned some of its Florida routes over to an air taxi operator. Between October 1967 and April 1970, local service carriers were replaced by air taxis at thirty-one points. Between 1964 and April 1970, trunks were replaced by air taxis at twenty-three points.[48]

Effects of Current CAB Route Policies on Carrier Subsidies

The purpose of the route policies described above has been to reduce the amount of federal subsidy paid to the local carriers. The final aspect of route policy discussed—the elimination of marginal stations—accomplishes this directly by eliminating services that generate insufficient revenues to cover their costs. The other policies seek to reduce the subsidy by internalizing it—by shifting its burden from the public in general to the customers of the local carrier and other carriers flying on denser, more lucrative routes.

The use of an internal subsidy to support a money-losing operation is generally disapproved of by economists on grounds of both efficiency and equity. With free entry, competition presumably would assure that city-pair markets offered, at most, a normal rate of return, thereby drying up

46. *Ibid.*, Chap. 7.
47. *Wall Street Journal*, Oct. 3, 1969, p. 2.
48. *Aviation Week and Space Technology*, Vol. 92 (June 29, 1970), p. 35.

the source of funds for internal subsidy. Hence a policy of internal subsidy requires control over entry and the deliberate fostering of monopoly power if it is to be successful. On equity grounds it is hard to top Caves's classic statement that "there is no reason why impoverished grandmothers flying from New York to Los Angeles should be the ones to subsidize well-off businessmen traveling between small towns."[49] Thus most economists would agree that if the public interest requires that certain services be maintained even if they do not generate enough revenues to cover their costs, the public that benefits from such service—whether the nation as a whole, a region, or a local community—should bear the cost.[50]

This proposal has the advantage that the extent of subsidization would remain fully apparent, and the requirement that appropriations be voted annually to cover costs of losing operations theoretically would require an annual determination that the benefits of the service exceed its cost.

That the Board has not agreed with this position has already been noted. The Board relied on a policy of internalizing the trunkline subsidy to eliminate what it felt was the political liability of carriers' making excess profits on some routes yet receiving government funds for serving others. Yet the Board's policy of transferring marginal stations from the trunks to the local carriers in the 1950s and early 1960s "re-externalized" the subsidy by shifting its burden from the "impoverished grandmothers" to the federal treasury. This was not its stated intention. Rather, its action reflected instead the trunks' realization that ridding themselves of the burden of supporting their unprofitable short-haul segments would substantially improve their financial position. Caves, writing in 1962, when the Board's trunkline transfer/suspension program was nearly completed, commented: "Internal subsidy, and the Pandora's Box of regulatory difficulties it brought to the Board, should not constrain public policy so much in the future."[51] He foresaw the time when this development would allow entry controls to be dropped.

49. Richard E. Caves, *Air Transport and Its Regulators: An Industry Study* (Harvard University Press, 1962), p. 436.

50. As Alec Nove recently has observed, care must be taken to separate internal subsidization from the long-haul, short-haul problem referred to above. If the impoverished grandmother referred to by Caves first flew from some small New England town to New York and thence to Los Angeles, the use of a portion of her long-haul fare to cover part of the cost of her short-haul segment would not necessarily involve an internal subsidy. In fact, the lack of such a transfer mechanism would result in the short-haul segment's "subsidizing" the long-haul segment. ("Internal Economies," *Economic Journal*, Vol. 79 [December 1969], pp. 847–60.)

51. *Air Transport and Its Regulators*, p. 411.

This was not to be, however. The Board's policy of strengthening local service routes in the 1950s and early 1960s was an attempt again to internalize the local service subsidy. It differed only from the current policy in that it did not go so far as to promote direct trunkline–local service competition. The subsidy was to be shifted to only those passengers who traveled on the denser routes of the local carrier. The 1966 policy shift implied that the groups bearing the burden were to be expanded to include trunkline passengers on routes where the local service carriers competed.

Ignoring the question of the desirability of an internal as opposed to an external subsidy, it is not clear that the Board's policy as it concerns the locals is a feasible one. Assume that a local service carrier serves route *ABCDEF*, as shown in Figure 6-1, and that its revenues do not cover its costs, thus necessitating the payment of a subsidy if it is to stay in business. Assume that a trunkline is flying route *BF* nonstop and is earning a rate of return on the route that is in excess of what generally would be considered "fair." Current Board policy would allow the local carrier to offer nonstop service over route *BF* in the hope that it could capture excess profits that could take the place of the federal subsidy. How could such profits be generated? The local carrier could cut prices, hoping to lure away the trunk's customers. However, it could expect the trunk to match its price cuts until price just covered marginal cost and in the long run af-

Figure 6-1. Schematic Representation of New Types of Authority to Operate among Six Arbitrary Points Granted to Local Service Air Carriers by the Civil Aeronautics Board in the Post-1966 Period

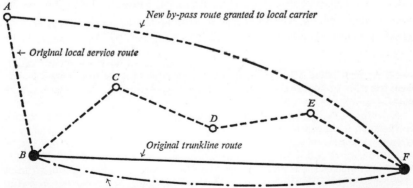

forded each carrier a normal rate of return. This is the result economists usually hope for from entry; yet in this case, it would spell failure for the Board's policy. The passengers flying route *BF* would be better off; yet no excess profits would be generated for internal subsidy purposes. The local carrier would still need to be subsidized if it were to fly route *ABCDEF*.[52]

Another possible strategy would be for the local service carrier to try to win a share of the market by offering service of better quality. Presumably the trunkline, if it is rational, is already providing service up to the point where the marginal revenue generated by an additional flight will cover that flight's marginal cost. The local carrier, believing that frequent service would stimulate total traffic and also attract traffic from its rival, might engage in a scheduling war by increasing frequency of service. Yet this would increase costs and might also be matched by the trunkline. Again the result probably would be a reduction in profits down to "normal" (or even below), this time because costs have risen more than revenues.

Third, the local carrier might request a fare increase, hoping that the trunk would be satisfied to surrender a share of the market if it could keep its profits constant. Again, however, the success of this strategy would depend on the acquiescence of the trunk, for the additional profits the trunkline earned as a result of the fare increase might merely provide it with additional funds with which to compete with the local carriers.

In short, if the local is to gain excess profits, the trunk must be willing to give them up. If it is not, the local might engage in actions that would eliminate the excess profits—such as a scheduling war or saturation advertising. This is the argument behind Western's claim that "placing locals in trunk markets won't save subsidy."[53]

An example of how allowing a weaker carrier to compete with stronger ones can actually weaken the carrier further is found in the case of Northeast Airlines, which, although it is a trunkline, had many "local service" attributes in the past.[54] In contrast to the strengthening of the other smaller

52. A price-cutting strategy would yield excess profits for the local only if its costs were less than those of the trunkline, but there is no reason to believe that this is the case.

53. *Aviation Daily*, Dec. 4, 1967, p. 181. George J. Stigler has argued that nonprice competition, if unchecked, may have the effect of eliminating monopoly profits. *The Organization of Industry* (Irwin, 1968), Chap. 3, "Price and Nonprice Competition."

54. The case of Northeast is conspicuously absent from Frontier's exhibit in the 1966 hearings, in which it shows how the Board's policy of "strengthening" the smaller trunklines helped them to eliminate subsidy. *Review of the Local Air Carrier Industry*, Hearings, pp. 197–209.

trunklines, the "strengthening" of Northeast involved primarily granting it routes in competition with the other stronger trunklines.

In the early 1940s Northeast served a number of cities in New England, primarily cities north of Boston. It was considered at that time to be one of the weakest of the trunklines. In June 1944 the Board chose Northeast over United, TWA, and Eastern to compete on an unrestricted basis with American on the Boston–New York route, stating that "the development of a substantial volume of traffic [by Northeast] should improve its financial position."[55] At that time the Boston–New York market was the nation's largest, and American was the only carrier in the market that offered unrestricted turn-around service. In the same case, Eastern was authorized to serve the market, but only on a severely restricted basis. Northeast began service in May 1945. For the first year it was able to offer high quality service and won a significant share of the market. In mid-1946 it acquired DC-4s for use in this market, even though this aircraft was much too large to use on any of its other routes. (Previously both American and Northeast had used DC-3s on the route.) American matched Northeast in the use of DC-4s and began to fight back to regain its lost share of the market. The quality of Northeast's service started to decline, and its share of the market dropped from 37 percent in September 1946 to 10 percent in September 1948. Furthermore, Northeast's entire operations suffered, for the carrier found itself trying to operate two airlines—a low-density service north of Boston and a high-density service between Boston and New York. The problem was compounded by the fact that Northeast was operating an inefficiently small fleet of DC-4s on its New York–Boston route. Northeast's financial position deteriorated, and its subsidy rose.[56]

The second attempt by the CAB to strengthen Northeast by giving it competitive routes occurred in 1956, when the carrier was awarded routes between New York, Philadelphia, and Boston, and Florida. The Board chose Northeast specifically to strengthen the carrier, saying that "extension of Northeast to Florida will, in our judgment, eliminate the carrier's current subsidy need of more than $1.5 million annually."[57] In doing so it overruled its examiner's contention that awarding the route to Northeast

---

55. *Civil Aeronautics Board Reports*, Vol. 4 (December 1942–June 1944), p. 695.

56. Northeast tried again in the spring of 1967 to improve its position in the New York–Boston market through a substantial increase in scheduling, matching Eastern and American both in frequency of service and in the use of jet aircraft. The plan failed, and by late 1969 the carrier had cut back its schedules.

57. *Civil Aeronautics Board Reports*, Vol. 24 (September 1956–March 1957), p. 100. Northeast was then the only trunkline receiving subsidy.

would increase rather than decrease Northeast's subsidy need because of the carrier's inability to compete effectively with National and Eastern— the carriers that were then serving the route.[58]

In fact, the examiner was correct. Although subsidy was withdrawn from Northeast in 1959 in anticipation of the profits it would earn from its Florida routes, the airline's losses grew steadily, and in 1963 the Board was forced to resume subsidy payments.

In late 1969 Northeast was again "strengthened" by the award of a non-stop Miami–Los Angeles route. At about the same time, however, the Board found the "final solution" to strengthening Northeast. It permitted Northeast to turn over its low-density, short-haul New England routes to Mohawk and to an air taxi operator. In short, the only way in which Northeast could really be strengthened was to allow it to drop the routes that were the initial source of its need for strengthening.

If prospects are slight for strengthening the local carriers by allowing them to compete directly with trunklines, another facet of the Board's route policy may have a better chance of producing profits for use in internalizing the subsidy—though with the attendant inefficiencies implied. Assume that the local carrier whose situation was described above, and was illustrated in Figure 6-1, feeds a considerable amount of traffic into point B, where the passengers board a trunk carrier for the journey to point F. Now assume that the Board grants bypass authority for the local carrier to fly directly from A to F.

The local carrier would now have a monopoly on route AF and presumably could benefit accordingly. To enhance its monopoly position the carrier could make connections at B difficult (by scheduling its arrivals at point B for just after the trunkline flight from B to F leaves) and by scheduling the rest of its route system so that traffic is fed to A rather than to F.[59] The trunk would have a much harder time retaliating against these actions by the local carrier. It could rearrange its schedules to make connections easier, but this move could easily be offset by the local.

58. *Ibid.*, pp. 102–3.

59. George N. Spooner, vice-president for market planning for Allgeheny, is said to have admitted that Allegheny scheduled its operations to maximize its own on-line connecting service. It is further reported that, "Frontier, among other locals, also is attempting to schedule its feeder flights so that it provides connections to its own service rather than to trunks as formerly." See Harold D. Watkins, "Locals, Trunks Vie for Short-Haul Traffic," *Aviation Week and Space Technology*, Vol. 93 (July 13, 1970), pp. 33ff. This tactic would also provide the locals with a competitive advantage in markets where they compete directly with trunks. Of course, fear that this might occur was one reason why the local carriers were created in the late 1940s.

For this policy to be successful in producing monopoly profits, the local should not overschedule its flights on route AF. But if B and F are both large cities, the trunkline would probably have many flights per day between them. If A and B are relatively close together, an attempt by the local carrier to increase load factors over segment AF by maintaining a low frequency might be offset by passengers' driving from A to B or by the entry of an air taxi into the AB market. In short, while the chances of generating monopoly profits appear to be greater when bypass authority is granted than when directly competitive routes are awarded, such profits are limited by the higher frequency of service offered to the trunk carriers between points B and F and by the possibility of entry by air taxis.[60]

Both the Board and the industry by late 1969 were beginning to realize that the route strengthening policy was not working as planned. In its December 8 issue, *Aviation Week* announced that a joint industry-CAB review of the local service subsidy problem was under way and admitted that "The theory [behind CAB route policy] was that increased revenues from new routes would offset the subsidy decline, but this has not been the case. Inflation of operating costs has been a primary factor in this adverse development, but also the airlines have found new routes do not produce immediate profits."[61] In May 1970 the same publication noted that the Board had modified its route strengthening policy to require that a local carrier seeking competitive authority prove that it would fully cover its return on investment on such service during the first year of operation. Prior to that, Board policy was said to require a forecast of profits only in the second or third year of operation.[62]

60. One reason given by the Board for authorizing bypass authority is that it relieves air congestion at major terminals. Ozark's routes bypass Chicago. Southern's routes avoid Atlanta, Piedmont's avoid Washington, D.C. Whether or not the trunk carriers react to this by cutting back frequencies over routes like BF depends on the importance to them of this traffic. It is clear, however, that the granting of bypass authority *does* affect congestion at the terminal points. In June 1970, Ozark, Piedmont, and Southern together were flying nine flights a day into already congested New York from places like Columbus, Georgia; Charlottesville, Virginia; and Champaign and Peoria, Illinois. Whether the loss of passengers at Atlanta, Washington, D.C., and Chicago, respectively, caused trunk carriers to reduce frequencies into New York by more than nine a day (if at all) is not known.

While creating more traffic hubs to relieve congested airports may well be a desirable policy, it would appear that a system of peak-load user charges would accomplish the task more efficiently.

61. *Aviation Week and Space Technology*, Vol. 91 (Dec. 8, 1969), p. 38.

62. Harold D. Watkins, "Local Service Airline Support Criticized," *Aviation Week and Space Technology*, Vol. 92 (May 25, 1970), p. 49. The author remarked that he had been informed by local service airline executives that most opportunities for competitive

An article by Watkins, referred to earlier (see note 33 to this chapter), carried a rough estimate that, as a whole, the locals might have *lost* as much as $20 million in 1969 on their competitive routes.

Inflation is not necessarily to blame for much of the current adversity of the local carriers. The findings in Chapter 3 showed the extent to which increases in competition can affect costs, even on routes that remain noncompetitive. To be sure, interest payments and heavy lease obligations, reflecting the increasing tightness of money in the economy during the late 1960s, are responsible for the current difficulties of many of the locals; but these obligations were undertaken in order to finance the acquisition of aircraft that the locals thought they needed in order to be competitive on their new routes.

Crew costs per hour on the DC-3 did rise from $36 in 1966 to $48 in 1968, but, as suggested in Chapter 3, this may have reflected attempts by the Air Line Pilots Association to spread the gains from the productivity of new jets to all its members and not just those flying new aircraft.[63] Thus, while the increase in the cost of inputs during the latter part of the 1960s affected the local carriers as it did all business firms, it is unreasonable to lay a major share of the blame for the poor performance of the locals on "inflation." Rather the locals' problems can be traced to the fact that capacity was growing faster than traffic, to the high costs of entering into major direct competition with the trunks on a large number of routes, and to the cost increases on noncompetitive routes brought about by the phasing out of the DC-3 and the use of equipment unsuited to the needs of these routes.

---

route expansion already had been exploited by them by the time the policy shift was announced.

63. An indication that this may have been the case is the fact that per-hour crew costs on the DC-9-10 rose only from $86 to $88 during the same period.

CHAPTER SEVEN

The Quality of "Local" Air Service and Its Cost to the Government

IN CHAPTER 2 the point was stressed that, except where a community is so isolated that any air service at all represents a substantial improvement in the transportation alternatives open to it, an air carrier must offer frequent, conveniently timed service if it is to capture any appreciable share of the potential short-haul travel market. While the local carriers today still serve many isolated communities, particularly in the West, the tremendous improvement in highways since the Second World War has moved most of the points they serve into the frequency-sensitive category. The response of the local service carriers to the increase in competition from the automobile has been to cut back frequencies in their shorter-haul markets and at their smaller stations in order to concentrate their attention and their equipment on markets where the airplane has a greater inherent advantage over other modes of transportation.

The Quality of Local Air Service

Recognizing their continuing need for government subsidy, and thus for good relations with Congress, the local carriers have been anxious to dispel any impression that they have been neglecting service to smaller communities. A report prepared in 1969 for the Association of Local Transport Airlines (ALTA), and intended for release to the public, said, "In keeping with their primary mission of providing the best and most efficient service to the smaller communities, the local airlines have constantly improved and expanded their service to those communities. Analysis of the airports served reveals that the local service carriers continue to give the smaller cities the

Table 7-1. Number of Airports Served by Local Service Air Carriers and Flight Departures per Station per Day, by Population of Cities Served, 1958 and 1968

Population of cities served	Number of airports served		Total annual flight departures (thousands)		Flight departures per station per day		
	1958	1968	1958	1968	1958	1968	Increase, 1958–68
100,000 or less	224	233	312	428	3.8	5.0	1.2
100,000–500,000	118	150	326	525	7.6	9.6	2.0
500,000–1,000,000	28	33	79	192	7.7	15.9	8.2
Over 1,000,000	31	44	144	456	12.7	28.4	15.7
All airports	401	460	861	1,601	5.9	9.5	3.6

Source: Systems Analysis and Research Corporation, "Public Benefits Provided by the Local Airline Industry: A Report on the Nation's Fast-Growing Local Airline Industry," Report No. 6, prepared for the Association of Local Transport Airlines (Cambridge, Mass.: SARC, 1969; processed), p. 10. The departure table in the source indicated that the data were for 1956 and 1966. A check of Civil Aeronautics Board data shows that they are for 1958 and 1968.

highest priority."[1] The carriers point to such factors as the increase in the average number of departures per station per day from 4.8 in 1954, to 6.1 in 1960, and to 9.5 in 1969 as proof of their continuing interest in their smaller stations. Yet even their data reveal to some degree the decline in the quality of service offered at these points. Table 7-1, compiled from data published in the report, reveals that the number of departures per day at cities with a population of 100,000 or less showed almost no increase between 1958 and 1968. (In 1969 only 15 of the 287 cities depending on a local service carrier for their only certificated, scheduled air service had a population of more than 100,000.) But an examination of Tables 7-2 and 7-3, which show passenger originations and average number of departures per day by city population for the 287 exclusively served cities, makes it clear that many of these small towns generate a considerable amount of traffic relative to their size. In 1969, 33 of the 144 cities with a population of less than 25,000 that were served exclusively by local service airlines originated more passengers over the twelve-month period than their listed population.[2] Forty-nine percent of the cities under 25,000 generated a volume of traffic that

1. Systems Analysis and Research Corporation, "Public Benefits Provided by the Local Airline Industry: A Report on the Nation's Fast-Growing Local Airline Industry," Report No. 6, prepared for the Association of Local Transport Airlines (Cambridge, Mass.: SARC, 1969; processed), p. 10.
2. Obviously some of these points were resort areas and military posts, where the listed population underestimates the traffic potential.

Table 7-2. Number of Cities Served Exclusively by Local Service Air Carriers, by Number of Passenger Originations and by City Population, 1969

Population of cities served[a]	Passenger originations per station						Total
	Under 7,300	7,300– 12,499	12,500– 24,999	25,000– 49,999	50,000– 99,999	100,000 or more	
Under 6,250	17	0	3	2	0	0	22
6,250–12,499	35	9	4	0	2	0	50
12,500–24,999	35	11	23	2	1	0	72
25,000–49,999	32	15	20	15	4	0	86
50,000–99,999	7	5	9	11	10	0	42
100,000 and above	4	2	2	2	3	2	15
Total	130	42	61	32	20	2	287

Source: Calculated from data in the appendix.

a. The population figures used were obtained from the *Rand McNally Road Atlas: United States, Canada, Mexico* (Chicago: Rand McNally, 1970). The Rand McNally figures are "from [the] 1960 Census and latest available estimates" (p. 104). In cases where an airport was designated as serving more than one community, the combined population of the designated communities was used. The designation of the cities served was that used in the CAB publication, *Airport Activity Statistics of Certificated Route Air Carriers, 12 months ended December 31, 1968* (1969). No attempt was made to include other adjoining cities that might supply traffic *except* where the listed airport was located on a military post (such as Fort Leonard Wood, Missouri, or Eglin Air Force Base, Florida) for which population figures were not available. The 287 cities, their population, and 1969 data on the number of passenger originations, the number of departures per day, and originations per capita are shown in the appendix.

Table 7-3. Number of Cities Served Exclusively by Local Service Air Carriers, by Number of Flight Departures per Day and by City Population, 1969

Population of cities served[a]	Flight departures per station per day							Total
	Under 3.0	3.00– 5.99	6.00– 8.99	9.00– 11.99	12.00– 17.99	18.00– 23.99	24.00 or more	
Under 6,250	10	10	2	0	0	0	0	22
6,250– 12,499	19	29	0	1	1	0	0	50
12,500– 24,999	19	33	17	2	1	0	0	72
25,000– 49,999	11	42	23	5	4	0	1	86
50,000– 99,999	4	13	10	4	8	2	1	42
100,000 and above	1	4	3	2	3	1	1	15
Total	64	131	55	14	17	3	3	287

Source: Calculated from data in the appendix.
a. See note a to Table 7-2.

was greater than half of their listed population. On the other hand, 42 percent of the 57 cities of more than 50,000 that were served exclusively by local carriers generated a volume of traffic equivalent to less than 25 percent of their population; and 19 percent of these cities generated traffic over the year that was equivalent to less than 10 percent of their population. The low level of traffic relative to population at these larger cities reflects the fact that better transportation alternatives are available there. In most instances the better alternative is an interstate highway.[3] In others air taxi service is available.[4]

It appears that the relatively more intensive use of air service by the smaller cities is not reflected in the level of flight frequency provided them.[5] To see if smaller, exclusively served cities indeed receive fewer departures than they are "entitled" to, a simple model was constructed to explain airline scheduling. It was assumed that an airline considers two factors in deciding how many flights to offer a station—the amount of traffic it is expected to generate and its population. As a proxy for expected traffic, the actual number of passengers originated by the station during the previous year was used. The data were those for the 287 stations served only by local carriers in 1969. The equation was estimated in logarithmic form.

ln (flight departures per station per year, 1969)

$$= 2.742 + 0.45 \ln \text{ (passenger originations per year, 1968)}$$
$$(24.32)$$
$$+ 0.086 \ln \text{ (population of city served)}.$$
$$(4.27)$$

$N = 287$, $R^2 = 0.74$, $F = 400.69$
The numbers in parentheses are t-ratios.
All variables are significant at the 1 percent level, as is the equation as a whole.

As would be expected from the discussion in Chapter 2, a strong relationship was found between flight departure levels and traffic. More interesting for the current discussion is the significant positive relationship found between population and flight departure levels. Of two cities generating equal amounts of traffic, the more populous one systematically was

3. Of the 18 cities with a population of 50,000 or more that generated fewer than 12,500 passengers in 1969, all but two lie within approximately an hour's drive of a large city that has a superior level of air service.

4. Of the 18 cities referred to in note 3, above, 10 were served by air taxis or intrastate air carriers in 1969. This includes the two airports where cities were more than one hour's drive from a large city with superior air connections.

5. In 1969, 33 percent of the exclusively served stations with a population of less than 25,000 received fewer than three departures a day. Eighty-three percent of such cities received fewer than six departures a day.

Table 7-4. Cities Served Exclusively by Local Service Air Carriers in 1969 and Also Served in 1959, Classified by Change in Average Number of Departures per Day and by City Population, 1959–69

City population	Change in average number of departures per day, 1959–69								Total
	Greater than −6.0	−6.00 to −3.01	−3.00 to −0.01	0 to +2.99	+3.00 to +5.99	+6.00 to +8.99	+9.00 to +11.99	+12.00 or more	
Under 6,250	0	0	9	1	0	0	0	0	10
6,250–12,499	0	0	19	11	2	0	0	0	32
12,500–24,999	2	2	21	17	1	1	1	0	45
25,000–49,999	1	8	27	20	3	1	1	1	62
50,000–99,999	2	6	10	7	2	5	3	1	36
100,000 and above	1	0	2	7	1	1	0	0	12
Total	6	16	88	63	9	8	5	2	197

Sources: *Flight Magazine*, Vol. 59 (June 1970), pp. 60–67, and Vol. 49 (June 1960), pp. 56–60, 105; *Rand McNally Road Atlas, United States, Canada, Mexico* (Chicago: Rand McNally, 1970).

offered more aricraft departures. Admittedly, the population variable does not have a very great impact; the larger cities generally receive at most only a few hundred more departures a year than do the smaller cities, but such behavior is not what would be expected from a group of airlines that claim that "their primary mission [is] providing the best and most efficient service to the smaller communities."[6]

Table 7-4 shows 1959 and 1969 flight frequencies for the 197 points which were served only by local carriers in 1969 and which had also been served in 1959. Over the decade average daily departures declined at 56 percent of these stations. They declined at 61 percent of the cities with a population below 25,000 and at 81 percent of the cities with a population of less than 50,000.[7] At many of the stations where declines occurred, the local carriers changed the scheduling of the remaining departures to free equipment for use on their higher-density routes. The flights that remained were inconveniently timed from the viewpoint of the travelers at the smaller towns, and thus the quality of service declined more than in proportion to the drop in frequency.

The response of traffic to this general decline in the quality of service was what one would expect from the findings in Chapter 2. At 17 percent of the

6. Systems Analysis and Research Corporation, "Public Benefits," p. 10.

7. On an average, departures per station did increase slightly over the 1959–69 period at these 197 stations. The average increase was 54 departures a year, or about 0.15 a day. This means that in 1969 this group of stations together received about 10,500 more departures than they did in 1959. Between 1959 and 1969 total local service departures increased by 608,000—from 986,000 to 1,594,000. The bulk of this increase went to stations that were served also by trunklines. At only 5 of the 87 cities of less than 25,000 population did departures rise by more than 3.0 per day. Departures increased by more than 3 a day at only 11 of the 149 cities with a population of less than 50,000.

197 cities, passenger originations in 1969 were below or near their 1959 level.

An excellent example of how a decline in service quality may affect traffic can be found in the case of Iowa City, Iowa, a community of 40,000 and home of the State University of Iowa. Service was inaugurated in Iowa City during 1959, and thus it does not appear in the sample referred to above. However, in 1968 it originated 9,433 passengers for Ozark Air Lines—an average of 26 per day and 7.2 per flight. During June 1968, Iowa City was served by two one-stop flights a day to and from Chicago. Flights departed Chicago for Iowa City at 9:35 a.m. and 7:10 p.m. Flights to Chicago left Iowa City at 8:29 a.m. and 4:28 p.m. The morning flight originating in Chicago continued on to Des Moines and Sioux City. Six days a week Ozark offered connections in Sioux City for a flight to Denver.[8]

In 1969 Ozark began its "by-pass service" to New York and Washington from Moline/Davenport/Rock Island (75 miles east of Iowa City on Interstate 80). At the same time it reduced the quality of service into Chicago. For Iowa City this meant the loss of one of its two daily round trips and a less convenient time for the remaining one. The new departure time from Chicago was 10:10 a.m., and the plane left Iowa City for the return flight at 3:30 p.m. Service to Sioux City was eliminated, as was the connection to Denver. The single flight remaining to Des Moines (150 miles west of Iowa City on Interstate 80) left at 11:59 a.m., with the return flight from Des Moines to Iowa City leaving Des Moines at 2:42 p.m. Traffic at Iowa City responded to this substantial drop in the quantity and quality of service by falling 56 percent between 1968 and 1969.

Iowa City is relatively fortunate, since it has good alternative forms of transportation to which its residents can turn when the quality of air service declines.[9] This is not true of such cities as Crescent City, California, or Hancock/Houghton, Michigan. These places are relatively small and isolated—one in the upper northwest corner of California and one on Michigan's upper peninsula. Departures at each declined over the 1959-69 period, yet traffic rose with the growth of each town, since even the reduced service provided by the local carriers in each case represented by far the best means of transportation available.

The picture presented here is clearly one of a significant decline in the already low quality of air service provided to cities that depend on the

8. Reuben H. Donnelley Corporation, *Official Airline Guide*, Quick Reference North American Edition (June 1, 1968).

9. Also, Iowa City is only 17 miles south of Cedar Rapids, a city served by United Air Lines and Ozark.

local service carriers for their only certificated air service. The responsibility for this deterioration of service rests in large measure on the Civil Aeronautics Board. The Board has never provided the local carriers with a sufficient incentive to use the kind of aircraft that would allow them to offer adequate service to their smaller stations. Indeed, with the limited exceptions noted above in Chapter 5, it has, through its route and subsidy policies, allowed or even actively encouraged the local service carriers to acquire aircraft that are suitable only for dense, longer-haul routes. Its removal of the intermediate stop restrictions, though necessary, was done in a way that encouraged competition between the local service carriers and the trunklines, rather than allowing the local service carriers the flexibility needed to serve their smaller points adequately. The Board's subsidy policy during the pre–class rate period actively encouraged the use of excessively large aircraft, and the class rate subsidy system, even when it has been "neutral" as among types of aircraft, has been administered in such a way as to encourage service cutbacks at the smaller stations.

With each new version of the class rate, the Board cut back on the number of daily trips it was prepared to subsidize, until under Class Rate IV (adopted in early 1967), it was prepared to pay subsidy for a maximum of two round trips a day. Class Rate V, established for fiscal 1971, was designed to encourage the continuation of service to smaller stations, though it was conceived of as only an interim measure. As far as direct service standards are concerned, the Board has said only that points generating more than five passengers a day should receive at least two round trips a day. It has never tried to control the scheduling quality to reduce a carrier's subsidy when it chose to provide flights at inconvenient times.

The Cost to the Government of Local Air Service

Just as the local carriers claim that they are as interested as ever in serving the smaller communities, so do they claim that the cost to the government of providing local air service has been steadily declining. Before the cost to the government of providing air service to communities that otherwise would be without it can be estimated, it must first be determined which cities would in fact lose air service if the subsidy were ended. It should be recognized at the outset, however, that it will be impossible to provide a completely satisfactory answer to this difficult question; only a rough indication can be made of the level of traffic a city might have to generate in order to cover the costs of serving it.

In Chapter 5, data were presented from a 1959 report by United Research estimating the minimum avoidable cost of serving an intermediate point with at least two round trips a day, using a DC-3 or a Convair 340 or 440. By assuming that the passengers paid the average local service fare, it was determined that such a station would have to have generated between 4,500 and 8,000 passengers a year, depending on the aircraft used. The same report contained an estimate that if subsidy had been discontinued in 1959, approximately half of the 530 points then receiving scheduled air service—roughly those generating fewer than 7,000 passengers a year—would have lost their service.[10]

Since 1959, both costs and fare levels have increased. The average local service fare in 1959 was $14.02. In 1968 it was $22.51, an increase of 61 percent.[11] Taneja and Simpson's results imply that the minimum average direct station cost in 1966 was approximately $30,000, or double the 1958 figure.[12] With this information and current aircraft operating cost figures, and following the United Research procedure, it was calculated that in the late 1960s an on-line intermediate station would have had to generate 7,700 passengers a year to cover the avoidable costs of providing it with two round trips a day using an F-27; if a Convair were used and the same level of service provided, the city would have to generate 9,000 passengers a year.[13] (These are the two aircraft used to serve the smaller stations now that the DC-3 has been phased out of the local service fleet.) Thus Watkins's characterization of points that generate fewer than 20 passengers a day (7,300 passengers a year) as "weak traffic points" and possible candidates for transfer or abandonment does not appear to be seriously out of line.[14]

Table 7-5 was constructed with these standards in mind. Traffic and subsidy data for 1969 were used even though many carriers claimed that this

10. United Research Incorporated, "Federal Regulation of the Domestic Air Transport Industry," Prepared for the U.S. Department of Commerce (Cambridge, Mass.: United Research, 1959; processed), pp. 27, 62.

11. This overstates the increase because of the increase in average trip length from 198 to 277 miles. On the other hand, using the average yield figure would understate the increase due to the taper in the fare structure.

12. N. K. Taneja and R. W. Simpson, "A Multi-Regression Analysis of Airline Indirect Operating Costs," FTL Report R-67-2 (Massachusetts Institute of Technology, Flight Transportation Laboratory, June 1968; processed), p. 52.

13. The aircraft operating cost data used are from the CAB publication, "Local Service Carriers' Unit Costs, Year Ended March 31, 1969," pp. 1, 2.

14. Harold D. Watkins, "Economic Problems of Locals Resist Jets, New Authority," *Aviation Week and Space Technology*, Vol. 92 (March 9, 1970), p. 177.

Table 7-5. Local Service Air Carrier Traffic at Exclusively Served Cities, Grouped by Number of Originating Passengers and Subsidy per Trip, 1969

Number of originating passengers per year	Number of cities	Number of originations (millions)	Total trips[a] (millions)	Subsidy per trip[b] (dollars)
All stations	287	4.75	9.50	3.79
Fewer than 25,000	233	1.92	3.84	9.37
Fewer than 15,000	189	1.08	2.16	16.66
Fewer than 10,000	158	0.69	1.38	26.07
Fewer than 7,300	130	0.45	0.90	39.98

Source: *Flight Magazine*, Vol. 60 (June 1970), pp. 48, 49, and 60ff.

a. Data on the number of arrivals and departures at exclusively served cities, and the number of trips between these points, are not available. Therefore, the number of trips is arbitrarily assumed to be double the number of originations.

b. The total subsidy paid to local service carriers in 1969 amounted to $35,981,100 (after adjustments).

level of subsidy was inadequate to cover the costs of the service they provided.[15] Traffic is shown for all stations that received their only certificated air service from local service carriers, even if they were not served for a full year. In the absence of data on the number of arrivals and departures at exclusively served cities and the number of trips between exclusively served points, the number of passenger originations was arbitrarily doubled to obtain an estimate of the total trips to and from exclusively served points. Thus the total-trips column of Table 7-5 is based on the assumption that all originations at exclusively served stations are round trips and that all trips had a jointly served station as one of the terminal points. While the former assumption is roughly true in the aggregate, the latter is not.[16] Subsidy per trip, computed using the trip data shown, is therefore an underestimate to the extent that trips between exclusive points involve double counting. Moving down to points that generate less and less traffic, this

15. Frontier, among other carriers, has claimed that even its 1969 subsidy was only about half of the amount actually required to continue to operate its low-density services. *Ibid.*

16. The CAB *Air Traffic Survey, March 1949* was examined by carrier to determine the percentage of arriving and departing passengers at points served exclusively by local service carriers that were traveling to or from another such point served by the same carrier. (No attempt was made to calculate the percentage of passengers traveling from a point served exclusively by one carrier to one served exclusively by another.) An average correction of 5.1 percent to total arrivals and departures was necessary to eliminate double counting resulting from such trips. The maximum correction required was 10.4 percent, the minimum, zero. The larger proportion of points served today that are exclusive points probably means that this correction would be greater today for total traffic generated by all such points.

assumption obviously becomes more and more fulfilled, and thus the degree of underestimation of subsidy per trip declines.

In 1969, local service carrier passenger originations were 23.4 million. Table 7-5 shows that even under the generous assumptions made here, the exclusively served stations were included in fewer than 41 percent of the total trips during the year. Furthermore, almost 60 percent of the originations at exclusively served stations occurred at the 54 exclusively served stations that originated more than 25,000 passengers during the year 1969. The 158 stations originating fewer than 10,000 passengers a year (well over half the exclusively served stations) originated a total of 0.69 million passengers and, under the assumptions used here, were involved in only 1.38 million trips, fewer than 15 percent of total local service trips originating or terminating at exclusively served stations. If it is assumed that all stations that originated fewer than 10,000 passengers a year in 1969 would not have been served if there were no subsidy, then the per-trip cost to the government of providing this air service was $26.07. If the cutoff point was instead 7,300 passengers a year (20 a day), then the per-trip cost to the government of local air service was $39.98.

The possibility was mentioned above that the assumptions used in deriving the column "total trips" may cause a downward bias in the calculation of subsidy per trip. There is also another source of downward bias. Obviously not all cities that originate fewer than 10,000 passengers a year would lose air service even if the local carriers chose to abandon all of them. It has been noted that unsubsidized air taxis already provide service at a number of these cities, and entry of this sort could be expected to accelerate with the abandonment of such points by the local carriers. The number of cities where the local service subsidies actually are responsible for the existence of scheduled air service may be far fewer than the estimates would indicate, and the per-trip cost to the government of providing such service may be correspondingly higher.

The cost to the federal government of providing air service at communities that would have been denied such service in the absence of federal support was certainly lower in 1969 than in the early 1960s, when the subsidy bill was higher and the number of marginal stations, expanded by the Board's generosity in the area cases, substantially higher. But was it lower than before the major CAB effort of "route strengthening"? Table 7-6, which gives the same data for 1954, is based on the same assumptions as Table 7-5 and provides a chance to make such a comparison.[17] These

17. The year 1954 was chosen because it was the first one for which individual station data were available. It also was the first year when service mail pay was reported sepa-

Table 7-6. Local Service Air Carrier Traffic at Exclusively Served Cities, Grouped by Number of Originating Passengers, and Subsidy per Trip, 1954

Number of originating passengers per year	Number of cities	Number of originations (millions)	Total trips[a] (millions)	Subsidy per trip[b] (dollars)
All stations	216	0.63	1.27	18.70
Fewer than 25,000	215	0.61	1.22	19.50
Fewer than 15,000	212	0.54	1.09	21.80
Fewer than 10,000	204	0.45	0.89	26.70
Fewer than 7,300	197	0.39	0.77	30.90
Fewer than 5,000	181	0.29	0.58	41.00

Sources: *Flight Magazine*, Vol. 43 (June 1955), pp. 35ff.; CAB, *Handbook of Airline Statistics, 1965 Edition*, p. 233.

a. See Table 7-5, note *a*.

b. The total subsidy paid to local service carriers in 1954 amounted to $23,807,000 (after adjustments)

tables suggest that, even allowing for growth of traffic and increases in fare over the intervening fifteen years, the cost per trip to the government of providing service to those points that would otherwise not have been served may not have declined, and in fact may actually have increased.

Unquestionably a major reason for this was the high operating costs of the excessively large equipment used by the local carriers to provide service to these points. The Systems Analysis and Research Corporation study that forecast a substantial need for smaller aircraft throughout the 1970s and projected the adverse effect that the use of larger aircraft would have on subsidy has been referred to above. SARC determined that aircraft with a capacity of less than 40 passengers (that is, smaller than F-27s or Convairs) should fly 61 percent of local service routings in 1975.[18] This level of use would require these aircraft to fly 71 million aircraft-miles in 1975, compared to the 44 million flown by the local service carriers' DC-3s in 1963. However, in 1969 the local service carriers together flew only about 3.3 million aircraft-miles using aircraft smaller than the 40-seat F-27. And in 1970 the Nord was eliminated from the local service fleet.

To estimate the effect that the use of excessively large aircraft had on the 1969 subsidy, the costs of operating three aircraft, the Convair 580, the Nord 262, and the De Havilland Twin Otter (shown in Table 7-7) may be

---

rately from subsidy. Finally, it was the last year before Allegheny Airlines and Mohawk Airlines introduced large piston aircraft.

18. A routing is the pattern flown by an aircraft during a day. In 1963, the year covered by the SARC study, DC-3s flew 46.5 percent of local-service routings. Systems Analysis and Research Corporation, "Economic Analysis of the Short-Haul Transport" (Cambridge, Mass.: SARC, 1964; processed), pp. 29, 60.

Table 7-7. Operating Costs at 90-Mile Average Stage Length for Convair 580, Nord 262, and De Havilland Twin Otter, and Seating Capacity, 1968
Costs in dollars per mile

Item	Convair 580	Nord 262	De Havilland Twin Otter
Direct operating costs	1.27	0.99	0.60
Indirect operating costs	0.95	0.74	0.45
Return on investment	0.33	0.22	0.24
Total operating costs	2.55	1.95	1.29
Seating capacity	53	24–28	15–20

Source: Derived by author using procedures described in text and basic data from the following sources: *Review of the Local Air Carrier Industry*, Hearings before the Aviation Subcommittee of the Senate Committee on Commerce, 89 Cong. 2 sess. (1966), pp. 136, 159; Civil Aeronautics Board, "Local Service Air Carriers' Unit Costs, Year Ended March 31, 1969," Attachment C, pt. 3, p. 1; brochures from De Havilland Aircraft of Canada, Limited; CAB, *Aircraft Operating Cost and Performance Report for Calendar Years 1968 and 1969* (August 1970), Vol. 4, p. 74.

compared. The Convair is one of the turboprop conversions of piston-powered aircraft discussed in Chapter 5 and is the one that, together with the F-27, provided most of the service at smaller stations during 1969. The Nord is the French-built turboprop 28-seat DC-3 replacement introduced into service by Lake Central Airlines in 1965. The Twin Otter is a small twin turboprop short take-off and landing aircraft developed by De Havilland Aircraft of Canada, Limited, and widely used by air taxi operators. It can seat up to 20 passengers for short hops, but generally is operated with 15 to 18 seats. The table compares operating costs for these three aircraft over a route system with an average stage length of 90 miles. Convair costs are those experienced by operators of this aircraft during 1968, adjusted to a 90-mile stage length.[19] The costs for the Nord were those experienced by Lake Central in 1968 before its merger with Allegheny. Lake Central's average stage length was 89 miles. Costs for the Twin Otter are based on those supplied to the author by the manufacturer. They correspond closely to costs reported by air taxi operators. For various reasons, some of which were outlined in Chapter 3, such operating cost levels probably could not be attained by a local service airline in practice, the most important reason being the way local service pilots are compensated.

19. The adjustment was made using Chart 3, p. 136, and Appendix F, p. 159, in *Review of the Local Air Carrier Industry*, Hearings before the Aviation Subcommittee of the Senate Committee on Commerce, 89 Cong. 2 sess. (1966). While the cost levels for the Convair 580 shown in this source have proven to be higher than those encountered in practice, there is no evidence to suggest that the general relationship shown between direct operating cost per mile and average stage length is inaccurate.

Therefore, operating costs for the Twin Otter should be taken as representative of the lowest cost required to provide a no-frills, low-density, short-haul service. As in the SARC study, it is assumed that indirect costs per mile for each type of aircraft are 75 percent of direct costs.[20]

Subsidy paid by the government includes an allowance for rate of return, so a rate-of-return element was calculated for each aircraft and included in total operating costs. Average investment per aircraft for the Convair 580 and the Nord 262 were taken from CAB data.[21] The aircraft cost (including full avionics and interior) for the Twin Otter was that being quoted in 1968 by the manufacturer. This figure was multiplied by 1.5, in accordance with CAB practice, in order to determine the average investment per aircraft. It was assumed that a 10 percent rate of return on investment would be allowed by the Board. The rate-of-return element per mile was calculated by dividing the annual rate-of-return element by the number of miles each aircraft was assumed to fly in a year. For the Convair 580 this was assumed to be 500,000 miles, for the Nord 262, 400,000 miles, and for the Twin Otter, 270,000 miles.[22] As Table 7-7 shows, for each aircraft-mile flown using a Convair 580 where a Nord 262 would have been the appropriate size aircraft, subsidy need was increased by 60 cents. The increase in subsidy need resulting from the use of the Convair 580 was $1.26 a mile over what it would have been if a no-frills, air taxi type of service could have been provided using a Twin Otter.

As was noted above, the SARC study estimated that in 1975, 71 million aircraft-miles should be flown using aircraft of approximately the size of the Nord 262 or the Twin Otter. This estimate was based on the assumption that all low-density routes that were flown in 1963 would continue to be flown in 1975. Certain of these routes have since been dropped, however.

20. SARC, "Economic Analysis of the Short-Haul Transport," p. 37. Recall that in Chapter 3 it was found in several cases that indirect cost components were positively correlated with the size of aircraft used.

21. CAB, "Local Service Air Carriers' Unit Costs, Year Ended March 31, 1969," Attachment C, Pt. 3, p. 1.

22. In 1968 Frontier's CV-580s, flying over a 131-mile average stage length and operating 6.97 hours a day flew 650,000 miles per aircraft; and Lake Central's Nord 262s, operating over an 89-mile stage length and operating 5.38 hours a day, flew 345,000 miles a year. The figure for the 580 over the shorter stage length probably would have been less, while the low figure for the Nord could have been raised through better equipment utilization. During 1967 Lake Central achieved a 6.22-hour a day utilization on its DC-3s. Equivalent utilization of its Nords in 1960 would have meant their flying about 15 percent more. The Twin Otter figure assumes a utilization of 1,800 hours a year (about 6 hours a day) and an average airborne speed of 150 miles an hour.

Therefore, to be conservative, it is assumed that in 1969 the local service carriers should have flown only 44 million aircraft-miles using smaller aircraft. This is the same number of miles they flew in 1963 using DC-3s and is only 62 percent of the SARC estimate of the number of aircraft-miles they should fly in 1975 using these smaller aircraft. Subtracting the 3 million aircraft-miles actually flown using smaller aircraft in 1969 leaves 41 million miles that were flown using aircraft that were too large. Even this conservative assumption implies that the 1969 subsidy need (including the rate-of-return element) was increased by a minimum of $25 million by the use of excessively large aircraft. This figure implies the use of Nord 262s rather than Convair 580s. If instead Twin Otters could have been used and indirect operating costs pared to air taxi levels, the increase in subsidy need resulting from the use of excessively large aircraft rises to $52 million.[23]

Perhaps SARC seriously overestimated the continuing need of the local carriers for smaller aircraft. Certainly it did not foresee the Board's change of policy in letting the local carriers compete directly with the trunks and the local carriers' subsequent rush to acquire jet equipment. Consequently the forecast of traffic growth in the denser markets is a serious underestimate. This failure, however, should not blind us to the true question— whether the local carriers still have a large number of markets that are best served by aircraft with less than 40-seat capacity. The current moves on the part of the Board and the local carriers to turn over many stations to air taxi operators who use aircraft such as the Twin Otter suggest that there are indeed a substantial number of such markets and that the estimate made here of the increase in subsidy needed as a result of the use of excessively large aircraft may not be far off the mark.

23. If it is assumed that there was no saving in indirect costs from the use of smaller aircraft, the increase in the direct operating costs and rate-of-return element alone increased the subsidy need by $16 million over what it would have been with the Nord 262, and by $31 million over what it would have been with the Twin Otter.

CHAPTER EIGHT

Policy Options Open to the Federal Government

THE GOVERNMENT TODAY is faced with a choice concerning its future support of short-haul, low-density air service. It has basically four policy options:

1. The local service subsidy could be eliminated over a short period and the local carriers be allowed to abandon any cities they wished. They would then be treated as trunklines for purposes of regulation. Unsubsidized air taxis would enter many of the abandoned markets, but many smaller cities would lose their only scheduled air service.

2. The federal government could commit itself to pay enough subsidy to compensate the local carriers fully for the short-haul, low-density services they provide, with the aircraft they currently use.

3. The Civil Aeronautics Board (CAB) could be directed to encourage local carriers to subcontract to air taxis service at smaller stations. The air taxis would be subsidized where necessary through the local carriers. The local carriers themselves would receive a "management fee" in return for administering the subcontracts.

4. The government could deal directly with air taxis and award long-term contracts (after competitive bidding) for these services where continued subsidy was deemed in the public interest.

Option 1: End the local service subsidy

If all local service subsidy were ended, how many points would lose service? In a 1970 speech Civil Aeronautics Board Member John G. Adams suggested that if "around 100 towns" were dropped, this "probably would end the federal subsidy program."[1] The estimate made here that a station

1. "Remarks of John G. Adams, Member, Civil Aeronautics Board, Before the Association of Local Transport Airlines" (speech delivered in New Orleans, May 1, 1970; processed), pp. 4, 5.

would have to generate 20 to 27 passengers a day (7,300 to 10,000 a year) to cover the avoidable costs of serving it suggests that between 165 and 200 towns would be dropped. This is based on the assumption that the local carriers would choose to drop only those stations where they do not cover the costs incurred using their present equipment. It is reasonable to suppose that, if they were given the chance, the local carriers might also choose to drop all cities that they felt could not eventually generate the level of traffic required to support service with "small jet" aircraft.[2] The approximate level of traffic required to support such equipment was revealed by the president of Eastern Airlines, Floyd D. Hall, when he asked for the CAB's permission to "swap" routes with other carriers. Hall claimed that Eastern made money at one-third of the 116 communities it served, broke even at another third, and lost money at the other third.[3] In 1968, the best of Eastern's poorest third cities (in terms of the number of passengers originated) generated approximately 25,000 passengers. During 1968, the smallest aircraft being used by Eastern to serve such cities was a 65-seat DC-9-10, a "small" jet which was widely used also by the local service carriers. If the local service carriers should indeed choose to drop all points that failed to generate at least 25,000 passengers, then (based on 1969 traffic figures) approximately 250 exclusively served cities would lose service.[4]

It has been suggested above that a city that was dropped by a local service carrier would not necessarily lose its scheduled air service. Unsubsidized air taxis would enter the market and provide some of the larger stations with service equal to, or superior to, that currently received from the local service carriers.[5] Although air taxis today serve many of these

2. In its June 1970 issue, *Flight Magazine* said: "As soon as practical, Frontier hopes to convert to all jet equipment." "Frontier's Reversing the Adverse," *Flight Magazine*, Vol. 59 (June 1970), p. 45.

3. "Route Swapping Proposed by Eastern Air President," *Wall Street Journal*, Vol. 174 (Oct. 3, 1969), p. 2.

4. If the 7,300 passengers-a-year standard were used, 130 of the 287 cities receiving their only certificated service from a local carrier would be dropped. If a 10,000-passengers-a-year standard were used, 158 cities would lose service. If the 25,000-passengers-a-year standard were used, 233 cities would be dropped. In the latter case, all but 7 of the 144 exclusively served cities with a population of less than 25,000 would lose their service.

5. Paul G. Delman, founder of Commuter Airlines, one of the largest of the air taxis, was reported to have said that the secret of success in the air taxi business is to choose a city with a population of 50,000 to 60,000 without air service (preferably a marketing, institutional, or industrial city) or one with about 75,000 that is getting poor service from certificated carriers. Such a city should lie within an hour's flying time of a "hub" airport. (Lynwood Mark Rhodes, "Those Brash Little Airlines," *Kiwanis Magazine*, Vol. 54 [March 1969], p. 25.) If the 50,000-population rule of thumb were indeed followed

markets, others are not entered for fear of retaliation by the local carriers if the air taxi demonstrated the existence of traffic potential. Once the local carriers had abandoned these markets, air taxis would be encouragd to experiment with offering service, particularly if the Board were to grant limited route protection in the form of a temporary (for example, five-year) nonrenewable exclusive franchise to the carriers first entering a market, with the provision that the rights would lapse if the carrier failed to offer continuous service.

In other cases, communities, states, or regions might enter into direct contractual relationships with local carriers to subsidize the continuation of air service in their areas. In fact, this is how some short-haul, low-density air service is paid for today in France. Trunklines that want to maintain feeder services might themselves subsidize either local service carriers or, more likely, air taxis. This is what happened when helicopter subsidies were ended in the early 1960s.

As in the case of replacement of local service carriers by unsubsidized air taxis, such nonfederal and trunkline subsidization probably would assure the continuation of scheduled airline service at the larger cities. There is no denying that the end of the local service subsidy would mean the end of all scheduled air service at a substantial number of smaller cities—cities that could not support even a limited unsubsidized air taxi service. These would include many of the more isolated communities that today use air service to a much greater degree relative to their population than do many larger cities.

Option 2: Pay subsidies to the local service carriers sufficient to support the current level of service using current equipment

Alternatively, the Board could admit that its program of subsidy internalization has failed and ask the Congress to appropriate subsidy funds sufficient to compensate the local service carriers for the costs they incur in

by air taxis, then the following net losses of air service would occur: If the local carriers dropped service to all points that failed to generate at least 7,300 passengers, the net loss would be 119 points (130 cities, less the 11 with a population of 50,000 or more, assumed to be served by air taxis). If service to all cities failing to generate at least 10,000 passengers were suspended, the net loss would be 144 points; if 15,000, 166 points; and if 25,000, 203 points. Better population data that included suburbs probably would increase substantially the number of cities with a population large enough to attract air taxi service.

operating their short-haul, low-density services. The attitude of the current CAB Chairman, Secor Browne, as expressed before the Senate Subcommittee on Aviation in mid-1970, indicates that such a proposal is being considered seriously.[6] It has been estimated that adoption of this solution would require the payment of approximately twice the $36 million paid in subsidy in 1969.[7] Furthermore, there would be little hope of a reduction in the subsidy within the foreseeable future. Some of the ways in which costs induced by competition spill over into noncompetitive routes were indicated in Chapter 3. Pilot salaries and wages of other personnel are based on productivity levels on dense routes, yet they apply on all routes. Company operating procedures are tailored to the dense, competitive routes but raise costs unnecessarily on thin, noncompetitive routes. Aircraft are purchased primarily with competitive routes in mind but are used on noncompetitive, low-density routes. As the importance to the local carriers of their competitive routes continues to increase, these spillover effects on the costs of operating the low-density services can also be expected to increase.

It is standard airline practice to transfer older equipment to use on poorer routes when newer, more productive equipment is purchased rather than to buy equipment specifically suited to serve such routes. In the mid-1960s, when Mohawk Airlines was considering whether to buy turboprop aircraft, or to convert its larger piston aircraft to turboprop power, or to retain its piston aircraft, it was told by a consultant that "well-managed airlines have never put substantial capital into their bottom layer equipment" and that Mohawk should not consider doing so.[8] Consequently, it is predictable that in the not too distant future the local carriers will begin to move some of their "small jets" onto their marginal routes.

The impact on the need for subsidy resulting from the use of Convair 580s where aircraft such as the Nord 262 or De Havilland Twin Otter would suffice has been estimated above. Applying the same set of assumptions as above to the DC-9-10, one discovers that total operating costs per

6. "Statement of Secor D. Browne, Chairman of the Civil Aeronautics Board" (testimony prepared for delivery before the Subcommittee on Aviation of the Senate Committee on Commerce, May 27, 1970; processed), pp. 7–9.

7. Harold D. Watkins, "Locals Expand with Mixed Results," *Aviation Week and Space Technology*, Vol. 93 (July 6, 1970), p. 25. The fiscal year 1970 subsidy was $33.8 million. The Board proposed to raise this figure to $58.6 million in fiscal year 1971. "Subsidy Increase Proposals by CAB," *Aviation Week and Space Technology*, Vol. 94 (Feb. 8, 1971), p. 23.

8. Wilbert A. Pinkerton, Jr., "Mohawk Airlines, Inc. (c): The FH-227 Purchase," T672 (Harvard Business School, 1967; processed), p. 46.

mile (including the rate-of-return element) are $3.54.[9] This is 39 percent more than the operating cost of the Convair 580.[10]

In short, unless past equipment replacement practices are discontinued or unless the Board establishes and is able to maintain a strong position against the use of jet aircraft on subsidized routes, the commitment of the Board and Congress, if the option being discussed should be adopted, will be a virtually open-ended one. If the Board and Congress should rebel at this, they would face the choice of forcing the carriers to subsidize such services themselves, which they are unlikely to agree to do, or allowing the local carriers to drop their marginal points—the same dilemma that is being faced today. Secor Browne was quite correct when he said that increasing subsidy would be no panacea but "little more than a method of providing time."[11]

Option 3: Subcontract local air service to air taxis

Another option open to the Board would be to encourage the local service carriers to follow the lead of Allegheny Airlines and subcontract service at their weaker stations to air taxi operators who would serve these points with smaller aircraft. Board Member Adams recently spoke approvingly of such a policy, though he was quick to declare that his support was not to be construed as a sign of Board endorsement. Adams referred to points generating fewer than 15 passengers a day—there were 120 such points, according to him—as "suitable candidates" for this type of substitute service.[12] He cited Allegheny's experience as evidence that the lower level of costs and the higher frequency of service made possible by the air

9. In 1968 the DC-9-10 cost $1.30 a mile to operate over a 210-mile average stage length. Correcting this figure to a stage length of 100 miles raises it to $1.60. Indirect operating costs come to $1.20 a mile. Average investment required for a DC-9-10 is $4.9 million. A 10 percent rate of return on this investment would mean $490,000 a year. In 1968 DC-9-10s in intra-Hawaiian operation, flying over an average stage length of 130 miles, flew 660,000 miles a year. Assuming that local service DC-9-10s flying over 100-mile average stage lengths could achieve this level of utilization (a generous assumption) leads to a rate-of-return element of 74 cents a mile.

10. Certain smaller pure jet designs, such as the Fairchild Hiller FH-228, the Russian Yak 40, or the West German VFW 614, claim operating costs at or below turboprop levels, but the local carriers have shown no interest in these aircraft.

11. "Statement of Secor D. Browne" (testimony before the Subcommittee on Aviation, May 27, 1970, p. 9).

12. "Remarks of John G. Adams, Member, Civil Aeronautics Board, Before the Association of Local Transport Airlines," May 1, 1970, pp. 6–7.

taxis' use of smaller equipment and by their substantial economies in the "indirect" cost area could drastically reduce or even eliminate the need for subsidy at many such stations. One should realize, as Adams apparently does, that Allegheny's success may not be a true indication of the results to be expected if such a plan were to be adopted on a significantly wider scale. Most of the cities at which Allegheny Commuter contracts have been let have a population of more than 25,000, and all, with the exception of Elkins, West Virginia, lie within a maximum of one to two hours' driving time of a large city that offers a high level of air service. Allegheny has used its Allegheny Commuter concept at those points where the improved frequency of service offered is most likely to stimulate traffic substantially.

Transfers to air taxis do not always work, however. In April 1970 Frontier Airlines turned over service at eight isolated North Dakota and Montana cities to Apache Airlines, an air taxi operator. By October, Apache had returned the routes to Frontier, claiming a $300,000 loss on the operation. Thereupon Frontier itself leased two Twin Otters and began using them to provide service to the cities.[13]

The Allegheny arrangement might well be expected to serve as a model for subcontracts if the option were chosen. Allegheny's contracts with air taxi operators run for a ten-year period. They specify the frequency of service to be provided and require the air taxi maintain at least a 95 percent flight completion average.[14] The air taxi operator uses the trademark "Allegheny Commuter" and is required to meet "Allegheny's standards of customer service." He must use a two-man flight crew (captain and first officer) and carry the same liability insurance as Allegheny—$100,000 per seat. In return Allegheny guarantees the air taxi operator a breakeven financial result during the first two years "based on a standard cost allowance"[15] and agrees to "resume flights with at least the same level of service in effect prior to Commuter service if the agreement is terminated."[16]

13. *Wall Street Journal*, Vol. 176 (Dec. 16, 1970), p. 32; *Aviation Week and Space Technology*, Vol. 94 (March 8, 1971), p. 131. According to the *Journal* article, the president of Apache Airlines accused the communities involved of sabotaging the transfer attempt in hopes of forcing Frontier to resume its service. No information is yet available as to the success of the Frontier operation with Twin Otters.

14. The ratio of flights performed to flights scheduled, not counting flights that are canceled because of adverse weather conditions.

15. For details of this cost allocation for one Allegheny contract, see *American Aviation*, Vol. 31 (October 1967), p. 51.

16. Allegheny Airlines, "Salient Points of the Contract," in *Allegheny Commuter* (Allegheny Airlines, 1969).

Air taxi operators may be expected to agree to such a contract only for stations where they feel there is a good possibility of eventually profitable operations. At points where there does not appear to be this potential, such as those points in Montana and North Dakota where Frontier's attempted transfer failed, it would be necessary to find a way to funnel subsidy funds to the air taxis through the local service carriers. Adams proposed that a plan be devised "to recognize reasonable subsidy payments or guarantees by local carriers to [air taxi operators] as legitimate operating costs of the local carrier. . . . The local service carrier would have the responsibility of administering the payments and of ensuring that the air taxi was performing the agreed level of service, agreed to . . . by the communities, the carriers, and the Board. The local service carrier could be paid for administration, and the total subsidy figure could be an amount necessary to make the air taxi whole [sic], with a reasonable profit. The incentive to the local carrier would be his opportunity to get rid of the drag on profits these loss points now place on him."[17]

Such a scheme would appear to have much to recommend it. It would take advantage of the economies afforded by the use of smaller aircraft, which, as has been seen, are far from trivial. In many cases it would mean a substantial improvement in the quality of service offered to smaller communities. There are certain problems, however, that do not appear to have been fully anticipated. Payments of "administration fees" to the local service carriers might easily serve as a vehicle for continued subsidization of this carrier group. The problem appears equal in difficulty to the problems encountered in the early 1950s, when mail pay was split into two component parts, "service mail payments" and "subsidy mail payments." It is hoped that congressional vigilance would serve to prevent such a thing from happening.

A second difficulty lies in the method of compensation used to subsidize the air taxi subcontractors. Air taxi operators are low-cost operators today only because their survival depends upon it. The current absence of subsidization for air taxi operations and the constant threat of entry are powerful spurs to cost consciousness. The previous chapters have stressed the effects a removal of such threats would have, as illustrated by the cost performance record of the local service carriers over the past twenty-five years. There is no reason to think that the urge to economize is any stronger

17. "Remarks of John G. Adams, Member, Civil Aeronautics Board, Before the Association of Local Transport Airlines," May 1, 1970, pp. 6–7.

among the air taxis than it was among the local service carriers during the early days of their operations or that this urge would persist any longer than it did with the locals once the pressure was removed. Allegheny's air taxi contracts now guarantee "a breakeven financial result during the first two years."[18] What will happen when air taxi costs begin to rise? One can expect air taxi pilots to want to improve their economic position, just as the early local service pilots did.[19] Nor are pilots likely to be the only employees seeking to benefit once an air taxi's future is secured by such a contract. What will be Allegheny's response when the air taxi operator tries to pass on these costs? It might terminate the contract and look for a new air taxi subcontractor for the route; the large number of air taxi operators and the ease of entry into the industry suggest that new candidates would not be hard to find. Alternatively, Allegheny might in turn press the CAB to increase its subsidy in order to maintain the existing air taxi subcontractor. If the Board refused and if Allegheny then terminated the contract, either Allegheny or the Board would be forced to pay the additional costs of operating the low-density route with the smallest aircraft Allegheny then had available, perhaps by that time a 100-seat DC-9-30. The approval in 1970 by the Board of a "temporary" $210,000 a month subsidy to Aloha Airlines, an intra-Hawaiian operator, after the official termination of subsidy for intra-Hawaiian operations and the "temporary" suspension of scheduled local-service subsidy reductions through fiscal 1971, suggests that the Board would not be deaf to Allegheny's plea for "temporary" help.[20] In short, while allowing local service carriers to subcontract service at marginal stations certainly will lower subsidy requirements in the short run, it will not by itself guarantee that those requirements will remain lower in the long run. To be successful, any subcontracting scheme must offer the greatest possible incentives for the subcontractors to remain efficient, low-cost operators. It should make maximum use of the fact that many entre-

18. Allegheny Airlines, "Salient Points of the Contract."
19. The Air Line Pilots Association (ALPA) has been fighting transfers to air taxis. In 1970 it filed a suit seeking to prevent one such shift by Mohawk even though it was authorized by the Board ("ALPA Suit Hits Service Shifts," *Aviation Week and Space Technology*, Vol. 93 [July 20, 1970], p. 25). There are reports that the union was successful in one attempt to prevent transfers. ("Where Others Get in Pilot's Seat," *Business Week*, No. 2061 [March 1, 1969], p. 92.) The ALPA considers such transfers a threat to local service and trunkline carrier crew jobs. If the transfers are allowed, the ALPA can be expected to try to organize air taxi pilots and, if successful, to push for wage parity with other pilots.
20. George E. Haddaway, "Rounding the Bend," *Flight Magazine*, Vol. 59 (June 1970), p. 38.

preneurs are willing to start small airlines and that the capital requirements for entry into the industry are relatively low. It must not be set up in such a way that the subsidy paid to the local service carrier is higher than a fair amount for administering the agreement. Finally, it must be constructed so that the consequences of a failure of a subcontractor to perform efficiently rest in part on the local service carrier administering the contract.

Option 4: Contract directly with air taxi operators and others to replace local service carriers at low-density points

One way to avoid some of the problems with the scheme just proposed would be for the Board to contract directly with air taxi operators and others to operate those short-haul, low-density air services whose continuation appeared to be in the public interest.[21] The local service carriers would be informed that their subsidies were to be ended and that they would be required to list any points they planned to drop. The record of the use of air service by these communities would be examined and a list drawn up of those points where the public interest dictated that federal support of air service should be continued. At each such point the minimum frequency of flights needed in order to provide adequate service would be established. Open bidding would then be allowed, with each bidder stating the minimum lump-sum annual payment he would need in order to perform the designated service. The low bidder would then receive a ten-year contract to operate the route. Fullfilment of the terms of the contract could be guaranteed by requiring the winning contractor to post a performance bond.

The winning bidder would be free to offer any additional service to the city in question that he felt was justified by traffic potential, but no additional subsidy would be paid. Contractors also would be free to arrange with the communities involved to subsidize additional flights. The government's commitment, in short, would be limited to establishing a basic level of air service at communities where existing transportation facilities clearly were inadequate. If the results of the bidding should indicate that an ex-

21. This proposal is similar in some respects to one advanced by Howard Ralph Swaine, in his Ph.D. thesis, "Subsidization of Local Air Services" (University of California, Los Angeles, 1965), and in an article published in the *Journal of Air Law and Commerce*, entitled "A Proposal for Control of Local Service Subsidies" (Vol. 31, Summer 1965), pp. 181–97.

cessive amount of subsidy support would be needed, the government could scale down the level of service required and at the same time reconsider the value of providing air service to the community in question.

Under such a scheme it would be unnecessary for the Board to specify the type of aircraft to be used or the amount of ground or in-flight services to be offered. It also would not be necessary to specify that only air taxis could bid for such routes. If a local service or trunk carrier felt that it could offer the specified frequency and timing of service to a particular point by adding it to its current routes, it should be entitled to bid. Presumably, however, most successful bidders would be air taxi operators.

Because of the large number of actual and potential air taxi operators, the winning bidder could not make exorbitant profits from a contract. Indeed, just the opposite might be expected. Bidders might be tempted to submit unrealistically low bids in order to "buy in," with the intention of "readjusting" their bids later in negotiations with the CAB. This is indeed what happened in the early bidding for air mail contracts, and it is alleged to have occurred more recently in connection with defense contracts.[22] In particular, recent experience with defense contracts indicates that no matter how ingeniously a contracting system is designed to encourage honest bidding and efficient contractor performance, it is bound to fail unless the agency administering the contract is prepared to force the winner of the contract to adhere to the provisions of his bid, regardless of the consequences. The performance of the CAB vis-à-vis the local service carriers over the last twenty-five years offers little grounds for hope that it would be firm enough with the carriers that submitted winning bids in a competition to provide short-haul, low-density air service.

Criteria for Choice

The case for a complete end to the "local service experiment" thus appears to be a strong one. No convincing evidence has been discovered that any substantial benefits accrue to the nation at large from the continued expenditure of federal funds to support local air service. Furthermore, the fact that total passenger originations either remained constant or declined between 1968 and 1969 at 67 percent of the points served exclusively by the

22. Richard E. Caves, *Air Transport and Its Regulators* (Harvard University Press, 1962), p. 124; and Donald C. Winston, "LOH Hearing May Spur Tighter Bid Rules," *Aviation Week and Space Technology*, Vol. 86 (March 13, 1967), p. 87.

local service carriers indicates that even the prime beneficiaries of the subsidy—the travelers who fly for considerably less than cost—believe that the value of the service provided is declining. Traffic was static or declined at 71 percent of the exclusively served cities of less than 25,000 population. In Chapter 4 evidence was presented suggesting that even prior to the establishment of the local service carriers and the postwar expansion of the trunklines, air service was within easy reach of a substantial proportion of the population. As early as 1938, the average population of cities that were not served was only 11,595, and the average distance from the nearest city with air service was only thirty-five miles.[23] When account is taken of the probable entry of unsubsidized air taxis at many points if the local service carriers suspended service to them, it is quite conceivable that 97 percent of the metropolitan population, that proportion that the local service carriers claimed to be serving in 1969, would still have easy access to scheduled air service even if the local service subsidy were ended.

Advocates of continued federal support for local air service point out that a significant, though declining, proportion of the population does not live in metropolitan areas.[24] They say that it is well recognized that the federal government has undertaken a commitment to provide certain essential services to all its citizens, regardless of their location, and contend that access to scheduled air service should be included among these services. This point of view was set forth by John F. Floberg, Chairman of the Conference of Local Airlines (the predecessor of the Association of Local Transport Airlines), who, in arguing for permanent certification for the local service carriers in 1955, said:

There are some things that neither the Civil Aeronautics Board nor the Congress of the United States can change, and included in those things are the geog-

23. The 260 points added to trunkline or local service carrier routes between 1938 and 1959 had an average population of 25,370 and were, on an average, sixty-six miles from the nearest point having air service. United Research Incorporated, "Federal Regulation of the Domestic Air Transport Industry," Prepared for the U.S. Department of Commerce (Cambridge, Mass.: United Research, 1959; processed), Table B-7.

24. See Systems Analysis and Research Corporation, "Public Benefits Provided by the Local Airline Industry: A Report on the Nation's Fast-Growing Local Airline Industry," Report No. 6, prepared for the Association of Local Transport Airlines (Cambridge, Mass.: SARC, 1969; processed), p. 4.

In 1950, 64 percent of the total U.S. population lived in urban areas (towns of over 2,500 population), and some 60 percent lived in Standard Metropolitan Statistical Areas (SMSAs). According to 1970 census figures, almost 75 percent of the population now lives in urban areas, and about 70 percent lives in SMSAs. U.S. Bureau of the Census, *Statistical Abstract of the United States, 1971* (1971), p. 16.

raphy and the population distribution of the United States. There is nothing that this committee or the Congress or the CAB can do to make the population of Gunnison, Colo., the same as that of Syracuse, N.Y., or the population of Tonopah, Nev., the same as that of Johnstown, Pa., or the population of Enid, Okla., the same as that of Norfolk, Va.

But, I would like to know who there is to say that the people of Gunnison, or Tonopah, or Enid, are not just as much entitled to airmail service as the people of Syracuse, Johnstown, or Norfolk, or at least who would have the temerity to say that they should be penalized merely because they happen to be in relatively sparsely populated areas.[25]

Floberg's statement serves the useful purposes of pointing up the political nature of the decision to expand air service beyond the level that the market will support. Yet, carried to its conclusion, it obviously is impractical, since its acceptance would lead to the expansion of scheduled air service to every hamlet with an airstrip long enough to accommodate an airline and the construction of such airstrips where they do not now exist.

Even if Congress should decide, for political or other reasons, to continue the local service subsidy, it is clear that better standards are needed to allow the Board to judge which cities benefit from local air service and which would suffer little or no loss if it were discontinued. The first step in drawing up such standards is to inventory the transportation alternatives open to cities that might lose service if the local service subsidy were ended.[26]

One possible rule of thumb would be to deny subsidy for air service to any city lying within a two-hour drive of a larger city that does have air service. There is no reason to expect the government to subsidize a high enough frequency of service that, on an average, it is quicker to fly than it is to drive for two hours.

Cities that pass that test should be required to meet additional criteria in order to continue to receive federal subsidy. At present a city must generate only five passengers a day to retain air service once it has been authorized. This standard is unrealistically low and should be doubled at least. Furthermore, as the costs of serving smaller communities increase over time, this standard should also be increased so that a city bears at least a constant share of the cost to the federal government of providing it with

25. "Statement of John F. Floberg," in *Permanent Certificates for Local Service Air Carriers*, Hearings before the House Committee on Interstate and Foreign Commerce, 84 Cong. 1 sess. (1955), pp. 15–16.

26. It is encouraging to note that the CAB staff is constructing an "isolation index," having as its components such factors as the proximity of a city to other cities with air service and to an interstate highway system. *Aviation Week and Space Technology*, Vol. 94 (March 1, 1971), p. 27.

scheduled air service. It has been argued here that if a city of 25,000 generates only ten passengers a day, this is because its air service offers little or no improvement over other transportation alternatives. On the other hand, a small town may generate only ten passengers a day merely because its total traffic-generating potential is low. Some minimum level of passenger originations per capita should also be required of cities seeking to retain subsidized air service. The number of stations that were served exclusively by local carriers in 1969 and that would be made ineligible for subsidy even if they were required to maintain a traffic level of only 0.25 originations per capita per year are shown below:[27]

1. Total number of exclusively served cities 287
2. Exclusively served cities that originated fewer than 3,650 passengers a year 77
3. Exclusively served cities that originated fewer than 0.25 passengers per capita population[28] 98
4. Exclusively served cities falling in *either* (2) or (3) 117

Cities failing to meet these tests would be either too small to justify even the lowest level of air service or so well endowed with transportation alternatives that a federally supported air service would be of little value to them.

Of the 158 cities that in 1969 generated fewer than 10,000 passengers, 51 pass the two tests shown above. What type of service should the government agree to support at such cities?

It is estimated that the cost of using excessively large aircraft is between $0.60 and $1.26 per route-mile, depending on the aircraft used. Primarily what the government pays for with the additional subsidy needed to cover these higher costs is more passenger comfort.[29] The three aircraft whose costs were presented in Chapter 7—the Convair 580, the Nord 262, and the De Havilland Twin Otter—are all equally capable of safe, reliable operation. All are turbine-powered; all are flown by two pilots. In fact, the mechanical simplicity and the short takeoff and landing characteristics of the Twin Otter make this aircraft, if anything, potentially safer and more reliable than are the other two. There are differences among these aircraft

27. From data in the appendix.
28. Includes ten that originated more than 10,000 passengers a year.
29. Subsidizing a larger aircraft than is warranted by average anticipated traffic levels also allows a carrier to achieve a higher probability of meeting peaks in traffic demand. However, the additional capacity required to yield significant improvements in this element of the quality of service (and the increased subsidy cost associated with providing this peaking capacity) is likely to be quite large. See George Eads, "Competition in the Domestic Trunk Airline Industry: Excessive or Insufficient" (1971; processed), pp. 11–28.

other than those of capacity. The Twin Otter is unpressurized and lacks washroom facilities. Also there are no facilities for serving food and beverages to passengers, since the aircraft is not designed to carry a stewardess. The seats do not recline, and they are narrower than standard airline seats. In short, the plane is designed to transport up to 20 passengers for short distances, with a minimum of frills. The Nord 262 is a standard airline aircraft with all the associated features. It is both pressurized and air conditioned. It has a small galley and is designed to carry a stewardess. Although its maximum passenger capacity is only 28, as against the Twin Otter's maximum of 20, the usable cabin space is twice that of the Twin Otter. While some of the estimated 66-cents-a-mile difference in operating costs between these two aircraft is due to the lower input costs faced by air taxi operators, a significant part is due to the cost of these additional features that add to the initial price of the aircraft, increase its mechanical complexity and maintenance costs, and add weight that must be carried regardless of the passenger load.[30] The Convair 580 has no comfort features that are not found on the Nord 262. Its increased operating costs are traceable solely to its larger size and greater mechanical complexity.[31]

It is obvious that a passenger faced with equal frequencies and fares would prefer to fly on a Convair 580 rather than on a Twin Otter. However, the experience of the air taxis in attracting traffic on aircraft like Twin Otters shows that a large portion of potential local service customers do not consider the extra features essential. It is reasonable to argue that if the federal government is going to subsidize air service at all, it should be willing to pay the additional subsidy required to provide a pressurized aircraft. This is true particularly for services operated in the mountainous areas of the West. The same may be true of air conditioning. It cannot be argued, however, that the government should pay the costs of stewardesses and of passenger food and beverage service on such short flights. Furthermore, no case can be made for the government's subsidizing the additional passenger comfort that results from the use of a larger aircraft, such as the

30. The original version of the Nord was available either as a pressurized or unpressurized aircraft. The unpressurized aircraft was priced at $350,000 and the pressurized version at $390,000, in both cases fully equipped. Anthony Vandyk, "Nord Goal, 300 Super Broussards," *Airlift, World Air Transportation*, Vol. 25 (February 1962), pp. 25–26.

31. For example, the larger turboprop aircraft, such as the Convair 580, have auxiliary power units (APUs) that provide internal power and operate the air conditioning system when the aircraft is on the ground. These APUs are small gas turbine-powered generators, whose turbine section is not much smaller than the engines that power the Twin Otter.

Convair 580, when a smaller aircraft like the Nord 262, which has all the necessary features to provide safe, dependable air transportation (and in addition some features that are not strictly necessary but perhaps desirable) offers enough capacity to take care of the expected traffic. The costs incurred through the use of large aircraft must be borne either by the passengers traveling on a route or by the airline using the aircraft.[32]

The supporters of continued federal subsidization of local air service should be required to demonstrate that either the current level of service or the type of service they want provides a substantial improvement in transportation alternatives open to the cities they believe to be "isolated." In doing this they must compare a relatively low-frequency air service with a highway system that has seen substantial improvement since the end of the Second World War, with much of this improvement being concentrated in the areas previously considered to be isolated. To the extent that the service they envision makes use of smaller, more economical aircraft, their task will be made easier. While a case can be made for federal support of a minimum level of air service at a number of relatively isolated cities, it is argued here that the number of cities where service is subsidized should be reduced substantially and that advantage should be taken of the economies of operation made possible through the use of smaller equipment, more efficient ground operations, and a reduced level of passenger amenities.

CAB Policy toward the Locals and Regulation of the Domestic Airline Industry

Besides its undeniable impact on the level of service received by the smaller, more isolated communities, a decision by the Board to follow any one of the above four options will affect the entire domestic airline industry. Caves, writing in 1962, saw as highly desirable the shift of marginal trunkline cities to the local carriers and the consequent rise in the local service subsidy, since it opened the way for relaxing entry controls in the airline industry.[33] However, the more recent attempt by the Board to internalize the local service subsidy (by giving carriers routes on which it hoped substantial profits could be made) required that entry controls be

32. Another possibility would be for the community served to pay the additional cost of using larger aircraft.

33. Richard E. Caves, *Air Transport and Its Regulators: An Industry Study* (Harvard University Press, 1962), pp. 410–11.

continued. It also meant that the Board, in deciding which carrier to favor with route awards, had to continue to base its choice in large part on the need of local service carriers for profit and not on the more desirable criterion of which carrier would provide the needed service at the least cost. This policy clearly was not in the public interest.

Under all four of the options suggested above, the total cost of subsidizing local air service would be borne by the taxpayer, though the burden obviously would differ, depending on the particular one chosen. Consequently, each would permit the relaxation of entry controls now required by the CAB's effort to internalize the local service subsidy. In addition to its obvious effects on the trunk and local service carriers, this would ease much of the growing pressure for bringing the air taxis under the umbrella of Board economic regulation. These carriers now constitute the only exempt segment of the domestic interstate air transport industry. Their presence has been tolerated because of their relatively minor impact on the rest of the industry. A CAB staff study published in November 1969 concluded that "[It is] doubtful that the air taxis, at least at this time, represent a substantial competitive threat to the local service carriers."[34] This may change, however, with the continued growth of the air taxis. Already there are some markets where air taxis do provide substantial competition, in terms of the number of seats offered daily, to both trunks and locals.[35] Furthermore, the air taxis are currently asking that the Board liberalize their authority and allow them to use larger equipment. Board approval of this request would increase substantially the competitive potential of the air taxis. This would be certain to evoke increased pressure for air taxi regulation from the regulated segments of the airline industry.

Pressure for air taxi regulation is coming also from the states. *The New York Times* reported in March 1970 that several southern states were seeking to regulate the fares and routes of air taxis and that two states, Texas and Arkansas, were already regulating such airlines.[36] The third source of pressure for regulation is the air taxis themselves. The financial losses being suffered by many of them, and in addition the "chaotic conditions" in the industry, evoke pleas for some form of "route protection."[37]

The arguments for regulation usually are couched in terms of safety.

34. Civil Aeronautics Board, Bureau of Operating Rights, "An Analysis of Scheduled Air Taxi Operations" (November 1969), p. 10.

35. *Ibid.*, pp. 7–10.

36. "Southern States to Study Regulating of Air Taxis," *New York Times* (March 9, 1970), p. 74.

37. For example, see Rhodes, "Those Brash Little Airlines," pp. 25–26.

The accident rate for air taxis, higher on a fatalities-per-mile basis than that of the scheduled carriers, is cited as a reflection of the cut-throat competition in the industry. These arguments evoke memories of the pleas for regulation of the trucking industry that were heard in the 1930s. It is now generally admitted, however, that the underlying motives for regulation of trucking were the desire of the large truckers to limit price competition and obtain route protection, the desire of shippers for rate stabilization, and the desire of Congress and the Interstate Commerce Commission to protect a system of rail rates that embodied internal subsidization.[38]

This experience should be kept in mind when proposals are made for economic regulation of air taxis in order to improve safety. It is important that the air taxis be required to conform to the same safety regulations that the certificated carriers must obey. Air taxis already are subject to safety regulation, and moves by the Federal Aviation Administration to tighten safety standards for these carriers indicates that improvement in safety can be anticipated.[39] On the other hand, regulations promulgated in the name of safety that only increase costs should be avoided. For example, the FAA has ruled that all air taxi aircraft having more than 19 passenger seats must have a cabin attendant. This means that operators of De Havilland Twin Otter Series 300 aircraft or the Swearingen FS-226 Metroliner, both of which can carry more than 19 seats, must either remove the additional seats or assign a stewardess to the plane. While the presence of a stewardess might have a marginal effect on passenger safety, the FAA should be required to demonstrate that its rule is a reasonable one and is the only way of achieving the desired safety goal.[40]

The experience of the local service carriers shows how difficult it is for a regulated firm to remain cost conscious in the face of adverse regulatory incentives. While the air taxis are low-cost operators today, they could not be expected to remain so for any extended period of time should "route protection" (other than perhaps in the limited form suggested above) and "stabilization" of the industry be undertaken by the Board. The growth of the air taxis provides the CAB with a rare second chance to encourage the development of an efficient, economical, short-haul, low-density air service. It is important that the Board learn from the mistakes it made in regulating the local service carriers. Otherwise this second chance also could be lost.

38. Ann F. Friedlaender, *The Dilemma of Freight Transport Regulation* (Brookings Institution, 1969), pp. 21–22.

39. "FAA Adopts Air Taxi, Commuter Rules," *Aviation Week and Space Technology*, Vol. 91 (Dec. 22, 1969), pp. 31–32.

40. *Ibid.*, p. 31.

And what of the local service carriers? Freed of their money-losing segments they would be strong potential competitors for the existing trunklines in many regional markets. They would be in a position analogous to the smaller trunks in the late 1950s after they were shorn of their local service–type routes. Some would survive and prosper as separate entities, some probably would be absorbed by trunklines, others might merge among themselves, and still others might fail. The Board should keep in mind that its mandate does not extend to protecting the economic health of all the carriers it has created but rather is "the encouragement and development of an air-transportation system properly adapted to the present and future needs of the foreign and domestic commerce of the United States."[41]

41. 72 Stat. 740, Sec. 102(a); 49 U.S.C. §402.

Cities Served Exclusively by Local Service Carriers, 1969, Ranked by 1969 Passenger Originations

City	Population[a]	Passenger originations	Originations per capita	Departures per day[b]
Peoria, Illinois	136,000	132,632	0.98	22.6
Erie, Pennsylvania	135,000	101,656	0.75	26.0
Green Bay, Wisconsin	85,000	95,669	1.13	26.2
Elmira, New York	45,000	94,300	2.10	27.5
Superior/Duluth, Minnesota	135,000	93,720	0.69	15.9
Fayetteville, North Carolina	55,000	92,307	1.68	18.9
Utica/Rome, New York	153,000	89,827	0.59	17.7
Sioux City, Iowa	87,000	86,672	1.00	22.8
Champaign/Urbana, Illinois	85,500	83,822	0.98	13.1
Santa Ana, California	132,500	81,076	0.61	8.2
Springfield, Illinois	88,000	78,527	0.89	15.7
Waterloo, Iowa	78,000	73,872	0.95	15.9
Kalamazoo, Michigan	86,000	65,953	0.77	10.9
Dothan, Alabama	31,440	61,968	1.97	15.0
Lafayette, Louisiana	61,000	60,802	1.00	13.7
Eglin Air Force Base, Florida	12,147	58,140	4.79	9.0
New Bern/Morehead City, North Carolina	21,300	57,801	2.71	12.3
Islip, New York	12,000	55,349	4.61	12.2
Gulfport/Biloxi, Mississippi	80,000	54,419	0.68	10.4
Oshkosh, Wisconsin	47,000	53,728	1.14	12.7
White Plains, New York	50,040	51,064	1.02	10.1
Eureka/Arcata, California	33,372	50,921	1.53	6.9
Yakima, Washington	44,200	49,390	1.12	14.1
Kennewick/Richland/Pasco, Washington	52,314	48,088	0.92	14.2
Wilmington, North Carolina	53,500	46,428	0.87	12.5
Marietta, Ohio/Parkersburg, West Virginia	61,644	45,737	0.74	9.9
Ithaca, New York	28,799	43,657	1.52	10.6

Sources: *Flight Magazine*, Vol. 59 (June 1970), pp. 60–67; *Rand McNally Road Atlas: United States, Canada, Mexico*, 46th Annual Edition (Chicago: Rand McNally, 1970).

a. 1960 population figures are for the central cities; that is, surrounding suburban areas are not included.

b. Departures per day = $\dfrac{\text{passenger originations}}{365}$ ÷ passengers originated per departure. The latter data are from *Flight Magazine*, cited in source above.

City	Population[a]	Passenger originations	Originations per capita	Departures per day[b]
Wichita Falls, Texas	98,000	43,178	0.44	5.3
Williamsport, Pennsylvania	41,000	41,256	1.01	8.8
Abilene, Texas	96,000	40,729	0.42	8.1
Lynchburg, Virginia	58,000	40,187	0.69	16.9
Bridgeport, Connecticut	152,000	39,606	0.26	10.4
Lake Charles, Louisiana	60,000	38,665	0.64	12.8
Minot, North Dakota	33,477	38,395	1.15	7.7
Joplin, Missouri	38,500	38,353	1.00	9.6
Winston-Salem, North Carolina	143,000	37,443	0.26	15.8
Harlingen, Texas	38,000	36,117	0.95	8.8
Kinston, North Carolina	24,819	35,628	1.44	10.1
Traverse City, Michigan	18,432	34,730	1.88	8.1
Decatur, Illinois	88,000	34,587	0.39	8.2
Mission/Edinburg/McAllen, Texas	71,581	34,081	0.48	8.0
Charlottesville, Virginia	41,500	33,900	0.82	9.1
Battle Creek, Michigan	41,000	33,070	0.81	8.4
Fairmont/Clarksburg, West Virginia	55,589	32,665	0.59	8.5
Junction City/Fort Riley/Manhattan, Kansas	44,700	31,408	0.70	8.6
New London/Groton, Connecticut	43,500	31,173	0.72	4.6
La Crosse, Wisconsin	47,500	30,973	0.65	6.6
Yuma, Arizona	28,005	30,000	1.07	9.3
Fayetteville, Arkansas	26,279	29,005	1.10	9.3
San Angelo, Texas	66,500	28,279	0.43	7.0
Santa Maria, California	33,500	27,247	0.81	5.4
Grand Canyon, Arizona	900	27,133	30.15	5.6
Fort Polk/Leesville, Louisiana	4,689	26,573	5.67	6.9
Columbia, Missouri	42,000	26,124	0.62	7.9
Dubuque, Iowa	64,000	24,561	0.38	8.4
Texarkana, Arkansas	22,000	24,549	1.12	7.6
Bradford, Pennsylvania	15,061	24,497	1.63	8.7
Burlington, Iowa	33,285	23,244	0.70	6.7
Farmington, New Mexico	23,786	23,164	0.97	9.6
Lewiston, Idaho/Clarkston, Washington	18,709	22,288	1.19	8.7
Columbus, Mississippi	24,711	22,244	0.90	7.0
St. Joseph/Benton Harbor, Michigan	30,891	22,062	0.71	7.1
Marquette, Michigan	19,824	21,591	1.09	3.4
Lafayette, Indiana	46,000	21,518	0.47	5.9
Aberdeen, South Dakota	23,073	21,394	0.93	7.2
Florence/Sheffield/Tuscumbia/Muscle Shoals, Alabama	58,218	21,377	0.37	6.0
Morgantown, West Virginia	22,487	21,157	0.94	8.7
Fort Leonard Wood/Waynesville, Missouri	2,455	20,713	8.44	6.3
Eau Claire, Wisconsin	38,600	20,431	0.53	6.4
Twin Falls, Idaho	20,893	20,288	0.97	7.4

City	Population[a]	Passenger originations	Originations per capita	Departures per day[b]
Redding, California	12,773	20,207	1.58	5.2
Hannibal, Missouri/Quincy, Illinois	65,000	19,799	0.30	5.8
Clearfield/Phillipsburg/State College, Pennsylvania	46,726	19,760	0.42	5.1
Herrin/Marion, Illinois	20,748	19,465	0.94	6.9
Waco, Texas	105,000	19,305	0.18	9.8
Anniston, Alabama	33,657	19,271	0.57	4.1
El Centro, California	19,280	18,978	0.98	7.8
Staunton, Virginia	24,900	18,960	0.76	6.3
Roswell, New Mexico	50,000	18,887	0.38	6.5
Jackson, Wyoming	1,437	18,849	13.12	3.9
Mason City, Iowa	30,711	18,663	0.61	6.1
Scottsbluff, Nebraska	14,400	18,079	1.26	7.3
Terre Haute, Indiana	70,000	17,548	0.25	7.9
Jamestown, New York	41,200	17,492	0.42	6.8
Pullman, Washington/Moscow, Idaho	26,740	17,470	0.65	7.1
Greenville, Mississippi	45,400	17,451	0.38	5.6
Walla Walla, Washington	24,536	17,016	0.69	8.5
Chisholm/Hibbing, Minnesota	24,875	16,791	0.68	6.8
Santa Fe, New Mexico	40,000	16,619	0.42	6.2
Pellston, Michigan	429	16,609	38.72	4.8
Rhinelander, Wisconsin	8,790	16,358	1.86	4.6
Klamath Falls, Oregon	16,949	16,345	0.96	5.3
Laredo, Texas	74,000	15,916	0.22	5.3
Myrtle Beach, South Carolina	7,834	15,787	2.02	5.8
Princeton/Bluefield, West Virginia	27,649	15,669	0.57	6.0
Wausau, Wisconsin	31,943	15,291	0.48	6.2
Grand Island, Nebraska	29,300	15,225	0.52	5.5
Stevens Point, Wisconsin	17,837	15,208	0.85	7.1
Hancock/Houghton, Michigan	8,415	14,815	1.76	2.8
Atlantic City, New Jersey	59,000	14,546	0.25	4.3
Temple, Texas	30,419	14,503	0.48	7.6
Durango, Colorado	10,530	14,446	1.37	5.7
Pueblo, Colorado	102,000	14,221	0.14	6.5
Salina, Kansas	47,500	14,171	0.30	6.3
Chico, California	14,757	13,956	0.95	5.5
Tuscaloosa, Alabama	74,000	13,693	0.19	5.5
Florence, South Carolina	28,000	13,559	0.48	7.1
Coos Bay/North Bend, Oregon	14,596	13,307	0.91	4.2
Escanaba, Michigan	15,391	13,285	0.86	5.5
Altoona, Pennsylvania	66,000	13,275	0.20	3.8
Owensboro, Kentucky	45,800	13,107	0.29	4.3
Clarksville, Tennessee/Hopkinsville, Kentucky	55,122	13,101	0.24	5.4
North Platte, Nebraska	17,900	12,853	0.72	5.4

City	Population[a]	Passenger originations	Originations per capita	Departures per day[b]
Valdosta, Georgia	30,652	12,588	0.41	3.4
Liberal, Kansas	13,813	12,513	0.91	4.6
Hickory, North Carolina	19,328	12,397	0.64	7.4
Lancaster, Pennsylvania	59,000	12,389	0.21	4.8
Topeka, Kansas	127,500	12,186	0.10	7.1
Watertown, New York	33,306	12,091	0.36	5.5
Iron Mountain, Michigan	9,299	12,026	1.29	5.0
Kilgore/Gladewater/Longview, Texas	59,334	11,497	0.19	7.3
Plattsburgh, New York	21,090	11,358	0.54	3.6
Jackson, Tennessee	34,400	10,528	0.31	5.7
Bloomington, Indiana	42,058	10,372	0.25	4.5
Sault Ste. Marie, Michigan	18,722	10,288	0.55	1.9
Tyler, Texas	58,000	10,275	0.18	6.9
Fort Dodge, Iowa	29,654	10,262	0.35	4.8
Bloomington, Illinois	38,000	10,188	0.27	3.1
Cape Girardeau, Missouri	28,200	10,080	0.36	4.1
International Falls, Minnesota	6,778	9,835	1.45	2.4
Manitowoc, Wisconsin	33,215	9,751	0.29	4.9
Watertown, South Dakota	14,077	9,735	0.69	7.6
Bemidji, Minnesota	9,958	9,605	0.96	4.3
Riverton, Wyoming	6,845	9,511	1.39	4.7
Huron, South Dakota	14,180	9,344	0.66	6.2
Brainerd, Minnesota	12,898	9,201	0.71	4.7
Alamogordo, New Mexico	21,723	9,114	0.42	3.8
Johnstown, Pennsylvania	44,000	9,068	0.21	3.3
Galesburg, Illinois	37,243	8,988	0.24	4.4
San Luis Obispo/Paso Robles, California	32,877	8,975	0.27	5.2
Saranac Lake, New York	6,421	8,761	1.36	1.8
Menominee, Michigan	11,289	8,711	0.77	5.6
Glens Falls, New York	18,580	8,695	0.47	4.2
Kalispell, Montana	10,151	8,311	0.82	2.0
Cedar City, Utah	7,543	8,298	1.10	4.4
Beloit/Janesville, Wisconsin	76,199	8,118	0.11	5.2
Tupelo, Mississippi	17,221	7,953	0.46	5.3
Ottumwa, Iowa	34,000	7,873	0.23	3.9
Athens, Georgia	41,059	7,834	0.19	3.4
Camden/El Dorado City, Arkansas	39,896	7,778	0.19	5.2
Gadsden, Alabama	54,000	7,690	0.14	3.5
Beckley, West Virginia	18,642	7,579	0.41	3.8
Clovis, New Mexico	28,000	7,552	0.27	3.4
Anderson/New Castle/Muncie, Indiana	159,869	7,526	0.05	4.0
Ironwood, Michigan	10,265	7,406	0.72	3.8
Flagstaff, Arizona	24,592	7,405	0.30	3.2
Rocky Mount, North Carolina	32,147	7,351	0.23	6.1

City	Population[a]	Passenger originations	Originations per capita	Departures per day[b]
Goldsboro, North Carolina	28,873	7,177	0.25	7.0
Massena, New York	15,478	6,981	0.45	3.1
Wenatchee, Washington	16,726	6,977	0.42	3.5
Hastings, Nebraska	23,500	6,865	0.29	3.5
Danville, Virginia	49,500	6,671	0.13	4.1
Hays, Kansas	11,947	6,518	0.55	3.5
Alamosa, Colorado	6,205	6,483	1.04	3.6
Albany/Corvallis, Oregon	33,595	6,469	0.19	4.0
Kearney, Nebraska	14,210	6,447	0.45	3.6
Hobbs, New Mexico	26,275	6,439	0.25	4.5
Thomasville/Moultrie, Georgia	34,010	6,385	0.19	4.9
Hurley/Silver City, New Mexico	8,823	6,307	0.71	3.8
Lancaster/Palmdale, California	33,212	6,306	0.19	4.0
Montrose/Delta, Colorado	8,876	6,271	0.71	3.5
Inyokern/China Lake, California	550	6,210	11.29	1.8
Gallup, New Mexico	14,089	6,086	0.43	3.8
Jackson, Michigan	49,000	6,079	0.12	3.8
Alpena, Michigan	14,682	6,078	0.41	2.6
Charleston/Mattoon, Illinois	32,699	6,041	0.18	3.1
Natchez, Mississippi	23,791	5,825	0.24	12.3
College Station/Bryan, Texas	38,938	5,761	0.15	4.3
Clinton, Iowa	34,300	5,748	0.17	2.9
Thief River Falls, Minnesota	7,151	5,747	0.80	3.8
Crescent City, California	2,958	5,742	1.94	3.3
Trenton, New Jersey	102,000	5,645	0.06	3.4
Mt. Vernon, Illinois	15,566	5,606	0.36	3.0
Pine Bluff, Arkansas	57,500	5,534	0.10	3.8
Big Spring, Texas	31,230	5,492	0.18	4.3
Williston, North Dakota	11,866	5,375	0.45	2.9
Harrison, Arkansas	7,015	5,356	0.76	3.7
Tahoe, California	600	5,122	8.54	0.8
Laramie, Wyoming	19,000	5,209	0.27	3.3
Carlsbad, New Mexico	25,541	5,071	0.20	4.5
Garden City, Kansas	11,811	5,030	0.43	3.4
Rock Springs, Wyoming	10,371	5,019	0.48	3.6
Rock Falls/Sterling, Illinois	25,949	4,712	0.18	3.3
Jonesboro, Arkansas	23,944	4,605	0.19	3.5
Victoria, Texas	33,047	4,554	0.14	2.6
McCook, Nebraska	8,301	4,456	0.54	3.5
Independence/Coffeyville/Parsons, Kansas	42,533	4,298	0.10	3.2
Prescott, Arizona	13,823	4,286	0.31	4.5
Norfolk, Nebraska	13,640	4,268	0.31	3.8
Ludington/Manistee, Michigan	17,745	4,203	0.24	1.9
Cortez, Colorado	6,764	4,173	0.62	3.5

City	Popu- lation[a]	Passen- ger origi- nations	Origi- nations per capita	Depar- tures per day[b]
Enid, Oklahoma	40,000	4,166	0.10	3.6
Iowa City, Iowa	40,467	4,127	0.10	1.9
Lufkin, Texas	17,641	4,084	0.23	3.1
Gunnison, Colorado	3,477	3,995	1.15	1.8
Worland, Wyoming	5,806	3,990	0.69	3.6
Fairmont, Minnesota	9,745	3,930	0.40	3.6
Oil City/Franklin, Pennsylvania	27,278	3,854	0.14	2.2
Steamboat Springs/Hayden/Craig, Colorado	6,591	3,792	0.58	1.9
Sun Valley, Idaho	317	3,790	11.96	4.5
Brownwood, Texas	16,974	3,583	0.21	3.6
Hot Springs, Virginia	200	3,578	17.89	2.6
Cody/Powell/Lovell, Wyoming	12,029	3,541	0.29	2.8
Ponca City, Oklahoma	24,411	3,492	0.14	3.5
Kingman, Arizona	6,021	3,477	0.58	3.5
Mitchell, South Dakota	12,555	3,446	0.27	4.3
Yankton, South Dakota	9,279	3,405	0.37	3.7
Greenwood, South Carolina	19,861	3,374	0.17	1.7
Chadron, Nebraska	5,079	3,371	0.66	3.3
Vernal, Utah	3,655	3,340	0.91	1.8
Worthington, Minnesota	9,015	3,311	0.37	3.6
Rockford, Illinois	143,000	3,264	0.02	3.2
Hutchinson, Kansas	38,000	3,217	0.08	3.4
Hattiesburg, Mississippi	37,500	3,208	0.09	3.3
Anderson, South Carolina	41,000	3,157	0.08	3.5
Moses Lake/Ephrata, Washington	17,847	3,138	0.18	3.4
Winslow, Arizona	8,862	3,023	0.34	3.8
Galveston, Texas	65,000	2,975	0.05	2.5
Corbin/London, Kentucky	11,154	2,962	0.27	3.4
Great Bend, Kansas	16,670	2,899	0.17	2.6
Blythe, California	6,023	2,846	0.47	3.2
Riverside, California	131,000	2,825	0.02	2.5
Stillwater, Oklahoma	23,965	2,741	0.11	2.9
Brookings, South Dakota	10,558	2,718	0.26	3.1
Oxnard/Ventura, California	97,269	2,704	0.03	2.8
Astoria, Oregon	10,800	2,668	0.25	3.0
Bend/Redmond, Oregon	15,276	2,584	0.17	2.7
Aberdeen/Hoquiam, Washington	29,503	2,564	0.09	3.1
Laurel, Mississippi	27,889	2,559	0.09	2.7
Wheeling, West Virginia	48,000	2,537	0.05	3.3
Ogdensburg, New York	16,122	2,534	0.16	2.3
Devils Lake, North Dakota	6,670	2,519	0.38	2.9
Alliance, Nebraska	7,845	2,511	0.32	3.4
Duncan, Oklahoma	20,009	2,394	0.12	2.9
Santa Rosa, California	41,615	2,390	0.06	2.8

City	Population[a]	Passenger originations	Originations per capita	Departures per day[b]
Columbus, Nebraska	12,476	2,367	0.19	3.4
Lima, Ohio	54,000	2,286	0.04	2.1
Logansport/Peru/Kokomo, Indiana	82,756	2,185	0.03	1.6
Winona, Minnesota	26,771	2,129	0.08	2.2
Pascagoula, Mississippi	17,155	2,085	0.12	3.0
Bartlesville, Oklahoma	30,000	2,071	0.07	3.2
Moab, Utah	4,682	2,036	0.43	2.9
Greenwood, Mississippi	20,436	1,996	0.10	2.9
Glasgow, Montana	6,398	1,946	0.30	1.8
Elizabeth City, North Carolina	14,062	1,909	0.14	3.1
Sidney, Nebraska	8,004	1,765	0.22	3.5
Goodland, Kansas	4,459	1,727	0.39	1.7
Oxford/University, Mississippi	9,483	1,704	0.18	3.1
St. Joseph, Missouri	75,000	1,692	0.02	3.6
Page, Arizona	4,500	1,687	0.37	1.8
Roseburg, Oregon	11,467	1,677	0.15	2.3
Wolf Point, Montana	3,585	1,676	0.47	1.8
Rutland, Vermont	18,325	1,616	0.09	0.7
Blacksburg, Virginia	7,070	1,457	0.21	2.3
Miles City, Montana	9,665	1,388	0.14	1.8
Kirksville, Missouri	13,123	1,384	0.11	1.0
Vicksburg, Mississippi	28,500	1,329	0.05	1.7
Cambridge/Zanesville, Ohio	52,562	1,328	0.03	3.0
Poughkeepsie, New York	37,000	1,243	0.03	0.6
Glendive, Montana	7,058	1,220	0.17	1.0
Olympia, Washington	18,900	1,212	0.06	2.8
Lamar, Colorado	7,369	1,184	0.16	1.5
Yuba City/Marysville, California	21,060	1,131	0.05	1.9
Paris, Texas	20,977	1,119	0.05	1.9
Havre, Montana	10,740	1,101	0.10	1.9
Borger, Texas	20,911	1,076	0.05	1.5
Crossville, Tennessee	4,668	1,062	0.23	2.6
Tacoma, Washington	152,000	985	0.01	3.0
Portsmouth, Ohio	31,500	977	0.03	2.4
Tullahoma/Shelbyville, Tennessee	24,123	952	0.04	2.9
Martinsburg, West Virginia	15,179	852	0.06	2.6
Muskogee, Oklahoma	38,000	787	0.02	1.8
Olean, New York	21,868	781	0.04	1.2
Lewistown, Montana	7,408	608	0.08	1.9
Baker, Oregon	9,986	575	0.06	1.6
Rupert/Burley, Idaho	12,415	546	0.04	1.9
Payette/Ontario, Oregon	9,552	293	0.03	1.3

Index

Aberdeen, S.Dak., 114
Abilene, Tex., 1
Adams, John G., 191, 195–97
Adams, Mass., 83
Aero Commander, 168
Aircraft: depreciation, 55–57, 93, 142–43; helicopters, 127–28, 193; maintenance, 55–58; operating costs, 38, 49–70, 134–39, 187–90; parts, 38–40, 58; piston, 53–54, 58, 64–65, 70, 125, 188; piston versus turboprop, 129–36; productivity variable, 32–35, 40; purchase by local carriers, 38–41, 45, 48, 106, 125–42, 149, 151, 194; size and subsidy, 129, 143, 183, 187–90; turboprop, 53–54, 58–59, 64–65, 70, 125, 127–28, 136–42, 147; used, 38–39, 55–56. *See also* Jet aircraft; specific aircraft
Air Line Pilots Association (ALPA), 176; crew scheduling, 53; wage formulas, 32–34, 51
Airlines. *See* Air taxi; Local service carriers; specific airlines; Trunk carriers
Air mail. *See* Mail pay
Airport, 2–3; consolidation plan, 148, 150. *See also* Stations
Air taxi: aircraft types, 188–90; CAB rulings, 5, 166–69, 206; charter, 167; contracting for, 195–200; crew costs, 35; flight frequency, 27–28; and local carriers, 35, 151–52, 167–69, 174, 192–93, 206; nonscheduled, 5; origin, 151, 166–69; pressure for regulation, 206–07; scheduled, 2, 5–6, 167–69; subsidy, 168
Air Transport Association Standard Method of Estimating Comparative Direct Operating Costs of Transport Airplanes (ATA formula), 50, 58
Air West: crew costs, 35; merger, 164–65; passenger expenses, 63
Albany, N.Y., 14, 83, 158
Albuquerque, N.Mex., 164

All American Aviation, 79, 109. *See also* Allegheny
Allegheny Airlines, 7, 131, 156; aircraft types, 132–34; air taxi contracts, 168–69, 195–96, 198; Allegheny Commuter, 168–69, 196; ground expenses, 36, 64, 67, 70; mergers, 3, 7, 164–65, 188; passenger expenses, 61–63; scheduling, 109; subsidy, 134; trunk competition, 14, 158, 161; trunk suspension effect, 114–15
Allison 501 engine, 138
Aloha Airlines, 198
ALPA. *See* Air Line Pilots Association
Amarillo, Tex., 1
American Airlines, 14, 113–14, 133; local carrier competition, 156, 158, 161, 173; merger proposal, 5
Apache Airlines, 169, 196
Association of Local Transport Airlines (ALTA), 177
ATA formula, 50, 58
Athol, Mass., 83
Atlantic City, N.J., 115
Augusta, Maine, 27
Austin, Tex., 1, 86–87, 108
Automobile, as local carrier alternative, 14–15, 17–19, 24–26, 177, 180. *See also* Bus; Rail travel
Averch, Harvey, 113*n*, 137*n*

BAC-*111*, 33–34, 45, 158
Baitsell, John M., 32, 53
Barnes, Leslie O., 133*n*, 156
Baumol, William J., 12
Beechcraft *18*, 79, 92, 98, 126
Beechcraft *99*, 128, 168
Binghamton, N.Y., 95
Boeing *247D*, 94, 96
Boeing *727*, 50
Boeing *737*, 50

217